Urban Studies:
A Canadian Perspective

Urban Studies:
A Canadian Perspective

edited by

N. H. Lithwick
Gilles Paquet

Methuen

Toronto   London   Sydney   Wellington

Library of Congress Catalog Card Number 68-8670

SBN   458   90480 5   Pb
SBN   458   99520 7   Hc

Printed and bound in Canada

  3   4   5   6   7   8   9   74   73   72   71

Contents

Part Three
Public Policy for City and Region

Conclusion

The Authors

R. T. Adamson
Executive Director
Central Mortgage and Housing Corporation

Harold Kaplan
Associate Professor of Political Science
York University, Toronto

N. H. Lithwick
Associate Professor of Economics
Carleton University, Ottawa

A. N. McKay
Research Economist
Department of Municipal Affairs of Ontario

Gilles Paquet
Associate Professor of Economics
Carleton University, Ottawa

Peter C. Pineo
Associate Professor of Sociology
McMaster University, Hamilton, Ontario

D. Michael Ray
Associate Professor of Geography
New York State University at Buffalo

D. C. Rowat
Professor of Political Science
Carleton University, Ottawa

D. W. Slater
Professor of Economics
Queen's University, Kingston, Ontario

Preface

This book emerged from an experiment in cross-disciplinary work launched in Ottawa under the auspices of the Canadian Political Science Association (Ottawa Chapter). During the academic years of 1965-1966 and 1966-1967 a series of seminars dealing with problems of cities and regions in Canada was presented at the Dominion Bureau of Statistics to a study group directed by the editors. This book, which we hope will be of interest to a larger public, is a compendium of these papers.

Many organizations and individuals were involved with the launching of this experiment. Most important among these is Alan Armstrong, the Executive Director of the Canadian Council on Urban and Regional Research, who has provided both moral and financial support for our own research in urban economics and has triggered our interest in greater interdisciplinary dialogue in the area of urban studies. We would also like to acknowledge the collaboration of the two research officers of the Council who have taken great interest in this effort, André Saumier and Robert Cournoyer. Our seminar participants have provided subtle encouragement and direction to our research in a number of useful ways. Finally we wish also to thank Audrey McCallum for her endless patience and care in typing and retyping major portions of this book.

Research Seminar in Urban Economics   N. H. Lithwick
Carleton University   Gilles Paquet
Ottawa, Ontario
Spring 1968

Introduction

1 Prolegomena to Urban Analysis

N. H. Lithwick
Gilles Paquet

The Rise of Urbanology

The trickle of interest in the city that began in the inter-war period now has turned into a flood. All around us there has been growing concern over the problems of the structure of cities, their functioning and their evolution, and in the "interconnectedness of city shape, city movement and city values".[1] Entire issues of the most widely circulated American magazines have been devoted to a panoramic view of the scope and the scale of the problems created by urbanization.[2] Thus, the public at large has been made aware of them. In Canada, the climax of concern was reached at the Federal-Provincial Conference on housing and urban development in Ottawa the week of December 11, 1967.

---

[1] David Riesman, "Some Observations on Community Plans and Utopia", *The Yale Law Journal*, Vol. 57, December 1947.

[2] *Scientific American*, September 1965; *Life*, December 24, 1965; *Saturday Review*, January 8, 1966.

This interest has been deepened by the conviction of scholars that urban issues will prove to be the most important problem of the second half of the twentieth century.[3] Revelations such as the fact that as many persons were urbanized in Quebec in the 1940's as in the entire preceding century, or that there were as many families with income below $3,000 in Montreal and Toronto as in the whole of the Maritime provinces have further awakened the Canadian public to the urban reality.

The field of urban analysis has been given a tremendous impetus by these developments. Many research projects have been launched and entire research institutes brought into being.[4] Partly because of the very recent emergence of academic interest and, as we shall show, partly because of some inherent difficulties in the analysis of complex systems such as cities, we have not progressed much beyond superficial pronouncements about the urban crisis facing our nation of cities.[5] Nevertheless, the newly acquired academic acceptability of urban analysis and the institutionalization of research in this field permit us to conclude that the birth of urbanology has taken place.[6]

Historical Antecedents and Current Analysis

The recency of these developments has led many urban scholars to feel that they were entering an entirely new field. But urban research has a very long history with very impressive credentials dating back to ancient Egypt, to the Greek *polis* and Roman *civitas*, through Pirenne's medieval cities, Renaissance Italy's cities and the cities of the industrialized

---

[3] For example, Wilbur R. Thompson, *A Preface to Urban Economics*, Johns Hopkins, Baltimore, 1965, p. v.

[4] Most impressive in this connection has been the work of Resources for the Future, Inc. through its Committee on Urban Economics.

[5] D. J. Elazar, "Are we a nation of Cities?", *The Public Interest*, Summer 1966.

[6] The ultimate consecration of this name was the *Time* cover of July 28, 1967, featuring Pat Moynihan, urbanologist.

world.[7] As a result we have a substantial stock of descriptive material, including comments, critiques and comparisons of diverse urban phenomena.

Even the antecedent for urban analysis as a discipline *sui generis* goes back at least fifty years. Some of this work developed within the boundaries of the traditional disciplines. For example, in sociology and ecology there was the work of Park and Burgess[8] which found its Canadian interpretation at McGill and Laval Universities.[9] Then there was the pioneering work of Christaller and Lösch in economic geography.[10] In addition, there were several attempts to deal with the urban problems at a cross-disciplinary level, including possibly the work of Bowley and the English authors of the demographic-socio-economic civic surveys.[11]

An important and venerable attitude toward the city has been to visualize it as a global society in the small, because it has "the advantage of mirroring the complexities of society within a frame that respect(ed)s the human scale".[12] Man has been led by this attitude to use the city as a laboratory in which to conduct his social experimentation. Thus, it has been "in terms of the city" that "Utopias from Plato to Bellamy have

7 Robert S. Lopez, "The Crossroads Within the Wall", in Oscar Handlin and John Burchard (eds.), *The Historian and the City*, MIT Press, Cambridge, Mass., 1966, pp. 27-43.

8 R. E. Park and E. W. Burgess, *The City*, University of Chicago Press, Chicago, 1925.

9 J. C. Falardeau, "Problems and First Experiments of Social Research in Quebec", *Canadian Journal of Economics and Political Science*, Vol. 10, No. 3, August 1944.

10 W. Christaller, *Die zentralen Orte in Süddeutschland*, Jena, 1933; A. Lösch, *The Nature of Economic Regions*, Southern Economic Journal, 1938, pp. 71-78.

11 A. L. Bowley and A. R. Burnett-Hurst, *Livelihood and Poverty*, G. Bell and Sons, London, 1915. For a very short but illuminating discussion of this approach and related ones, see L. Chevalier, "Le Problème de la Sociologie des Villes", in G. Gurvitch (ed.), *Traité de Sociologie*, Tome I, Les Presses Universitaires de France, Paris, 1958, Section 3, Ch. 3.

12 L. Mumford, "Utopia, the City and the Machine", in F. E. Manuel (ed.), *Utopias and Utopian Thought*, Houghton-Mifflin, Boston, 1966, p. 3.

been visualized".[13] The consequences of this attitude have been mixed. On the one hand, the need for public policy at the urban level has long been appreciated.[14] On the other, however, the need for a comprehensive understanding of the reality has not been recognized and anything with sufficient aesthetic or fiscal appeal has sometimes been palmed off as urban policy.

Thus, despite long-standing interest in and concern for the city, it has remained a particularly elusive entity. The urban landscape has been examined but the urban phenomenon is still very poorly understood. And while the complexity of the problem is acknowledged in scores of books, nowhere does one find a strategy for the analysis of the urban unit in all its complexity.

This book then is an attempt to find avenues that might lead us toward a global concept of the city.

An Approach to Global Analysis

If, despite the need for a global approach to the urban unit, research has remained partial in scope, the reasons must be clearly understood. All too often research workers are accused of having too narrow a focus on the problem, or their disciplines are viewed as being too compartmentalized to permit cross-disciplinary dialogue. The real difficulties lie on a more basic plane, namely the weakness of the conceptual apparatus for dealing with these complex problem areas or meta-problems.[15]

In a number of ways the problems facing anthropology are analogous to those facing the urbanologist. In both cases the *globality* of the socio-economic-cultural system is fundamental.

---

[13] *Ibid.*

[14] In Canada, an early plea for such policy can be found in Canada, Commission of Conservation, *Report on the Fifth Annual Meeting*, report no. 16: Preliminary Report of the Committee on Town Planning Legislation, Bryant Press, Toronto, April 1914.

[15] The notion of meta-problem has been introduced by Michel Chevalier, *Stimulation of Needed Social Science Research for Canadian Water Resource Problems*, Working paper, Science Secretariat, Ottawa, 1967.

Anthropologists have responded to this problem by introducing the concept of "total social phenomenon" which captures the globality factor at the theoretical level.

Dans ces phénomènes sociaux 'totaux', comme nous nous proposons de les appeler, s'expriment à la fois et d'un coup toutes sortes d'institutions: religieuses, juridiques et morales — et celles-ci politiques et familiales en même temps; économiques — et celles-ci supposent des formes particulières de la production et de la consommation, ou plutôt de la prestation et de la distribution; sans compter les phénomènes esthétiques auxquels aboutissent ces faits et les phénomènes morphologiques que manifestent ces institutions.[16]

> In these total social phenomena, as we intend to call them, all sorts of institutions are expressed simultaneously: religious, judicial and ethical — pertaining both to the family and the body politic; economic — involving particular forms of production and consumption, or rather of collection and distribution; without mentioning the aesthetic phenomena which characterizes these artifacts, and the morphological phenomena through which these institutions are manifested. (our translation)

One could not easily capture the complexity of the urban phenomenon more accurately. It may be possible to eliminate the conceptual bottleneck in urban research by drawing on the experience of anthropologists. However, we cannot lean too heavily on them since Mauss himself, after examining superficially these "total social phenomena", was unable to produce effective tools with which to analyze them.

In part the failure to move beyond the descriptive elegance of total phenomena to its effective analysis is due to the highly aggregative nature of the concept and the global units

---

[16] Marcel Mauss, "Essai sur le Don. Forme et raison de l'échange dans les sociétés archaiques", *Année Sociologique*, 2de Série, 1923-24, t. 1, reprinted in Marcel Mauss, *Sociologie et anthropologie*, Les Presses Universitaires de France, Paris, 1950.

with which it is concerned. Since there is a dearth of tools even for simple aggregation problems, the fact that a break-through has not been made should not surprise us.

By decomposing the aggregative unit into three stages it is possible to fully comprehend the degree of complexity involved. Our particular mode of decomposition is of some interest since at several stages significant advances in aggregation have been made.

The first stage is the aggregation within disciplines, which involves the moving from micro units (individual elements) to macro units (collective elements). This area remains a source of our greatest problems. Even in economics the difficulty has not been overcome.

The second stage involves the integration of various disciplines. So much has been said against cross-disciplinary work that pinning expectations on it might seem naïve in the extreme. However, the independent convergence of many disciplines on the use of systems analysis and its usefulness in examining problems of a cross-disciplinary nature offer real possibilities for important insights into global-type problems. One can cite, for example, the universality of the power formula known as the Pareto law in economics and as the Zipf law in linguistics, and which led to all sorts of rank-size rules. The application of the principle of allometry in the examination of the relative growth of urban and rural components of the whole system is another example.[17]

At both stages, however, meaningful analysis has been retarded by the persistence of superficial classification schemes. The role of this intellectual bottleneck can best be seen by reviewing the zoology books of the eighteenth century. Zoologists of the day used to classify animals by the number of legs or by similar "apparent" criteria. This led experts who were at the mercy of this classification scheme to regard a

---

[17] See G. K. Zipf, *Human behaviour and the principle of least effort*, Addison-Wesley, Cambridge, 1949; R. S. Naroll and L. V. Bertalanffy, "The principle of allometry in biology and in the social sciences", *General Systems*, Vol. I, 1956.

whale as a fish and a bat as a bird.[18] The shift of attention to more fundamental structural features rapidly led to superior classification schemes in the sense that much more of reality could now be understood. In economics, an analogous shift to more useful classification schemes emerged in the work of John Maynard Keynes. Hicks has stressed that the real breakthrough into aggregative analysis resulted from the way in which Keynes decided to aggregate markets into two classes according to their fundamental mode of operation — price-adjusting and quantity-adjusting.[19]

Our contention is that the way to approach globality, which requires an aggregation stage and an integration stage, is to shift the discussion from the level of superficial analogies to basic functional homologies between the many dimensions of the urban phenomenon.

An examination of the components of that phenomenon by a process which would parallel the disassembling of a drum by a child in an attempt to understand the source of the noise would not be particularly useful. Global (total) phenomena can be tackled only at the multi-dimensional level. Any attempt to reconstruct it from partial views would be like attempting to reconstruct a snowstorm from the dew of flakes melting in one's hand (Updike). The analytical process must always preserve globality.

A Global Approach to the City

Our attempt has been to search for the highest common factor among all the dimensions within which previous approaches to the urban unit have been undertaken. This immediately forced us to move from the superficial differences to the functional correspondences. In part this was reflected in a growing recognition by the different analysts that there existed

---

[18] This discussion borrows heavily from the argument proposed by R. Callois, *Méduse et Cie*, Gallimard, Paris, 1960.

[19] J. R. Hicks, "Methods of Dynamic Analysis", in *25 Essays in Honour of Lindahl*, Economisk Tidsckrift, Stockholm, 1956.

some such correspondences in their constructs. In other words, beyond the *ceteris paribus* approach of each discipline there seemed to be a more fundamental level of reality that could enable appropriate aggregation and integration for a cross-disciplinary treatment of the urban unit as a global phenomenon.

From each discipline, as the reader will see, we have succeeded in capturing this effort to go beyond the superficial descriptions. In this process, there has been a convergence from all quarters toward the use of new concepts such as network, system, pattern — all of which may be regarded as an attempt to proceed toward this elusive functional level.[20]

Despite this shift to more functional classification schemes, particularly within the relevant disciplines, the integration stage remains unsatisfactory. For example, economics and geography have moved toward more functional schemes but have done so largely independent of each other. Thus, the geography of urban units has been collapsed into questions of distance, while the economics have been reduced to an examination of quantities. It is only with the stress on totality that some moves toward integration have been possible.

An example of this unfinished process of shifting to a functional classification might be the debate on the classification of land use. The problem is important and has been regarded as an "essential prerequisite of any satisfactory treatment, scientific or practical, of land".[21] However, even though the cost of a defective land use classification for public policy has been estimated as very high, we are still without a satis-

---

20 For instance, the convergence toward systems analysis (on which we will say more in the next part) is clear in geography, economics, sociology and political science. In all but economics, the importance of systems analysis has been acknowledged by the fact that it has now reached the textbook level. The isolationism of economics and the Marxian influence which has stressed the asymmetrical impact of economic activity on the other levels of reality might be partly responsible for this cultural lag and the lesser interest in cross-disciplinary work.

21 R. T. Ely, "Characteristics and classification of land", *Outline of Land Economics*, Vol. 1, Edwards, Ann Arbor, 1922, p. 44.

factory scheme.[22] If too often the classification has been limited by the triviality of the model which generated it the lack of functional classification may well lead in turn to very ineffective model building.

We are forced to realize that the shift to a functional classification is merely a shift to what has been called the underlying or subterraneous reality. To extract this subterraneous reality, new approaches and techniques have proved most useful. General systems analysis and cybernetics have been at the forefront, providing somewhat complementary techniques.[23] These approaches are set directly at the level of wholes and methods of exploration derived from them are already in use. One, factor analysis, deserves some attention as a way to generate a simple structure of factors which would be relatively invariant.[24]

The Role of this Book

We have mentioned that to arrive at cross-disciplinary research, there must be a stock-taking of the literature and the model-building can follow. This book is designed as a survey of the literature on a reduced scale. It presents a sampling of the approaches to the urban phenomenon by the various relevant disciplines. We shall try at the conclusion to evaluate the prospects for developing cross-disciplinary approaches to the urban reality.

One must be careful, in presenting a sampling of the literature, to avoid distorting the whole picture. Thus, we

---

[22] The problem will be discussed at length in our monograph on *Taxation and Urban Land Use*, prepared under a grant from the Canadian Council on Urban and Regional Research.

[23] The former focuses its attention on the functioning of articulated structures while the latter gives an insight into the relationships between the nodes of the network. See the Yearbooks of the Society For General System Research and O. Lange, *Wholes and Parts*, Pergamon, Warsaw, 1965.

[24] On factor analysis, see P. Horst, *Factor analysis of data matrices*, Holt, Rinehart and Winston, New York, 1965.

shall attempt to place our various studies within the corpus of the existing literature on urbanology.

For the purposes of discussion one might separate the literature into three segments:

(a) work on the urbanization process
(b) work on the nature of the city
(c) work on the functioning of the city.

The urbanization process is a crucial factor for sociologists. In their models urbanization is the link between the traditional or folk society and the industrial society. However, they have never made the process explicitly a tool of analysis. In the first place the urbanization process is never really clear. The sociologist has to explain the urban drive in terms of economics. Most of the time he has used the notion of economic function in order to preserve his hegemony on the findings. However, if we forget about the remote past to concentrate on the evolution of society in the last couple of centuries, we might say that Shigeto Tsuru is right in emphasizing that "the economic rationale for the growth of cities can best be described in terms of a conceptual framework which separates as 'external economies' those positive contributions to the rise of productivity which cannot be directly attributed to the individual accounting unit in the system".[25] This enables the research worker to go beyond the usual parallel between urbanization and industrialization. Although the most important externalities may have been captured in the city as an industrial centre, more recently this has not always been the case nor is it a trend which will necessarily be preserved. Moreover, the notion of external economies or diseconomies can be very readily extended to cover a much broader field. For instance it might be suggested that this concept could very easily capture and measure the interaction between individuals which defines urbanism as a way of life. Sociologists have often attempted to define the city in terms

---

25 S. Tsuru, "The economic significance of cities" in Oscar Handlin and John Burchard (eds.), *op. cit.*

of the size of the population aggregate, or in terms of density of settlements, or in terms of the heterogeneity of the inhabitants, social interaction and group life. This last dimension might be regarded as more satisfactory and more accurate for perceiving urbanism as a way of life as the other two are greatly dependent on local circumstances.[26]

This position of the problem fits neatly into current economic thought, for it has enabled economists to proceed with the analysis of urban problems in recent years in the context of a notion of "public economy".[27] Some of the most recent works have indeed emphasized this private-public dichotomy as the key economic factor. In this context the urbanization process becomes the condition of emergence of a large set of externalities which will be examined by the sociologist and the economist along different lines but according to the same fundamental assumption. This type of inquiry has generated some very interesting work in recent years, and we might say that very slowly the demographic notions of urbanization are fading away. This book will give the reader a chance to examine the urbanization process through the eyes of both economists and sociologists. In Part One there will be an attempt to examine the process through which urban externalities permeate the region around a city. In Part Two, a sociologist will examine more carefully the importance of these social externalities in the process of urbanization.

A second segment of the literature deals with the nature of the city proper. This literature has been developed mostly by geographers and sociologists. Both groups have long been interested in the spatial and temporal patterns of cities. A large number of schemes have been suggested to define the

---

[26] A useful density measurement in North America like 50 people per square mile might be very misleading in Japan where intensive farming means often as many as 1,000 people per square mile.

[27] An example of this literature is the present publications of the Committee on Urban Economics, Resources for the Future: H. G. Schaller (ed.), *Public expenditure decisions in the urban community*, Washington, 1963; J. Margolis (ed.), *The public economy of urban communities*, Washington, 1965.

functions of cities, their optimal location and spacing, their optimum size, their demographic structure, their class composition, and their organizational and institutional structures.[28] On this front, a fantastic amount of work has been done but an integrated theory has not yet emerged. In most cases, we are faced with useful observations and much descriptive material which pave the way to future analytical schemes. More recently geographers have developed the most ingenious descriptive schemes and have carefully devised empirical regularities. Functional classifications of cities have been elaborated, anatomization of city functions have been proposed, but as yet no unifying theme exists. Sociologists have been satisfied to examine a host of specific relationships between diverse characteristics of the urban population and urban life. This has led, for instance, to the definition of certain trends in ghettoing activity, to the singling out of the importance of the neighbourhood, to the emergence of recreation as a whole field of investigation and to the study of the relationship between these characteristics and political behaviour.

Economists have too often been tempted to look at the city as a factory; sociologists have become deterministic; and political scientists have dealt with the city as an artifact.

An easier question at this stage, and one which lends itself to analysis especially by economists and political scientists, is the problem of the functioning of the city. Again the notion of externality which is at the crossroads of economics and political science is one of the key issues. Economists have examined carefully the behaviour of economic agents in the private and in the public sector. They have also attempted to shift the debate to a slightly higher level, and they have even suggested the fundamentals of an urban policy. This venture was bound to be somewhat less than perfectly successful because any urban policy model can be meaningful only after one has carefully defined the economic actors and their

---

[28] See P. K. Hatt and A. J. Reiss (eds.), *Cities and Society*, Free Press, Glencoe, Ill., 1957.

interaction in a dynamic context. Two papers in Parts One and Two will attempt to throw some light on this problem and the papers in Part Three will proceed to policy discussion directly.

However, as mentioned earlier, political scientists have also been very interested in the functioning of cities. A paper in the second part will examine the problem of the optimal structure and functioning of cities from a political point of view.

But what about land economics, transportation, the housing market, the construction industry, the problem of location of industry, the ethnic pattern of locational choice, the data bank issue, the administration of cities, the problem of urban poverty, the cultural features of urban life and the social psychology of the suburbanites? These and many other crucial problems will not be dealt with here but have been extensively studied in Canada as well as elsewhere. One must admit that too often these papers are spread among a diversity of journals and are not easily accessible to the casual reader.[29] This set of studies will, it is hoped, begin to overcome the problem of scattered reference sources. We hope to compile a reader on urban problems in Canada in the near future.

The Organization of the Book

The book is divided into three parts. In each, the editors have attempted to introduce succinctly the general set of issues in order to put the papers in perspective. The introduction to each part often complements the papers and indicates a few of the issues in dispute with references to the general theme.

The three parts of the book correspond roughly to the usual partitioning of the problems of cities. In the first part, the possibilities arising from a cross-disciplinary approach are examined. This involves only economics and geography. The second part proposes some modern samples of urban analysis.

---

[29] See, however, Canada Council on Urban and Regional Research, *Urban and Regional References*, Ottawa, 1964, as a first step in assembling a bibliography of research.

Economist, sociologist, and political scientist each presents his tools of analysis. The third part deals with urban policy at both the general and the specific level.

In the conclusion, the editors attempt to draw together the threads of the different arguments in order to suggest the priorities for urban research in Canada.

Part One

Toward
a Cross-disciplinary
Approach

This section of the book attempts to capture the process of convergence of economics and geography toward a middle ground where urban analysis can be fruitfully discussed. Only these disciplines are considered because they have the greatest potential for such integration at this stage. The work in this part surveys an already extensive literature in order to define the trend in dealing with the urban problem.

The three chapters which follow examine the emergence of an economic-geographic perspective from the viewpoint of economists (Chapter 2) and from the point of view of a geographer (Chapter 3) before attention is focused on a problem which appears to lie right at the crossroads of economics and geography — the problem of urban land use (Chapter 4). Although the authors have tackled their problem in different ways, both sides tend to converge rapidly toward a common ground.

In Chapter 2, N. H. Lithwick and Gilles Paquet stress the

economist's perspective. They focus their attention on the
question of land coefficients of different types of economic
activity and show how this concept can be used in conjunction with the geographer's distance variable to explain
changes in the spatial distribution of economic activity. This
approach builds on the Innis-Easterbrook work on centre-
margin interaction and on the frame of reference sketched
by O. D. Duncan *et al.* in *Metropolis and Region*, published
in 1960 by Resources for the Future.

In Chapter 3, D. Michael Ray approaches the problem of
city-region interaction from the viewpoint of geography. He
also deals with the work done by geographers on urban
growth. His point of departure is the concept of distance,
but his survey of the literature reveals at the same time the
value and the limitations of an approach restricted to accessibility considerations. In particular, the primitive notion of
location which ignores the space-using characteristics of economic activity leaves much of the spatial patterning unex-
plained. However, the wide application of the accessibility-
oriented approach and the imaginative hypotheses which can
be derived from it make it difficult to understand why economists have ignored the spatial dimension for so long.

Chapter 4 has an integrating vocation. In the face of the
somewhat narrow conceptualizations of economics and geography, there is a need to construct new concepts which clearly
belong to this common ground at the fringes of the two
disciplines. One such concept is the notion of urban land
use. In their bibliographical essay, Lithwick and Paquet
attempt to specify the genealogy of a meaningful concept of
urban land use. Moreover they suggest a classification scheme
to present the work already done on the problem of land use
and land value. It appears that the development of a number
of economic-geographic concepts is the way to a genuine
cross-disciplinary approach.

The purpose of Part One is therefore both methodological
and bibliographical, although no attempt is made to provide
an exhaustive coverage of a very extensive literature. Moreover

it contains substantive new material on the central place structure of eastern Ontario. Fundamentally we wish to make a case for a refurbished conceptual apparatus which will go beyond the juxtaposition of economic and geographic categories into the development of new economic-geographic concepts. Obviously this could be extended to a broader set of disciplines.

2 Urban Growth and Regional Contagion

N. H. Lithwick
Gilles Paquet

Introduction

This study is an attempt to use the tools of urban economic analysis to shed light on several of the key issues arising from the interaction between city and region.[1] These issues have been considered almost exclusively from the perspective of the regional analyst. It is our contention that as a result the scope of regional policy as now conceived has been severely limited, both because the notion of the region lacks specificity and because the methodology of the regional approach is essentially descriptive and static.

We shall first attempt to give the concept of region some analytical content from which a mechanism for understanding

---

1 The interaction between city and region is a generic term which covers a variety of situations. One may be dealing with a unitary city or with a complex system of cities. And the direction of influence may run predominantly from city to region or vice versa. In order to clarify our discussion, we shall use the following notation: case I, unitary city where the predominant influence runs from city to region; case II, unitary city where the predominant influence runs from region to city; case III, a complex system of cities where the city system is dominant; case IV, a complex system of cities dominated by the hinterland. In this chapter we shall restrict ourselves to the unitary city cases (I and II) and we shall focus our attention on the process of regional contagion — that is, the process through which the city permeates the region (case I).

city-region interaction might be derived.[2] This "model" will then be tested via an attempt to explain the spatial pattern of Canadian economic development. For this purpose, a brief description of the process of economic growth is presented, followed by an analysis of its impact on city-region relationships in Canada. The emphasis on economic structure reflects the biases of the economist. The specific contribution of the urban economist is the consideration of the spatial impact of these structural interdependencies. To the geographer's concept of distance or accessibility, we shall bring the notion of quantity of land or availability[3] in an attempt to discover the spatial implications of this mechanism.

Defining a Region

We are interested at the outset in arriving at a non-empty concept of the region. The notion of region that currently dominates the work of the regionalist is very similar to what Perroux calls a "homogeneous space"[4] — an area that has some element of homogeneity. While even early work stressed

---

[2] This problem has received some attention over the years. One might single out the great impact on Canadian historiography of N. S. B. Gras' concept of the city-centred region and metropolitan dominance in his *Introduction to Economic History*, Harper and Bros., New York, 1922. This has been a recurrent theme in Harold Innis' work — understandably so, since his staples approach was almost congruent with certain forms of metropolitanism. The linkages between the growth pole and its polarized economic space apply equally well to the analysis of the relationships between an urban centre and its hinterland. The similarities between what has become known as the economic-base theory and the staples approach are striking. J. M. S. Careless, "Frontierism, Metropolitanism, and Canadian History", *Canadian Historical Review*, No. 35, 1954; H. A. Innis, *Essays in Canadian Economic History*, University of Toronto Press, Toronto, 1956, passim; R. W. Pfouts (ed.), *The Techniques of Urban Economic Analysis*, Chandler-Davis, West Trenton, N.J., 1960. In more recent years, the same idea has been revived by demographers, and geographers interested in urban analysis. O. D. Duncan *et al.*, *Metropolis and Region*, Johns Hopkins, Baltimore, 1960.

[3] W. Bunge, *Theoretical Geography*, Gleerup, Lund, 1962. Spacelessness is perhaps the weakest link in central place theory.

[4] François Perroux, "Economic Space: Theory and Applications", *Quarterly Journal of Economics*, Vol. 64, February 1950.

homogeneity in several dimensions (for example the work of Weeks and Sametz)[5] factor analysis and the computer now enable the research worker to deal with more complex types of homogeneities.[6] This does not, however, affect the substance of the issue. The word REGION in this sense may be very loosely defined to cover such large aggregates as the Prairies and the Atlantic Provinces[7] in the name of some implicit but rarely defined homogeneity. The same notion is used to deal with sub-provincial entities (Eastern Ontario) or to generate units through the reduction of alternative property-spaces.[8] In all these cases, a region is nothing more than a result of a classification scheme which is nowhere made explicit.

A rather different idea of the region emerges through a refinement of the homogeneity characteristic. The simplest possible scheme is based upon the differentiation between cause and effect, or leader and follower — or more specifically, between the pole and the polarized area. The urban base theorists initially perceived the usefulness of this dichotomy, although they made no serious attempt to go beyond a description of it and the extrapolations based on the simple ratios

5 E. P. Weeks and Z. W. Sametz, *The Economic Zoning of Canada* (1953), *Economic-Administrative Zoning of Canada* (1954), Department of Defence Production Monographs.

6 D. M. Ray and Brian J. L. Berry, "Socio-Economic Regionalization: A Pilot Study in Central Canada", in S. Ostry and T. K. Rymes (eds.), *Regional Statistical Studies*, University of Toronto Press, Toronto, 1966.

7 Economic Council of Canada, *Third Annual Review*, Queen's Printer, Ottawa, November 1966, Chapter 7.

8 The notion of property-space captures the representation in n-dimensions of any given entity. Given n characteristics of a given region more or less arbitrarily selected, one could represent this region as a point in an n-dimensional space. This notion is a simple extension of the Cartesian coordinate system. An IBM card would be a useful physical representation of such an n-dimensional space. Allen H. Barton has shown how we can start with such a property-space and reduce it to fewer dimensions down to a single dimension. This would provide a typology of these entities. If we were to start with n characteristics for a set of regions, we would end up through such a reduction process with a single ordering of regions along one dimension. This would provide a typology of region. See A. H. Barton, "The Concept of Property-Space in Social Research", in P. F. Lazarsfeld and M. Rosenberg (eds.), *The Language of Social Research*, The Free Press, Glencoe, Illinois, 1955.

growing system.[18] On the other, there are
the economy as a highly aggregated market-
explain the trend rates in the aggregates.[19]
es are unsatisfactory for our purposes because
y spaceless. That is, the marketplace being
geographical context; the transactions might
aking place on the moon. Hence the frustra-
ists in such fields as urban and regional

many other criticisms that can be levelled
o approaches is their neglect of such crucial
ructure of industry through which resources
into final goods and services, the distribution
g resource owners, and so forth. We therefore
roduce a disaggregated model of economic
e of revealing the internal workings of an

degree of disaggregation necessarily depends
tions to be answered. Since we are primarily
broad spatial questions, we shall use a level
on that coincides with the major industrial
economy — namely, *primary* or resource indus-
y or manufacturing industries; and *tertiary* or
ies.[20] It will become apparent that a finer
of markets might readily be introduced into
r more specific spatial questions than we raise

ected the concept of market because much of
ysis has been devoted to an understanding of
nd supply are brought into equilibrium within
ket, and how changes in one market affect

is category would be the work of Von Neumann.
cal growth theorists such as Robert Solow operate at this
post-Keynesians such as Sir Roy Harrod.
ies have been used extensively by Colin Clark in his
Economic Progress, Macmillan, London, First edition,

derived therefrom.[9] Certainly the functional relationships between the pole and its polarized area were only recently analyzed.[10]

An advance beyond this limited conception was made by geographers. Central place theory represents an attempt to tie cities and their periphery into functionally meaningful wholes. By this approach a region is defined as a structure of central places. These "urban systems" can be regarded as an X-ray of the region. Certain regional scientists have attempted to examine the evolution of these systems in different Canadian regions.[11] Indeed, Benjamin Ward has stated that the only way to produce a non-empty theory of regional development is to deal with a *region as a structure of cities*.[12]

Our own approach begins with the latter conception of a functional region. We shall continually stress the economic dimension of the region, despite the fact that we recognize other dimensions of that unit. Furthermore, the region will be viewed as a structured reality — that is, it is assumed to have a meaningful and well-defined economic structure. This position leads us to reject the conception of homogeneous space, which is the foundation of most attempts at region-building. Hopefully this avenue holds more promise than the static, rather sterile bookkeeping that has been passed off as regional work in recent years.

Our concept of the city derives from our understanding of the process of economic development, which we shall outline in the next section. Development is too often viewed in a spaceless context, and thus the role of the city is assumed away. As urban economists, we recognize the fundamental complementarity between industrialization and urbanization,

[9] R. W. Pfouts, *The Techniques of Urban Economic Analysis, op. cit.*

[10] Some reference to such work is made in R. W. Pfouts (ed.), *op. cit.* but the most interesting study along this line is by C. M. Tiebout, *The Community Economic Base Study*, Committee for Economic Development, New York, December 1962.

[11] G. Hodge, "Urban Systems and Regional Policy", *Canadian Public Administration*, Vol. 9, No. 2, June 1966.

[12] B. Ward, *Greek Regional Development*, Center of Economic Research, Research Monograph No. 4, Athens, Greece (undated).

the joint product of which is the possibility of specialization and exchange, which in turn lead to the rapid growth of technology that is the main source of economic growth.[13] Thus the city can be defined in terms of some arbitrarily specified threshold of "externalities".[14] One fascinating question that arises from this postulate is the degree to which the ascription of a large portion of modern growth solely to industrialization masks both the unique contribution of urbanization and the joint contribution of the two.

City-Region Interaction

In moving from the definition of region to the analysis of the interaction between city and region, it is useful to note the levels at which work by economists, political scientists, geographers and sociologists has been carried out. One can focus first on the direction of influence between a city and its hinterland, and in addition on the complexity of the structure of city systems.

The degree of complexity of the city systems will directly determine the operational regional unit. At this stage of our work we prefer to concentrate on some of the aspects of the interaction between city and region at the level of the unitary city. This has the advantage of providing us with the smallest possible meaningful regional unit. Once again the aspects of this interaction that we shall stress are the economic, but this is not to deny the relationship between city and region in intellectual and cultural spheres as well.[15]

We shall attempt to perceive how the economic structure

---

[13] "The growth of the modern city and the march of the industrial revolution are joint products of a single cultural strand—specialization." Eric E. Lampard, "The History of Cities in Economically Advanced Areas", in J. Friedmann and W. Alonso (eds.), *Regional Development and Planning*, MIT Press, Cambridge, 1964, p. 331.

[14] S. Tsuru, "The Economic Significance of Cities", in O. Handlin and J. Burchard (eds.), *The Historian and the City*, MIT Press, Cambridge, 1966.

[15] For instance, J. Friedmann, "Cities in Social Transformation", *Comparative Studies in Society and History*, Vol. 4, November 1961.

---

of the city and the
functionally related
that a city as a pro
which polarizes the
must recognize also
significantly on the
aspect has been em
concept of economic
changes in *city-regio*

Our emphasis on
region is an explicit
these units. A city m
recreation; it is also
Similarly a region is
unit. In this paper w
scheme enables us to
more meaningful set
method.[16]

We will first exar
between city and regi
the "regional relations
tive, these relationshi
mechanism. Furthermo
explaining *changes* in
following section such

The Process of E

Economists have taken
the analysis of economi
one hand, there are tho
single market situations

---

[16] See A. Chaîneau, "Un Mod
çais", *Revue d'Economie P*

[17] R. E. Dickinson, "The Reg
and A. J. Reiss, Jr. (eds.), C
Illinois, 1957.

---

conditions for a
those who view
place and seek t

Both approach
they are entirel
examined has nc
just as well be
tion of econom
economics.

Among the
against these tv
factors as the s
are transformed
of income amor
propose to in
growth, capabl
economy.

The optimal
upon the ques
concerned with
of disaggregati
segments of the
tries; *secondar*
service industr
differentiation
the analysis fo
here.

We have se
economic anal
how demand
a given mar

---

[18] Included in th
[19] The neo-class
level, as do th
[20] These industr
Conditions o
1940.

equilibria in related markets. Since this notion of related or linked markets will be the focal point of our subsequent analysis, it bears some elaboration. Essentially the relationships between markets are of three sorts: forward linkages, backward linkages and final demand linkages.[21] The first relates to the impact of a commodity on markets using it, the second to its impact on the markets for primary and intermediate inputs being used to produce it; and final demand relates to the impact of the spending of incomes paid to input owners on all final demand markets. Thus any change in the demand for or supply of a commodity will affect those markets linked to it through all three channels.

This interdependence of markets is best summarized in an input-output table. This table relates all markets to all primary inputs, to all intermediate users and to all final users.

In economics, we are concerned with the use of primary inputs to satisfy society's final demands. The industrial sector can be viewed as the transformer through which demands are channelled and inputs are distributed to meet them via the provision of goods and services. This can be schematized as follows.

TABLE 2-1

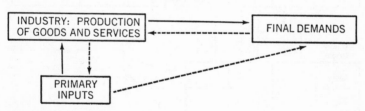

The service and commodity flows are described by the solid arrows; the financial flows by broken arrows. The fact that

---

[21] The first two concepts have been most fully elaborated by A. O. Hirschmann, *The Strategy of Economic Development*, Yale University Press, New Haven, 1958. The third is due to M. H. Watkins, "A Staple Theory of Economic Growth", *Canadian Journal of Economics and Political Science*, Vol. 29, May 1963.

incomes paid to inputs finance final demands is represented
by the broken arrow between these cells.

An input-output table is a detailed description of these
relationships. Primary inputs include labour, capital and land;
final demands include consumption, investment, government
and foreign demands. The industrial transformer-distributor
is of particular interest because it can be broken down into
as fine a level of industrial detail as is required. For our
purposes, we shall be content to specify three industrial
classes: primary (resource-based), secondary (manufacturing)
and tertiary (services). The detail is organized in the following
table.

TABLE 2-2

The sum of the income of primary inputs is National
Income. Its disposition between sectors of final demands and
between types of goods and services is shown in the final
demand matrix.

Most critical is the transformer-distributor. To clarify its meaning, we have inserted some letters for easy recognition. The level of final demand for the output of primary industry by consumers is denoted by A. However, this does not constitute all of the output of that industry, since some goes to manufacturing such as industrial raw materials (B), some goes to tertiary industry (C), and some goes abroad under aid programs (D). For purposes of exposition, we assume that no output goes to the government and investment sectors. The total output of primary industry is thus $(A+B+C+D)$ and the share to final demand is $(A+D)$.

The production of this output depends on the volume of inputs used. This industry may use h units of labour, i units of capital and j units of land. It also uses inputs from manufacturing (k), such as tractors, and from tertiary (l), such as government extension services. The payments for these primary and industrial inputs (payments to h, i, j, k and l) is equal to the revenue derived from selling the output $A+B+C+D$ (profit is included in the payments to primary inputs). It is this income which permits spending.

As we shall show, an economy's final demands shift from primary to secondary to tertiary commodities as income grows. This leads to a restructuring of the transformer-distributor from one where the centre of gravity is first at the top left-handed cell $(A+B+C+D)$, to one where it is at X and eventually to where it is at Y. This restructuring leads to a change in the input mix required, since the technologies in the three sectors are quite different. This in turn affects the level and distribution of income, and ultimately society's spending decisions.

This framework can be used to examine the process of growth in terms of its industrial impact and resource use as well as in terms of the aggregates. The neo-classical approach is based largely on an examination of the interaction between primary inputs and final demand, with the industrial impact all but ignored. Consequently any possibility of spatial analysis is eliminated. As we shall show in the next section, the more detailed framework permits us to deal with this problem because industries do have specific locational requirements.

Let us first sketch the process of economic growth in Canada using this framework. The initial impact on the economy resulted from the foreign demands upon Canada's resources or "staples". This led to an accumulation of capital and labour capable of providing these resources, and so the first type of market for resources was developed. As the demand for these exports grew, the incomes of the owners of these inputs grew apace. This led to a set of final demands which, in the early stages, focused primarily on food. Food supplies could be provided domestically because of the growing labour force and the accumulation of savings out of rising incomes. As a result, the agricultural market began to emerge. As would be expected from Engel's law,[22] the increase in incomes that resulted from the expansion of first resources and then of agricultural markets were devoted increasingly to the acquisition of manufactured non-food commodities. At the outset the supply of manufactured goods came mainly from abroad, but as the labour force and stock of capital continued to grow and the domestic market achieved an adequate scale, manufacturing began to replace importing. The process has continued, with an increasing proportion of domestic income being spent first on manufactured goods, and then on services. Technical changes and capital accumulation in manufacturing and primary industries led to a displacement of the labour force, which then found employment in the provision of these tertiary outputs. Canada's most recent experience has seen the very rapid growth of these service markets.

In our input-output table, we see a gradual transition in the importance of these three sectors from left to right. Lacking input-output tables for all but one year (1949) we can trace these changes only through an examination of the changing final demand weights of these three sectors. These are summarized in the following table.

---

[22] The tendency for the share of agricultural goods in consumption to decline as income rises was first noted by C. L. Ernst Engel in 1895.

TABLE 2-3

STRUCTURE OF FINAL DEMAND IN CANADA
1870-1965

Year	Share in Output*		
	Primary	Secondary	Tertiary
	%	%	%
1870	51	25	24
1920	29	32	39
1926	23	26	51
1965	14	32	54

*The measures of output are not exactly comparable. The first set (1870-1920) are based on GNP and are derived from M. C. Urquhart and K. A. H. Buckley, *Historical Statistics of Canada*, Macmillan, Toronto, 1965, Series E214-E244. The latter (1926-1965) are based on GDP and are from the DBS *National Accounts, Income and Expenditures*. Primary includes all resource industries; Secondary, manufacturing and construction, and Tertiary, the rest.

The changing centre of gravity of the economy from resource industries to manufacturing and then to services is readily seen in Table 2-3. While this superficial description of growth merely illustrates how the bare bones of the conventional growth models can be given substance, the implications of this approach are critical for the analysis of the spatial distribution of economic activity.

City-Region Interaction in Canadian Economic Development

The impact of economic development on the spatial distribution of economic activity is dramatic. It leads to changes in the structure of cities and regions and thereby to changes in the optimal spatial arrangement between and within them.[23]

23 Brian J. L. Berry, "City size distribution and economic development", *Economic Development and Cultural Change*, Vol. 9, July 1961. This constitutes, however, only a limited aspect of the problem. See also G. Hodge, *op. cit.*

In analyzing the impact of development on urbanization — that is, these changes in the relationship between city and region as the city grows from a trade centre stimulated by hinterland development (case II) to an urban node polarizing an area (case I) — we have probably underemphasized the converse process, namely, the impact of urbanization on economic development. This section examines how a simple linkage model applied to some historical examples reveals the reversal of city-region relationships as development proceeds, and the growing importance of cities as sources of growth.

The critical result of the changing structure of industries in the course of economic development is the fact that this leads to coincident shifts in the location of economic activity. So long as an economy is devoted to resource exploitation, economic activity is largely tied to the spatial imperatives imposed by these resources. In Canada, the critical staples such as fur, timber and wheat were diffused across the continent. Therefore, isolated markets developed with relatively weak linkages to other domestic markets. In such a situation, the regions of economic activity were defined by the limits of resource availability. The emergence of towns can be explained in terms of central place theory as centres servicing the resource developers. The nature of the resources, however, made the linkages within the regional economy weak relative to external ties.

For example, because of backward linkages to the markets for capital equipment and labour regional towns were usually bypassed in the labour and capital scarce economy of the early period. These linkages were basically with European and United States factor markets, with some impact on the main domestic ports and railheads that serviced the flows of these inputs.

Forward linkages had some impact on regional towns because of their collecting function. But once again, the key forward linkages were the foreign markets for the resources, and, indirectly, the domestic port cities.

Final demand linkages had their major impact on regional

towns, particularly in markets for consumer goods. In the earliest stages most consumer goods were imported. The ports, and then the towns, served primarily as distribution centres. As income and population in the dynamic resource activities expanded, port cities could begin to substitute domestic production for imports; even regional towns could follow suit in activities with low level economies of scale.

The emergence of towns and port cities, therefore, was dictated in the first instance by the dynamics of their resource base. The location and growth of the urban centres depended directly on the region defined by the resource activity.

As incomes grew, however, these relationships began to shift. The more rapidly a service centre grew in response to final demands, the greater became its role as a market place for the primary inputs, labour and capital. This permitted the establishment of forwardly linked markets as well, which by and large were part of the manufacturing sector. These in turn had forward and backward linkages, and so, in regions with healthy resource development, the cities that emerged became self-sustaining growth poles.[24] The reasons for the collection of secondary and tertiary industries in dense spatial clusters are clear: economies of scale in production and distribution, strong industrial interdependence in secondary activity, the availability of sophisticated labour and capital markets with their high degree of mobility, and so on. In contrast, regional towns based on static resource activity remain to this day service towns with little self-sustaining power. As incomes grew, the share of resources in final demand declined rapidly, as we have seen. More and more final demand was focused on manufacturing and related service industries. The result is that most urban centres are no longer dependent on their regional hinterland. The linkages in an urban milieu are entirely intra- and inter-urban. Forward linkages to users and backward linkages to suppliers are all part of the urban

---

[24] The critical level has been described as a ratchet mechanism by W. Thompson in his *Preface to Urban Economics*, Johns Hopkins, Baltimore, 1965, pp. 21-24.

complex. The non-urban proportion of our population is now too small to serve even as a major market for urban products, and certainly its role as a supplier of primary inputs, particularly labour, is limited. Similarly, final demand linkages are extremely weak as very little of the urban consumer's income flows back to resource industries. When the 1961 input-output table becomes available, the exact degree of this shrinking of the resource sector, and hence the expansion of urban activities, will become known.

What is clear from this analysis is that, despite their original dependence on regional economic viability, cities are now the determinants of that viability. In areas where cities have failed to emerge, depressed rural conditions prevail, whether around the coal mines of Nova Scotia, the wood lots of New Brunswick or the rural slums of Eastern Ontario. This lesson must be well understood, for those who argue for industrial development to offset rural depression miss the mark entirely. The problem is lack of cities, not industries. To thrive, industries require the full range of urban amenities, such as convenient transportation, skilled labour and ready markets. An industry placed in a depressed area will function only at the level of its environment; it will not raise the economic level of the surrounding area. Because manufacturing industries locate in cities, economic growth has been attributed to industries. However, as we have seen, there are overriding economic reasons for their location in urban environments. A good many consultants and regional development officers ignore this fact at their peril.

In highly productive, advanced economies, a new shift is taking place that may have revolutionary locational impacts. The growth of manufacturing activity has come to depend more and more on two primary inputs: labour and technological change. The market for activities producing these inputs is thus a key backward linkage for the current growth poles, and has been of increasing importance since about 1950.

The main institutional locus of this marketplace has been the university and the research and development laboratory.

These are "footloose" industries because both forward and backward linkages have very little space friction. Scientists and academics are highly mobile, and information which is the key output of their activities can be transmitted at zero or low cost. Since these and the final demand linkages are very powerful, and since these activities are likely to become major growth poles, their locational pattern will be crucial. Probably they will locate in cities because of a variety of service linkages, but there is no measure of the type of city that will be chosen. Indeed, it is often claimed that such factors as climate and nearness to the ocean are the most important locational variables.[25] An additional implication is that the tie between these activities and the urban hinterland will become increasingly weak, the latter coming to be almost entirely dependent upon its urban nexus.

Spatial Implications: Regional Contagion

The preceding analysis has revealed the structural changes inherent in a developing economy. Because of the differing locational requirements of the various activities, a necessary change in the relationship between city and region emerges. The polarized area becomes the growth pole and vice versa. In this section we shall examine the spatial implications of this reversal.

The analytical tool that can most usefully help explain these changes is based on a land use classification procedure. Conventional land use classification schemes rooted in the thinking of the 1920's have proved to be quite inappropriate for other than descriptive purposes. One possibility is to classify markets by their spatial adjustment mechanism. The one overriding dichotomy is between availability or quantity-adjusting and accessibility or distance-adjusting markets. This points up the fact that different types of markets have different

25 D. Allison, "The University and Regional Prosperity", *International Service and Technology*, April 1965.

spatial needs as reflected in the relative importance of quantity of space and proximity to certain loci. If one could determine the coefficients for these elements and their paths through time for various activities, one could obtain an operational mechanism for tracing the path of spatial development.

A second instrument that we shall have space only to suggest is based upon the changes in the nature of externalities in the urban unit. In the early stages the externalities provided by the city are mainly on the production side. Gradually, as the city becomes more and more self-sustaining, in the course of development, externalities on the consumption side grow in importance. As the shift to the consumption of services proceeds, an increase takes place in the consumption of those services required equally by all urbanites. Therefore participation by government in the life of the city becomes increasingly necessary. When this process is grafted to the spatial changes wrought by development, conflicts between political and geographic boundaries emerge. Thus one might observe increasing urban isolation with diminishing contagion throughout the region — an example of a dual economy type of development — or one might see urban sprawl across the face of the region. Let us apply these concepts to our model to examine the implications in more concrete terms.

Perhaps the critical differences between city and region can be traced to the essential differences in the spatial constraints in urban as opposed to regional economies.

In the latter the location problem is primarily one-dimensional; the only variable is proximity or distance. When we turn to the urban unit, a second dimension emerges — the problem of the quantity of space, which in this context becomes a scarce resource also. Thus, locational decisions of firms as well as households are complicated by the need to select an optimal combination of quantity and distance. This problem is particularly difficult to handle both theoretically and practically.[26]

---

[26] A recent commentary suggested that the residential land use market was really *availability adjusting*. This was ascribed by the commentator to the agrarian vision of North American urbanites. D. J. Elazar, "Are we a nation of Cities?" *The Public Interest*, Summer 1966.

Consequently, we are faced with urban units that are congested at the core and suffering costly urban sprawl at the fringes, as individuals and firms attempt to achieve optimal balance between their taste for proximity to the city centre and for ever larger amounts of land which can be satisfied only at the fringe.[27]

The implications of economic and industrial growth for the urban-rural penumbra is the invasion of rural areas by the urban unit. As cities grow, the demands for increased space lead to settlement beyond the legal boundaries of the city. This creates both political and economic problems.

The political problem has to do with the growing estrangement between the boundaries of the legal entity and the functional entity. The emergence of new legal entities, or the expansion of formerly rural townships into suburban entities, to service this population spillover leads to a host of inefficiencies in the duplication of municipal services and the use of land. Unfortunately, the pursuit of political power prevents rapid adjustment to changes in the urban reality and results in high long-run costs to society. The search for broader governmental units has been the main response to this problem. Paradoxically, the name for these units is "Regional Government". The wheel appears to have come full circle. Regions are now entirely urban oriented.[28]

The economic problem has to do with the roles of speculators at the urban fringe. Since the adjustment process for most urban land users appears to be most heavily directed to the quantity side rather than the location side (the exception being commercial units that are almost exclusively location-adjusting), the process of urban growth leads to ever-increasing

---

[27] Given the nature of the amenities valued by firms and households, the notion of accessibility may or may not involve a high price for proximity to city centres. Certain businesses need a location in the central business district, others need to be part of a cluster which may or may not be located at the city centre. See L. K. Loewenstein, "The Location of Urban Land Uses", *Land Economics*, Vol. 39, November 1963. The same argument would hold for diverse sets of households for, depending on their composition and socio-economic characteristics, they might value differently proximity to various amenities.

[28] See Harold Kaplan's paper on Metropolitan Toronto, Chapter 6.

demands for space. The desire for proximity also precludes the availability of such space within the urban unit. As a result, the value of land at the fringe undergoes rapid inflation making it a natural asset for speculation. Favourable tax treatment of such land encourages the process and thus more land at the fringe of the city is held idle. Since the flow of this land into the hands of developers is artificially constrained, the direction of the city's growth is determined in a less-than-optimal manner. And so ribbon development and sprouting hamlets requiring costly extensions of municipal services have plagued urban planners for decades. To the extent that this process takes place in outlying townships, and often is encouraged for selfish fiscal reasons by them, the political and economic problems are merged, rendering solutions even more difficult.

These are but two examples of the multitude of issues that can be analyzed within the framework of a developmental model with spatial dimensions. Several attempts to derive some of the relevant coefficients suggest that this approach might provide substantial analytical power.[29]

Implications and Limitations of the Approach

This mechanism has a variety of interesting features which have not been discussed at any length here. For example, it has rather serious implications for both understanding and analysis of regional problems. Central place theorists have accustomed us to the partitioning of urban systems into types of trade centres. However, if the very nature of the relationship between city and region changes through the process of

[29] J. Rannells, *The Core of the City*, Columbia University Press, New York, 1956. The author is one of the first to perceive the relationship between quantity and distance and to try and define some general patterns. See also L. K. Lowenstein, *The Location of Residences and Work Places in Urban Areas*, Scarecrow Press, New York, 1965. This focuses primarily on the accessibility attribute, and is thus in the tradition of most location theory. It is the attempt to derive patterns of location by type of industry that makes this work of particular interest.

development, as we have argued, then a new dynamic mechanism must be provided to study these relationships over time.

Our analysis implies that whereas cities were largely dependent upon regional development for their initial growth, in Canada this process has reversed through the dynamic changes in industrial structure in the course of economic development. The industrial focal points of economic growth are found in an urban environment, and the economic health of a region is now a function of the viability of the city within it. To the extent that there are no cities, regions tend to be depressed, except where profitable resource activities persist, such as in northern Ontario, the Prairies and British Columbia.

Furthermore, the degree of remaining linkages between city and region serves to define the economic potential of a region. Where the region serves as a backwardly linked market to cities, supplying labour services in particular, there will be income spillover beyond the city's boundaries. Some agricultural activity serving the city may also prosper if comparative advantages exist; but in the light of Engel's law and the rapid rate of growth of agricultural technology, one should expect a rapid decline in the importance of this form of economic activity.

Thus the problem of rural poverty grows apace. Increasingly regions find themselves in a deteriorating economic position and this has led to a demand for a regional development policy. As we have seen, the implementation of industry as a solution misses the point, since industrialization can lead only to self-sustaining growth in an urban marketplace where industrial interdependencies are maximized.

However, we would need an expanded volume to deal with the whole situation. The process of intercourse between periphery and centre is only part of the picture.

The junction of these urban areas (or more accurately of these urban nodes) will define an urban system. The *"effet d'agglomération"* and *"effet de jonction"* examined by Chaîneau were only a first useful approximation. Hodge's hierarchy of trade centres and Berry's distribution of city sizes were also only first approximations. The real work on the spatial dimension (both at the unique and the structure-of-cities level) remains to be done.

An important dimension of our preliminary work here at the unique city level is that of establishing the structure of the elementary region. It is then possible to proceed to partitioning a nation's total space into a maximum number of structured units. However, such a process may not succeed in accounting for the whole spatial dimension of the nation. It may also happen that the sum of these "agglomerations" will be different from the whole "urban system". Therefore, one should be very careful not to infer too much from Case I analysis.[30] However, none of these problems appears to be insurmountable. For if one can account in this way for only 25 per cent of the physical or banal space, about 95 per cent of the population will probably be represented. As for the second problem, it only means that the *effet d'agglomération* is not sufficient to explain the whole process, as has already been recognized by Chaîneau.

Another important limitation is the one mentioned at the beginning concerning our emphasis on the economic aspects of the *city-region* relationship. The civilization effect of cities, the cultural effect, the participation in the jet set and the paraphernalia of *external benefits* flowing from the cities to the hinterland have been largely ignored. A more thorough analysis would require that the Tsuru argument be tackled completely. According to Tsuru,[31] a city *would* grow up to the point when external malefits plus direct malefits would, at the margin, just equal external benefits plus direct benefits. The student would then be able to link the size of the city to the degree of publicness of a city's output-mix. The degree of publicness could then be mapped on a spatial dimension. The idea of "range of a good" produced by some central place theorists is a first step in this direction.

---

[30] See p. 18.
[31] S. Tsuru, *op. cit.*

Conclusion

It appears from our analysis that many of our present problems in both the urban and the regional environment stem from what may be called an agrarian or peasant view of economic reality. The changes brought about on the spatial organization of society as a result of economic development make this view archaic and irrelevant. Since it prevails in the hearts and minds of our policy-makers,[32] it is little wonder that we have been notoriously unsuccessful in coping with both our urban and our regional problems.

This paper has kept the discussion at a fairly general level in order to suggest a series of hypotheses capable of throwing some light on the penumbra between *city* and *region*. Our approach has asymmetrized the problem insofar as it has linked the relationship between *city* and *region* to the stage of development.

---

[32] A calculation of the average number of employees in various federal government departments in the first quarter of 1966 validates this contention. The number of employees in the departments concerned with primary industries is 16,300 (Agriculture, Fisheries, Forestry, Mines and Northern Affairs), whereas in industry-related departments, the number is 14,800 (Industry, Trade and Commerce, Labour, and the Unemployment Insurance Commission). This is remarkable considering that less than 15 per cent of the GDP originated in the primary industries. DBS, *Federal Government Employment*, April 1966, Table 11, pp. 32-35.

3 Urban Growth and the Concept of Functional Region[1]

D. Michael Ray

Introduction

Urban growth is dependent upon the number and types of goods and services provided for functional regions and is related to the size and population of the functional regions served. The usual cliché is that cities do not thrive where people merely take in one another's washing. "Cities do not grow up of themselves. Countrysides set them up to do tasks that must be performed in central places."[2] The tasks set reflect geographic location. There is, therefore, a sequential relationship between geographic location, urban functions, functional regions and urban growth. The form of sequential relationship is traced in this bibliographic essay by examining

1 The research on industrial location in Ontario was supported by the (American) Social Science Research Council. The research on consumer travel behaviour was conducted at the University of Ottawa with the assistance of students of the Department of Geography, including Gary Nadon, Brendan M. Hamill and Carl Smith.

   Additional maps and diagrams were prepared at Spartan Air Services by Robert Carstens with support from the Agricultural and Rural Development Administration. I also gratefully acknowledge the valuable comments and criticisms received from Drs. Brian J. L. Berry, Chauncy D. Harris, Harold M. Mayer, Gerard Rushton, Leroy Stone and Maurice Yeates.

2 Mark Jefferson, "The Distribution of the World's City Folks: A study in Comparative Civilization", *Geographical Review*, Vol. 21, 1931, p. 453.

the nature and type of urban functions and functional regions, and by reviewing the contribution of location theories to understanding the size and spacing of urban functions and urban places. The relationship is then illustrated by focusing attention on one area, Eastern Ontario, where urban growth has been retarded by the slow expansion of manufacturing industry and is dependent largely upon the central place functions performed.

Urban Functions

The relationship between urban growth and functional regions is clarified by partitioning urban functions into activities that are city-serving, or non-basic activities, and those that are city-forming or basic.[3] Non-basic activities are those services and functions that a city provides for its resident population and are not shaped by the location of the city. "Basic urban functions involve the processing or trading of goods or the furnishing of goods and services for residents or establishments located outside of the urban area."[4]

Basic activities show greater contrasts among urban places than do non-basic activities and thereby serve as a valuable guide to functional classification.[5] Examination of basic functions indicates four distinct types of city: (1) *central places*

[3] The economic base concept is reviewed by Harold M. Mayer, "A Survey of Urban Geography", in Philip M. Hauser and Leo F. Schnore (eds.), *The Study of Urbanization*, Wiley, New York, 1965, pp. 83-86; Wilbur R. Thompson, *A Preface to Urban Economics*, Johns Hopkins Press, Baltimore, 1965, pp. 27-30; and O. D. Duncan, *et al.*, *Metropolis and Region*, Johns Hopkins Press, Baltimore, 1960, pp. 23-36. Five studies on the economic base of cities are reprinted in Harold M. Mayer and Clyde F. Kohn (eds.), *Readings in Urban Geography*, University of Chicago Press, Chicago, 1959, pp. 85-126.

[4] Mayer, *op. cit.*, p. 83.

[5] For a review of urban classification systems, see Robert H. T. Smith, "Methods and Purpose in Functional Town Classification", *Annals of the Association of American Geographers*, Vol. 55, September 1965, pp. 539-548.

which provide retail and other tertiary services to their trade areas; (2) *transportation centres*; (3) *manufacturing centres*; and (4) *special-function centres*, such as government, administrative, religious or military centres.[6]

The distribution of basic functions among cities is related to the spatial elasticity of demand for those functions. The spatial elasticity of demand is the measure of distance decay, or the rate at which supply of a good or service from a city declines with distance from that city. Where the elasticity and hence the distance decay are high, as in the case of low-order retail services, the function has a ubiquitous distribution. For high-order manufactured goods, the distance decay is low, and the function becomes sporadic and found in only a few urban places.

Urban places with economic functions of a ubiquitous nature can be expected to serve only small functional regions, to have a limited growth potential and to have a regular distribution pattern. Accelerated urban growth depends upon the ability of a city to develop "national-market activities" which have a low distance decay. Walter Isard relates the population rank of a city within a country to the number of national-market area activities which it captures, while at the same time retaining all its "non-national" activities.[7]

The concept of basic functions thus stresses the economic ties which bind a city to its region and which links urban growth to the size of the region. Unfortunately, urban economic base studies have not generally been concerned with identification of the areas to which basic functions export, nor with the concept of functional region.[8] The section which follows reviews the concept of region and the factors influencing the location of boundaries of functional regions.

---

[6] Chauncy D. Harris and Edward L. Ullman, "The Nature of Cities", *Annals of the American Academy of Political and Social Science*, Vol. 242, November 1945, pp. 7-17, reprinted in Mayer and Kohn, *op. cit.*, pp. 277-286.

[7] Walter Isard, *Location and Space Economy*, MIT Press, Cambridge, Mass., 1956, pp. 55-60.

[8] Duncan *et al.*, *op. cit.*, p. 33.

The Concept of Functional Region

The area over which an urban centre provides services and functions is termed a functional or nodal region, or simply market area or hinterland. More generally, a functional region is "an area in which one or more selected phenomena of movement connect the localities within it into a functionally organized whole".[9] Except for the smallest urban centres and for the lowest-order functions, the market area includes other urban places as well as rural areas.

The "outer range" or "farthest possible range" of a functional region is defined as the point at which transportation costs to the consumer or producer reduce effective supply or demand to zero. The distance of the outer range from the urban centre depends on the spatial elasticity of demand, or distance decay, of the function. The lower the distance decay, the greater the agglomeration or concentration of industry and the larger the economic region.

The higher the distance decay, the less likely it is that the economic region will extend to the outer range. As functions disperse to produce a true network of regions rather than concentrating in a punctiform agglomeration, the more likely it is that the "real range" will be set by competition from other urban centres offering the same function. The real range occurs at the line where total costs for a service or good from two competing centres (that is, the cost of the good at each centre plus transportation costs) are equal. The line along which alternate centres can provide a function at equal cost is termed the "line of indifference".

A review of location theories in the next section suggests

9 Brian J. L. Berry and Thomas D. Hankins, *A Bibliographic Guide to the Economic Regions of the United States*, Department of Geography Research Series No. 87, University of Chicago, Chicago, 1963, p. x. See also Derwent Whittlesey, "The Regional Concept and the Regional Method", in P. E. James and C. F. Jones (eds.), *American Geography: Inventory and Prospect*, Syracuse University Press, Syracuse, 1954, pp. 21-68; and Richard S. Thoman and Gerald McGrath, "Regional Statistics and Their Uses: A Geographic Viewpoint", in S. Ostry and T. Rymes (eds.), *Regional Statistical Studies*, University of Toronto Press, Toronto, forthcoming.

that the line of indifference delimiting a functional region is rarely sharp. Complicating factors, such as multi-purpose travel behaviour, tend to produce a decreasing allegiance away from the region's urban centre until a zone of indifference is reached.

Furthermore, both the outer range and the real range of a function may be changed by pricing policy. An equalizing delivered-price system, or single or multiple basing-point systems of pricing practically eliminate market boundaries and may extend the range to the national market area.[10] Basing-point price systems have been used extensively by processing industries to retain their locational advantage and to maintain their market area in face of possible competition from firms at new locations.[11] Basing-point price systems have now been declared illegal by the United States Supreme Court, and the market areas there can be expected to become more sharply defined.[12]

An examination of the relationship between functional and other types of regions shows that the size and shape of market areas and functional regions is not determined by economic factors alone. Functional regions are conceptually distinct from the two other types of regions recognized by geographers but they are not independent of them.

The other two uses of the term "region" that geographers distinguish are the general region and the homogeneous or formal region. The first is most frequently used in Canada in a general sense to refer to an administrative unit or contiguous group of units, such as a province or a group of counties or municipalities. A homogeneous region is "an area within which the variations and co-variations of one or more selected characteristics fall within some specified range of variability

10 See Melvin L. Greenhut, *Plant Location in Theory and Practice*, University of North Carolina Press, Chapel Hill, N.C., 1956, pp. 23-83, and Appendix V, pp. 308-316.

11 Gardner Ackley, "Price Policies", *Industrial Location and National Resources*, National Resources Planning Board, Washington, 1942, pp. 302-303.

12 Frank A. Fetter, "Exit Basing Point Pricing", *American Economic Review*, Vol. 38, 1948, pp. 815-827.

around a norm, in contrast with other areas that fall outside the range".[13]

Functional regions are affected by the homogeneous and administrative regions in which they are located. Brian Berry, for example, has established that different systems of cities and different sizes of functional regions can be identified for different homogeneous agricultural regions by the different farm population densities supported in each agricultural region.[14] This study shows that Eastern Ontario may be divided into two homogeneous cultural regions and that the boundary of some functional regions is displaced from the line of economic indifference to the cultural boundary.

The boundaries of homogeneous physical regions, instead of delimiting the functional boundaries of existing towns, may lead to the establishment of new urban places to perform transportation functions at break-of-bulk points, such as coastlines, or to trade between the contrasted products of different physical regions.[15]

The boundaries of political regions tend to restrict functional regions. Lösch illustrates this effect by mapping the financial sphere of influence, or functional region of El Paso, on the United States-Mexican border.[16] The reduced market area south of the border accords with his theoretical statements.[17] Mackay succeeded in measuring the reduction in interaction across the Quebec-Ontario and Quebec-United States borders.[18]

---

[13] Berry and Hankins, op. cit., p. x.

[14] Brian J. L. Berry, "Cities as Systems Within Systems of Cities", Papers and Proceedings of the Regional Science Association, Vol. 13, 1964, pp. 147-163.

[15] Gordon East, The Geography Behind History, Nelson, London, 1938, pp. 91-92.

[16] A. Lösch, Die raumliche Ordrung der Wirtschaft, translated by W. H. Woglom and W. F. Stolper as The Economics of Location, Yale University Press, New Haven, 1954, p. 448.

[17] Ibid., p. 341.

[18] J. Ross Mackay, "The Interactance Hypothesis and Boundaries in Canada: A Preliminary Study", Canadian Geographer, No. 11, 1958, pp. 1-8. Julian V. Minghi reviews studies of political boundaries as locational factors in "Boundary Studies in Political Geography", Annals of the Association of American Geographers, Vol. 53, 1963, pp. 407-428.

Although the size and shape of functional regions is modified by non-economic factors, economic location theories do contribute to an understanding of the distribution of functions among urban places and of the interrelationship between urban growth and functional region. Location theories should relate urban functions to location; unfortunately, research has tended to treat function and location as separate problems.

Location Theories

The location theories reviewed in this section, central place theory and industrial location theory, apply to only two of the four main urban types noted earlier, namely, central places and manufacturing centres. These two types are the most important, however. Eric Lampard, for example, divides the history of definitive urbanization into two phases, classic and industrial, with central places dominating in the first phase, and the second phase witnessing the rise of the industrial city.[19] The theoretical review attempts to explain differences in the size and spacing of central places and manufacturing centres. It emphasizes one common element in the two bodies of theory, namely: distance decay or the spatial elasticity of demand.

Central Place Theory

The foundations of central place theory were laid by Walter Christaller in 1933.[20] Brian Berry and Allen Pred have summarized the six main features of Christaller's theory as follows:

>   (1) The main function of a city is to be a central
>   place providing goods and services for the market

---

[19] Eric Lampard, "Historical Aspects of Urbanization", in Hauser and Schnore, *op. cit.*, pp. 519-554.

[20] Walter Christaller, *Die Zentralen Orte in Suddeutschland*, Gustav Fischer Verlag, Jena, 1933. Christaller's concepts were introduced to the English language literature by Edward Ullman, "A Theory of Location for Cities", *American Journal of Sociology*, Vol. 46, May 1941, pp. 835-864, reprinted in Mayer and Kohn, *op. cit.*, pp. 202-217.

area; therefore, cities are located central to the maximum profit area they can command.

(2) The greater a city's centrality, the higher its order.

(3) Higher order places offer a larger range of goods and services, but are more widely spaced than lower order places.

(4) Low order places offer goods purchased frequently or convenience goods.

(5) A hierarchy of central places exists.

(6) Three hierarchies may be organized according to,
   (a) a market principle,
   (b) a transportation principle, and
   (c) an administrative principle.[21]

Lösch elaborated Christaller's work by demonstrating that Christaller's hexagonal market areas were optimal for consumers and entrepreneurs.[22] He also showed that Christaller's three hierarchies of market areas were special cases of the ten smallest hexagonal market areas that combine to form an economic landscape with six city-rich and six city-poor sectors around the regional capital.[23]

Brian Berry and William Garrison have shown that Christaller's theory is more limited than Christaller thought, because not all cities are primarily central places; it is also more general than Christaller believed because it applies to shopping centres within cities.[24] This broader application of central place theory emerges when it is reformulated in terms

[21] Brian J. L. Berry and Allen Pred, *Central Place Studies: A Bibliography of Theory and Applications*, Regional Research Institute, Philadelphia, 1965, pp. 3-4.

[22] Lösch, *op. cit.*, pp. 105-114.

[23] *Ibid.*, pp. 114-137.

[24] Brian J. L. Berry and William L. Garrison, "A Note on Central Place Theory and the Range of a Good", *Economic Geography*, Vol. 34, October 1958, pp. 304-311 and Brian J. L. Berry and William L. Garrison, "Recent Developments of Central Place Theory", *Papers and Proceedings of the Regional Science Association*, Vol. 4, 1958, pp. 107-120.

Figure 3-1. Relationship of Trade Areas of Central Places to Total Population Served and to Gross Population Densities.

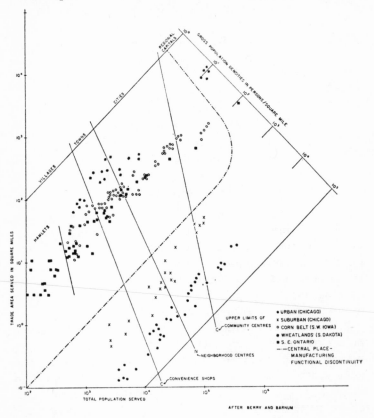

AFTER BERRY AND BARNUM

of its two essential concepts, "range of a good" and "threshold". The outer range of a good is the maximum distance that persons travel for that good. The inner range of the good is the distance enclosing the minimum number of consumers required to support the function. Threshold is "the minimum amount of purchasing power necessary to support the supply of a central good from a central place".[25] The number of establishments providing a function that can

25 *Ibid.*, p. 111.

be supported in an area is equal to the total purchasing power divided by the threshold. For higher order functions, requiring large thresholds, fewer establishments can be supported. A hierarchy of central places and of shopping centres within central places emerges which is indicated by the number of central functions that a central place or shopping centre contains, and by the total market area and total population which it serves.

Figure 3-1 illustrates the relationship of trade area served to total population served for systems of central places in six homogeneous regions.[26] The structure of these systems shows a remarkable consistency. The hierarchy of the central places in all regions, except Eastern Ontario, has been identified by use of a direct factor analysis. The upper limits of the groups of villages, towns, cities and regional capitals are linked by straight lines which intersect the Eastern Ontario system at the points suggested for it by changes in central functions performed.

Examine the central place systems for the agricultural regions in Figure 3-1. The higher the gross population density, the smaller the functional region but the larger the population served by a centre at a given level of the urban hierarchy. Thus, the spacing of these central places increases as the farm population density, which supports the basic urban functions, decreases. Moreover, the central place systems for these agricultural regions are grouped closely together, except for their regional capitals which tend to have much higher ranges and which serve much larger populations. The shopping centres for Chicago and suburban Chicago are also separated from the central place systems in the agricultural regions. It may be postulated that this separation is produced by the additional functions, primarily manufacturing, but also transportation and special functions, which the regional capitals and urban and suburban Chicago have acquired. The

---

[26] Figure 3-1 is copied from B. J. L. Berry and H. Barnum, "Aggregate Relations and Elemental Components of Central Place Systems", *Journal of Regional Science*, Vol. 4, Summer, 1962, Figure 2, p. 40, with the Eastern Ontario central places added.

separation may be termed, therefore, a "functional discontinuity". Urban places may cross this boundary and extend their area or population served only by obtaining these additional functions.

The lowest total population served by a level of the hierarchy in Figure 3-1 may be used as a measure of "threshold" or "condition of entry", provided that it is assumed that purchasing power is homogeneously distributed. The maximum range of each level of the hierarchy coincides with the threshold value of the next higher level of the hierarchy. The range of any level of the hierarchy cannot long exceed the threshold of a higher level before the additional functions that can be supported by the larger population are acquired, and the central place advances to the next higher order of the hierarchy. The growth of central places is limited by the size of the population in the maximum profit area that each place can command. An equilibrium necessarily exists between the size and the spacing of the central places.

The equilibrium in a central place system between the size and spacing of the central places is attained when the demand density per unit area lifts the range of the good above the threshold. Where the range of a good includes less purchasing power than the threshold value, activities are mobile. James Stine has illustrated this case in a study of travelling merchants and periodic markets in Korea.[27] The *distance* between the market centres that a mobile merchant must serve is dependent on the range of the good. The *number* of market centres he must serve is dependent on the threshold. Activities survive only where the cycle of the merchant's movements is short enough to offer to the customer the requisite frequency for that service and where the marginal costs of serving the additional markets to reach the threshold value do not exceed the resulting marginal revenue. Mobile markets are replaced by permanent markets and a

---

27 James H. Stine, "Temporal Aspects of Tertiary Production Elements in Korea", in Forrest R. Pitts (ed.), *Urban Systems and Economic Development*, School of Business Administration, University of Oregon, Eugene, Oregon, 1962, pp. 68-88.

regular pattern of central places crystallizes when the increase in the demand density per unit area lifts the range of the good above its threshold.

Changes in retailing technology, in population density and in income after the equilibrium between range and threshold is established and permanent markets or central places created produce shifts in the equilibrium.[28] Few studies of changes in central place systems have been made and all have encountered serious difficulties because of data deficiencies and because of changes over time in types of function and institutions providing central functions.[29] Nevertheless, these studies suggest that villages will share the same fate as hamlets, now in the final throes of decline, as a result of advances in technology and the consequent improvements in transportation and increased specialization in retailing.

The provision of central functions in larger but fewer stores is paralleled in metropolitan areas. Berry finds that a 5.87 per cent decrease per year in the number of retail establishments in Chicago can be attributed to technological trends.[30] These technological effects are modified by changes in population density and income. Changes of one per cent in real income have produced an average 0.87 per cent change in number of establishments. The net effect of technology and income changes in Chicago has been to produce a 2 per cent decline in retail establishments in higher income communities,

---

[28] Brian J. L. Berry, *Commercial Structure and Commercial Blight*, Department of Geography Research Series No. 85, University of Chicago, Chicago, 1963, pp. 161-177.

[29] Jacob Spelt, *Urban Development in South Central Ontario*, Van Gorcum and Company, Assen, Netherlands, 1955; H. Carter, "Urban Grades and Spheres of Influence in Southwest Wales", *Scottish Geographical Magazine*, Vol. 71, 1955, pp. 43-48; H. Carter, "The Urban Hierarchy and Historical Geography", *Geographical Studies*, Vol. 3, 1956, pp. 85-101; R. E. Dickenson, "The Distribution and Functions of the Smaller Urban Settlements in East Anglia", *Geography*, Vol. 17, 1932, pp. 19-31; R. E. Dickenson, "Markets and Market Areas of East Anglia", *Economic Geography*, Vol. 10, 1934, pp. 172-182; Brian J. L. Berry, "The Impact of Expanding Metropolitan Communities Upon the Central Place Hierarchy", *Annals of the Association of American Geographers*, Vol. 50, 1960, pp. 112-116.

[30] Berry, *Commercial Structure and Commercial Blight*, p. 173.

a 4 per cent decline in low income communities, and a 5 per cent decline in transition communities with falling socio-economic status.

By undermining villages and hamlets, as well as convenience shops in larger urban centres, changes in retailing technology are producing an effect on the growth of central places similar to Wilbur Thompson's "urban size ratchet" in the growth of metropolitan centres.[31] Central places that have failed to reach "town" or higher status can expect future functional development only if technological effects are off-set by a growing population and increasing socio-economic status in the functional region that they serve.

The focus by Berry and Garrison on the key concepts in central place theory of range of the good and threshold has been used to stress the relationship between growth of central places and number of central functions, and to reveal the equilibria within systems of central places between central functions and population of functional regions. Further insights on the relationship between city and region are obtained by reviewing range of the good in the framework of the broader concept of distance decay within which range of the good may be embodied.

Distance or interactance decay measures the decline in the demand for goods and services at an increasing distance from a central place. Distance decay is equivalent, therefore, to the spatial elasticity of demand. Distance or interactance decay is the structural element of the interactance or gravity concept which states that interaction between two masses is proportional to their sizes and inversely proportional to some function of their distance apart.[32] The interactance concept was first applied in central place studies by W. J. Reilly in 1929 to delimit the line of indifference, or the functional boundary between competing central places.[33]

---

[31] Thompson, *op. cit.*, pp. 21-24.

[32] See Walter Isard *et al.*, *Methods of Regional Analysis: An Introduction to Regional Science*, MIT Press, Cambridge, Mass., 1960, pp. 494-499.

[33] W. J. Reilly, "Methods for the Study of Retail Relationships", *University of Texas Bulletin*, No. 2944, 1929.

Clearly, the aggregate movement of consumers into a central place for all goods and services decreases with increasing distance from it. A central place offers all services with thresholds below the total purchasing power of the population located within its maximum functional region. But not all services are provided to all customers within that maximum functional region from a single central place. Other smaller central places nest within its maximum functional region to provide low-order services. The empirical study of Eastern Ontario in this paper shows, for example, that city-level central places do not provide food, auto repair, banking and other low-order services to all of their medical and dental service regions. The frequency and intensity of aggregate consumer travel to cities drop beyond the ranges where they can perform hamlet, village, and town level functions.

Distance decay has also been observed in the pattern of consumer travel behaviour for single services. J. D. Nystuen found in an analysis of consumer travel in Cedar Rapids, Iowa, that distance decay was higher for single purpose trips than for multipurpose.[34] The average distances travelled for multipurpose shopping trips was greater because householders may bypass the nearest store offering one service they need and instead "attempt to get maximum return from total travel effort needed to fulfill all the purposes combined on the trip".[35]

More recently, Gerald Rushton has determined the effect of differences in family income and in grocery expenditures on travel grocery purchases in Iowa State and has developed a space preference model which reveals a decreasing allegiance to a central place with increasing distance from it.[36] Applying this model to the town of Humboldt, Iowa, he predicts

---

[34] William L. Garrison *et al.*, *Studies of Highway Development and Geographic Change*, University of Washington Press, Seattle, 1959, p. 213.

[35] *Ibid.*, p. 212.

[36] Gerald Rushton, *Spatial Pattern of Grocery Purchases by the Iowa Rural Population*, Studies in Business and Economics, New Series No. 9, University of Iowa, Iowa City, 1966.

that beyond five miles of Humboldt, more than 25 per cent of families have a secondary grocery expenditure town and near the boundaries of Humboldt's functional region for grocery services, more than 75 per cent of the families have a secondary expenditure town.[37]

In summary, growth of central places is related to the equilibrium between the population served and the functions acquired. The greater the population that can be served from a central place in competition with other places, the higher the order of the functions that can be supported. Higher order functions have higher thresholds and are more widely spaced. The equilibrium between the population served and functions acquired is translated into an equilibrium in the size and spacing of cities. Both equilibriums are shifting ones, primarily because of changing technology. An urban ratchet effect may be observed in which central places with only hamlet or village status are usually slipping back, while higher order centres have their growth achievements locked in. A functional discontinuity is evident between the ranges and population served by regional capitals and metropolitan and suburban shopping centres, and by other central places in agricultural regions. This suggests that a marked growth of an urban place and its functional region occurs when central place functions are supplemented by manufacturing and other activities. The acquisition of manufacturing activity and the acceleration of urban growth may be explained by the industrial location theories reviewed in the next section.

Industrial Location Theories

The contribution of industrial location theories to understanding urban growth is limited by their restricting assumptions and by their concern with the location of individual establishments. These theories cannot be extended easily to explain regional patterns of manufacturing location in the real-earth space.

---

[37] *Ibid.*, p. 59.

Alfred Weber, in his seminal work, was concerned primarily with determining the location of lowest production costs for an establishment serving a single city market with inelastic demands.[38] An industrial plant would deviate from the point of lowest aggregate transportation costs and labour costs to serve two or more city markets only where the deviation costs are exceeded by the agglomeration economies, or economies of scale. Weber treats agglomeration economies as a local factor operating within the general framework formed by the regional factors, transportation and labour costs.[39]

Later studies extended the market from a single point to a straight line and dealt with the interdependence of two establishments under non-elastic and elastic market conditions.[40] Fetter was the first to determine the size and shape of market areas for given plant locations on a homogeneous plain.[41]

Lösch has criticized the unrealistic assumptions and the unusual locational problems in these studies and goes on to develop a three-level typology of industrial concentration and size of economic region. The highest level is termed a "puncti-form agglomeration" and occurs where the individual locations of the function coincide in a single urban centre or group of centres to serve the national market. Lösch gives the example of "factories producing men's collars, practically all of which are situated in Troy, New York, but whose market includes the whole of the United States".[42] An intermediate level of concentration, identified as "areal agglomeration",

---

[38] Alfred Weber, *The Theory of Location of Industries*, 1909, translated by Carl J. Friedrich, University of Chicago Press, Chicago, 1929. Reviews of this and other studies are contained in William L. Garrison, "Spatial Structure of the Economy", *Annals of the Association of American Geographers*, Vol. 44, 1959, pp. 232-239 and 471-482; and Vol. 50, 1960, pp. 357-373.

[39] *Ibid.*, p. 124.

[40] H. Hotelling, "Stability in Competition", *The Economic Journal*, Vol. 39, 1929, pp. 41-57, and A. Smitties, "Optimal Location in Spatial Competition", *Journal of Political Economy*, Vol. 49, June 1941, pp. 423-440.

[41] F. Fetter, "The Economic Law of Market Areas", *Quarterly Journal of Economics*, Vol. 38, 1924, pp. 520-529.

[42] Lösch, *op. cit.*, p. 11.

is subdivided into belt locations and district locations. In belt locations, the market network is compressed, (for example, the market for cotton gins is compressed into the cotton belt). In districts the centres are compressed but the markets are separated. An example is coal mines in a coalfield. The lowest level of concentration is for such commodities as bread. Lösch describes bakeries as having no concentration and "forming a true network of regions".[43]

Lösch's typology may be interpreted as selecting three critical stages in distance decay, or range of the good, with the highest distance decay for bakeries, and a low distance decay for men's collars.

Figure 3-2. Market Potential in Canada.

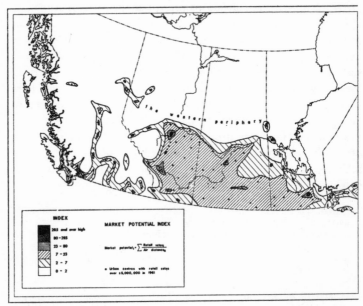

Harris applied the concepts of distance decay and gravity or interactance to measure aggregate accessibility from any

---

[43] *Ibid.*

point to the total market.[44] The measure, termed "market potential", is defined mathematically at a point (P_i) as the sum (Σ) of each market (M_j) divided by its distance (d_{ij}) from that point; that is, market potential at $P_i = \Sigma_j \left(\dfrac{M_j}{d_{ij}} \right)$ where the distance for measuring self-potential (d_{ij}) is an assigned constant. The point of highest market potential for the United States is New York and for Canada, Toronto (see Figure 3-2).[45] These two points offer the greatest accessibility to the national markets and national market area activities can be expected to gravitate toward them accelerating their rate of growth.

There is evidence that market is growing in importance as a factor in industrial location and that the amount of second-

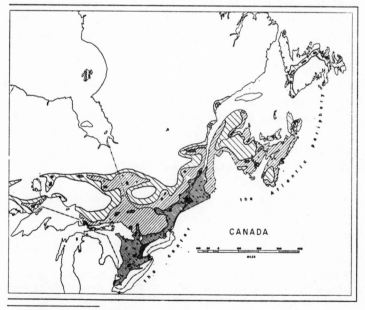

[44] Chauncy D. Harris, "The Market as a Factor in the Location of Industry in the United States", *Annals of the Association of American Geographers*, Vol. 44, December 1954, pp. 315-348.
[45] The distance decay exponent of 1.42 used in Figure 3-2 has been determined by an analysis of Canadian commodity flows.

ary manufacturing industry that an urban centre can acquire depends on its market potential. The growing importance of market is attributed by Harris to increased fabrication in finished products, greater efficiency in the use of raw materials, and improved transportation.[46] George Borts finds that differences in regional growth patterns are to be "explained by a difference in production functions or in the demand for a region's exports", and his findings provide "strong support for a model of regional growth based on the demand for a region's exports".[47] Victor Fuchs endorses the role of markets in determining changes in the location of industry.[48] Duncan finds that secondary manufacturing is highly correlated with population-potential and that deviations of manufacturing from market accessibility are attributable to the locational pull of mineral deposits.[49]

The market potential concept, introduced into industrial location theory by Harris, cannot entirely explain regional patterns of secondary manufacturing location. In particular, it does not take into account source of capital and industrial organization on location. Kenneth Hare has stressed the crucial importance of finance capital in economic development, and notes that the origin of finance capital is a more powerful determinant of location than the so-called "geographic" factors.[50] Origin of capital is particularly important where location decisions are made by head offices of multi-establishment firms. These location decisions will reflect the locations of the head office and its establishments for, as

46 *Ibid.*

47 George H. Borts, "The Equalization of Returns and Regional Economic Growth", *The American Economic Review*, Vol. 50, June 1960, pp. 319 and 343.

48 Victor F. Fuchs, "The Determinants of the Redistribution of Manufacturing in the United States Since 1929", *The Review of Economics and Statistics*, Vol. 44, 1962, pp. 167-177.

49 Duncan *et al.*, *op. cit.*, pp. 126-128, pp. 165-166, pp. 209-226, and Otis D. Duncan, "Manufacturing as An Urban Function: The Regional Viewpoint", *Sociological Quarterly*, Vol. 1, April 1960, pp. 75-86.

50 F. Kenneth Hare, "A Policy for Geographic Research in Canada", *Canadian Geographer*, Vol. 8, 1964, p. 115.

Lösch has said, "we are largely free to select our location. This is influenced, though not dictated, by our place of origin".[51]

The empirical section of this paper uses the concept of "economic shadow" to measure accessibility to finance capital and entrepreneurship.[52] Like range of the good and market potential, economic shadow employs the distance decay concept. It states that the likelihood of a manufacturer establishing a branch plant in a city is inversely proportional to that city's distance from the manufacturer. For example, the numerical difference between the ninety-eight branch plants in Metropolitan Toronto controlled by head offices in Chicago and the twenty-eight controlled from Los Angeles is largely explained by the greater distance of Los Angeles from Toronto. The primary element of economic shadow is sectoral affinity which states that branch plants tend to be located in the sector lying between the head office and the primary market centre within a region. Industrial interactance between a part of a region and a city beyond that region is impeded wherever the primary market centre of the region becomes an intervening opportunity. An "economic shadow" is thus cast over the area lying beyond the spatial sector linking a head office to the primary regional market centre. Urban growth may be retarded in areas of high economic shadow, irrespective of their market potential and accessibility to the national market. Urban growth is concentrated instead on what John Friedmann and William Alonso term "development axes".[53]

Despite the many gaps in the literature, it has been possible to trace the sequential relationship among geographic location, urban functions, functional regions and urban growth. Urban growth depends ultimately on geographical location and accessibility. In the early phases of definitive urbanization, the economic foundations of urban growth are low order

51 Lösch, op. cit., p. 1.

52 D. Michael Ray, Market Potential and Economic Shadow, Department of Geography, Research Series No. 101, University of Chicago, Chicago, 1965.

53 John Friedmann and William Alonso (eds.), Regional Development and Planning, MIT Press, Cambridge, Mass, 1964, p. 3.

central place functions. Geographic location is then to be interpreted merely as the degree of centrality to the surrounding rural area. Urban growth accelerates where special functions, such as transportation, administrative, mining, religious and military are acquired. The growth of these functions must also reflect geographic location. Resources and attributes of an area can be developed beyond local demand only if the area is favourably located in relation to other centres of population, even though all other requirements for its growth may be fulfilled.

Technological developments, primarily by improving transportation and reducing the friction of distance, and by increasing income and demand density, permit the establishment of higher order central functions and the creation of a hierarchy of networks of market regions. The geographic location and centrality of an urban place must then be measured in terms of larger areas including other urban places.

Once technological developments give rise to the industrial city, geographic location must be interpreted in terms of sub-national and national market areas. Higher order manufacturing has a low distance decay and becomes concentrated into areal and punctiform agglomerations. The ability of an urban centre to capture national and sub-national market area activities and to enjoy sustained growth can be measured by its market potential. Nevertheless, urban growth is retarded in areas of high economic shadow. These relationships are illustrated in the study on eastern Ontario which follows.

Eastern Ontario

United States Branch Plants in Southern Ontario

Eastern Ontario lies in the Canadian heartland, which comprises the densely populated St. Lawrence Lowlands and southern Ontario, and which contains over half the eighty

Canadian cities with populations over 10,000. The heartland stands out as a plateau of high market potential (see Figure 2-2), and all but two of the cities over 10,000 are classified by J. W. Maxwell as having manufacturing as their dominant function (see Table 3-1).

TABLE 3-1

FUNCTIONAL CLASSIFICATION OF CANADIAN CITIES

Region	Central Place	Trans-portation	Manufac-turing	Other	Total
Periphery	7	5	18	5	35
Heartland	1	—	43	1	45
Total	8	5	61	6	80

Note: Maxwell uses the minimum requirement approach of Ullman and Dacey to measure functional structure and to classify the cities. The study is for all urban areas with population over 10,000

Source: J. W. Maxwell, "The Functional Structure of Canadian Cities: A Classification of Towns", *Geographical Bulletin*, Vol. 7, No. 2, 1965, pp. 79-104.

Southern Ontario has led Canada since Confederation in levels of urbanization and manufacturing. Data released by the Dominion Bureau of Statistics show that Ontario has generally been a decade ahead of any other region in Canada in achieving given levels of urbanization and, in 1961, was the only province with more than three-quarters of its population classified as urban (see Table 3-2).

TABLE 3-2

CENSUS YEARS IN WHICH CANADA AND THE MAJOR REGIONS HAD REACHED OR SURPASSED SELECTED LEVELS OF URBANIZATION

	Levels of Urbanization[1]				
	25%	35%	50%	65%	75%
Canada					
Maritimes	1891	1901	1931	1961	—
Quebec	1901	1921	1961	— [2]	—
Ontario	1881	1891	1911	1941	1961
Prairies	1911	1951	1961	—	—
British Columbia	1891	1891	1911	1951	—

[1] The level of urbanization is measured by the percentage of population classified as urban.

[2] In this table, the dash indicates that the area in question had not attained the pertinent level of urbanization as of 1961, according to the source data.

Source: Table released by the Dominion Bureau of Statistics, Demographic Analysis and Research, Census Division, from the census monograph on urban development in Canada.

The considerable postwar growth of secondary manufacturing industry in Canada has been concentrated in parts of southern Ontario, particularly the Toronto metropolitan area and southwestern Ontario. In comparison, eastern Ontario's industrial growth has been retarded.

The sharp contrast between the rates of growth for southwestern Ontario and Toronto metropolitan area and for eastern Ontario is not confined to manufacturing. Factor analyses of socio-economic characteristics reveal the interdependency of rates of economic growth, population growth, age and sex structure, cultural characteristics, and housing conditions. They indicate that the regional contrasts in rate of economic development constitute the fundamental factor in the geography of Ontario.[54]

Donald Kerr and Jacob Spelt have shown that these contrasts cannot be explained satisfactorily in terms of internal factors, such as market potential, labour costs or labour stability. They conclude that other factors must be responsible for regional differences in rates of industrial location and economic growth.[55] A more recent study finds a high correlation coefficient between manufacturing and market potential $(r = .87)$ but with systematic overpredictions for eastern Ontario, and underpredictions for southwestern Ontario and Toronto.[56] These regional differences are related to "the regional impact of United States capital and entrepreneurship operating through an economic-shadow effect on Ontario manufacturing and development".[57] The failure of eastern Ontario to achieve more rapid economic development is due largely to the factors affecting the location of branch plants of United States subsidiaries.

One half of the manufacturing in Canada is owned and controlled by United States nationals.[58] American ownership

[54] D. Michael Ray and Brian J. L. Berry, "Socio-Economic Regionalization: A Pilot Study in Central Canada", in Ostry and Rymes, *op. cit.*; Brian J. L. Berry, "Identification of Declining Regions: An Empirical Study of the Dimensions of Rural Poverty", in W. D. Wood and R. S. Thoman (eds.), *Areas of Economic Stress in Canada*, Industrial Relations Centre, Queen's University, Kingston, 1965, pp. 22-66; William H. Bell and Donald W. Stevenson, "An Index of Economic Health for Ontario Counties and Districts", *Ontario Economic Review*, Vol. 2, September 1964.

[55] Donald Kerr and Jacob Spelt, "Some Aspects of Industrial Location in Southern Ontario", *Canadian Geographer*, No. 15, 1960, pp. 12-25.

[56] Ray, *op. cit.*, pp. 76-88.

[57] *Ibid.*, p. 15.

[58] Dominion Bureau of Statistics (DBS), *Canada's International Investment Position 1926-1954*, 1956, pp. 9-47. Harry G. Johnson, *The Canadian Quandary*, McGraw-Hill, Toronto, 1963. United States Department of Commerce, *U.S. Business Investment in Foreign Countries*, Office of Business Economics, Washington, 1960; and Raymond Mikesell (ed.), *U.S. Private and Government Investment Abroad*, University of Oregon, Eugene, 1962. An establishment is generally considered to be foreign controlled where 50 per cent or more of the voting stock is held in any one foreign country. Exceptions occur. See Canada, DBS (1956), *op. cit.*, p. 24.

of the automobile and rubber industries is almost complete although, by contrast, American ownership of the beverage, textile, and steel industries is negligible.

The location of United States branch plants is related to their need to maintain close contact with the parent company, particularly in the early stages of their organization. Among larger, wholly-owned United States subsidiaries in Canada, for instance, more directors live in the United States than in Canada (see Table 3-3). American branch plants "tend, therefore, to be located in regions which are near the parent company and the main industrial centres of the northern United States from which, in many cases, they draw complex parts, technical services or management and supervisory advice",[59] and are concentrated in Southern Ontario, the closest and most accessible part of Canada to the United States manufacturing belt.

TABLE 3-3
RESIDENCE OF DIRECTORS OF 105 DIRECT INVESTMENT COMPANIES

Residence of Directors	Wholly-Owned Subsidiaries	Partially-Owned Subsidiaries	Total
United States	219	155	374
United Kingdom	11	38	49
Canada	199	284	483
Total Directors	429	477	906

Source: Irving Brecher and S. S. Reisman, Royal Commission on Canada's Economic Prospects, *Canada-United States Economic Relations*, Queen's Printer, Ottawa, 1957, p. 134.

---

[59] Royal Commission on Canada's Economic Prospects, *Canadian Secondary Manufacturing Industry*, D. H. Fullerton and H. A. Hampson, Ottawa, 1957, p. 46. Unfortunately, they do not elaborate. A DBS survey of some 771 establishments of the larger United States controlled firms in Canada showed that these larger firms alone provided nearly one third of the manufacturing employment in Ontario, but less than a twentieth in the Atlantic provinces. DBS, 1956, *op. cit.*, pp. 90-91.

Examine the relationship between the number of Ontario subsidiaries and the number of manufacturing establishments in each Standard Metropolitan Statistical Area (SMSA) and the distance of these SMSA's from Toronto shown in Table 3-4.[60] In general, the number of Ontario subsidiaries controlled from any United States city is directly proportional to the number of establishments in that city and inversely proportional to its distance from the province. These relationships, when written mathematically as an interactance or gravity model, give accurate estimates of the number of subsidiaries controlled from each United States city.

Figure 3-3. The Ontario Location of United States Subsidiaries.

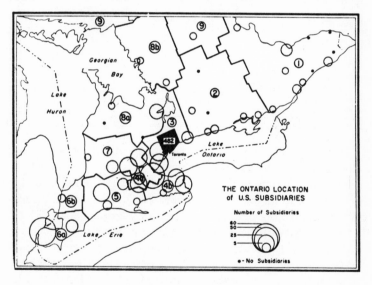

---

[60] The data used to test the economic shadow concept are the addresses of United States manufacturing parent companies and their Ontario subsidiaries. All parent companies in the United States Standard Metropolitan Statistical Areas (SMSA's) with 40,000 or more manufacturing employees have been cross-tabulated by their Ontario address. This sample numbers a thousand parent companies, two thirds of all United States parent companies with Ontario subsidiaries.

Figure 3-4. The Location of United States Parent
Companies with Ontario Subsidiaries.

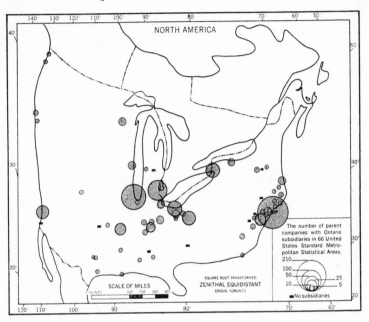

It follows that economic development within Ontario must
closely reflect the economic health of those United States
regions contiguous to the province. Compare the maps of the
Ontario locations of United States subsidiaries and the location of United States parent companies (Figures 3-3 and 3-4).[61]
The proximity of the American Midwest industrial concentration to southwestern Ontario compared to the distance
between the New York region and eastern Ontario is reflected
as a contrast between the number of subsidiaries in southwestern and eastern Ontario.

Two other factors are evident in the location of United
States subsidiaries in Ontario. Figure 3-5, which links by

---

61 The square roots of the graticule co-ordinates have been used to draw
  this map. The importance of any United States industrial centre to
  Toronto is directly proportional to its proximity on the map.

Figure 3-5. Industrial Desire Lines.

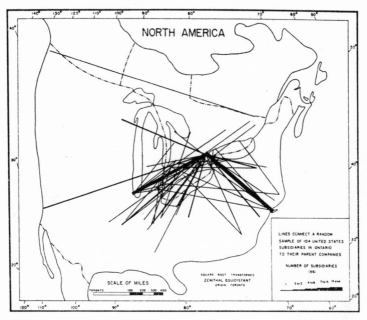

desire lines the location of a hundred Ontario subsidiaries, selected at random, to their parent companies in the United States, reveals a pattern of geographic *sectoral affinity*; subsidiaries tend to be located in the geographic sector that links the parent company to the primary Ontario market centre, Toronto. Of 210 Ontario subsidiaries with parent companies in the New York metropolitan area, 179 are in Toronto or locations closer to New York. Toronto provides the optimal market location for American subsidiaries and few subsidiaries locate beyond it. An Ontario city suffers economic shadow whenever Toronto constitutes an intervening opportunity between it and a United States city.[62] Toronto impedes eastern Ontario's interactance with all United States industrial centres except those in New England and adjacent states.

[62] S. A. Stouffer, "Intervening Opportunities and Competing Migrants", *Journal of Regional Science*, Vol. 2, Spring 1960, pp. 1-26.

TABLE 3-4

THE LOCATION OF UNITED STATES SUBSIDIARIES
IN SOUTHERN ONTARIO BY SUB-REGIONS

United States SMSA	A	B	1	2	3	4a	4b	5	6a	6b	7	8	9	Total Ontario
Akron	698	336			9	2	1	1			1			14
Boston	5,665	690		2	8	4								14
Buffalo	1,820	96		1	10	2	17	1			3			34
Chicago	13,508	702	5	7	98	11	3	6	5	6	4	2		147
Cincinnati	1,776	660	2		12	2		2						18
Cleveland	3,898	306	1	1	28	9	6	1	1		2	1		50
Columbus	835	506			7			1		1		6		15
Detroit	6,468	340	4		26	6	1	3	37	3	9			89
Los Angeles	16,910	3,496			28	1		1	1	1	3			35
Milwaukee	2,298	693			10	1			1			1		13
Minn.-St. Paul	2,433	1,111	2		13			1				1	2	19

	A	B	1	2	3	4a	4b	5	6a	6b	7	8	9	Total
Newark	4,425	539			14				1	1			2	2	20
New York	39,396	557	7	7	145	12	8	11	3		11	3	3	210
Philadelphia	8,124	534	1	2	19	5	1	2			2	1		33
Pittsburgh	2,479	363			19	4	5				7			38
Rochester	1,015	152			10		2					1		13
St. Louis	3,150	1,065	2	1	13	2	4	1			1		5	29
Toledo	742	409	7		1	1			3		2	1	1	15
Total	24	28	469	62	42	40	54	15	48	18	6			806

Source: Compiled from a list of parent company addresses supplied by the Ontario Department of Economics and Development.

Note: A = Number of manufacturing establishments 1958. B = Distance from Toronto by air (km).

1 = Eastern Ontario	3 = Metropolitan Toronto	6a = Lake St. Clair: Border
2 = Lake Ontario	4a = Burlington	6b = Lake St. Clair: Lambton
	4b = Niagara	7 = Upper Grand River
	5 = Lake Erie	8 = Georgian Bay
		9 = Northern Ontario

These regions are mapped in Figure 3-12 which shows the distribution of subsidiaries by county.

Hence, sectoral affinity parallels the effect of economic inter-actance to augment the contrast between the number of subsidiaries in southwestern and eastern Ontario.

A third element is apparent from a comparison of the Ontario location of the thirty-five Los Angeles and the thirty-four Buffalo subsidiaries (see Table 3-4 and Figure 3-5). Buffalo has ten subsidiaries in the Toronto region compared with twenty-eight for Los Angeles. Seventeen of Buffalo's subsidiaries are in the adjacent Niagara region. A pattern of *sectoral penetration* occurs in which the distance that a parent company penetrates into Ontario to locate a branch plant is directly proportional to the distance of the parent company from Ontario.[63] The Detroit manufacturer can evade the Canadian tariff barrier and the prejudice against foreign products by locating a branch plant across the St. Clair River. The marginal benefits of locating closer to the centre of the Canadian market may not compensate for losing the convenience of operating the subsidiary close to the parent company. The marginal effort required by the Los Angeles manufacturer to locate in Toronto rather than near Windsor is negligible for land and negative for air transport.

The corollary of sectoral penetration is that the more distant the United States centre from Ontario, the greater the proportion of its Ontario subsidiaries that are located in Toronto (see Table 3-5). United States cities closer than 400 miles to Toronto have a relatively low concentration of subsidiaries in Toronto. There is a sharp increase in the percentage of all subsidiaries in Toronto for cities located more than 1,000 miles from Toronto.

Sectoral penetration augments the contrasts between eastern and southwestern Ontario because of the greater proximity of the Midwest industrials than the New York industrials to Ontario.

---

[63] Roy I. Wolfe, in *Parameters of Recreation Travel Behaviour in Ontario: A Progress Report*, Ontario Department of Highways, Toronto, 1966, finds similar characteristics in American recreational travel behaviour in Ontario.

TABLE 3-5

ONTARIO AND TORONTO SUBSIDIARIES CONTROLLED BY UNITED
STATES PARENT COMPANIES LOCATED WITHIN TEN
DISTANCE BANDS FROM TORONTO

Distance Band	Total Number of Subsidiaries	Toronto Metro Area	
Road Distance of Parent Company From Toronto (miles)	Controlled by Parent Companies Located in Each Distance Band	Subsidiaries	
		Number	Per cent
0 - 200	47	20	43
201 - 300	165	68	41
301 - 400	76	41	54
401 - 500	467	312	67
501 - 750	67	35	52
751 - 1000	56	32	58
1001 - 1250	5	4	80
1251 - 1500	11	8	73
1501 - 2000	0	0	—
2001 +	49	38	85
Total Sample	943	558	59

Areas of Economic Shadow, Intervening Opportunity and Competing Industries

The three elements, which together constitute the economic shadow concept, may be reviewed by examining the maps of the location of the Ontario subsidiaries controlled from six United States cities (Figures 3-6 to 3-11). Ellipses have been produced on these maps by drawing one arc, with its centre at Toronto, through the United States city and the second arc, with the United States city as centre, through Toronto. These ellipses are used to define areas of economic shadow, intervening opportunity and competing industries.

> *The area of economic shadow* is the area in Ontario which lies beyond the ellipse and hence beyond the area of sectoral affinity. This is termed the economic shadow area because it appears unlikely that any Ontario subsidiary will be located farther from the parent company than Toronto, or farther from Toronto than the parent company.

> *The intervening opportunity area* is the part of Ontario falling within the ellipse which is, therefore, closer to the United States city than Toronto. It is the area of sectoral affinity.

> *The competing industries area* is the area in the United States part of the ellipse; it is closer to Toronto than a particular United States city.

Compare Figures 3-6, 3-9 and 3-10; the closer the United States city is to Ontario, the smaller is the concentration of the subsidiaries in Toronto. The more widely spaced the United States cities, the less satisfactory is any interchange of ellipses. The Minneapolis-St. Paul ellipse (Figure 3-7) would exclude most Syracuse subsidiaries (Figure 3-11). The area of intervening opportunity changes with each United States city. Only ellipses from the northeastern United States include eastern Ontario (Figures 3-10 and 3-11). No ellipses cover eastern Ontario exclusively, although most of the Niagara

Peninsula is included in all ellipses. Many ellipses include only southwestern Ontario and exclude northern and eastern Ontario (see Figures 3-6, 3-7, 3-8 and 3-9).

Figure 3-6. Los Angeles Subsidiaries and Economic Shadow.

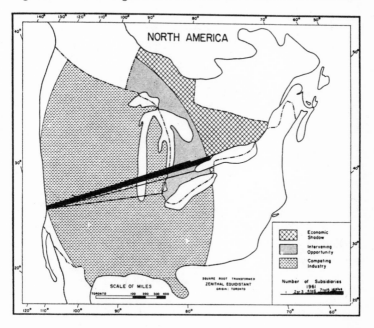

Compare these six figures with Figure 3-5 showing industrial desire lines and note how few desire lines cross eastern Ontario. The impact of economic shadow on regional economic development in eastern Ontario is evident.

The Pattern of Economic Shadow in Southern Ontario

The economic shadow values, based on distance decay and sectoral penetration, have been computed and mapped in Figure 3-12. The higher the numerical rating, the greater the possible contacts with United States industrial centres and the lower the economic shadow. The regional contrast between

Figure 3-7. Minneapolis-St. Paul Subsidiaries and Economic Shadow.

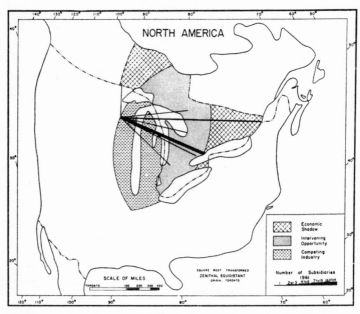

Figure 3-8. Chicago Subsidiaries and Economic Shadow.

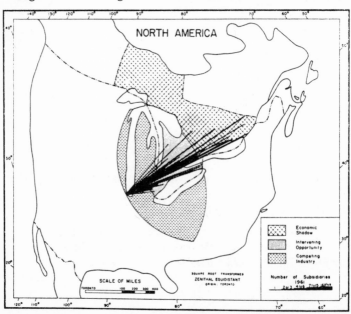

Figure 3-9. Detroit Subsidiaries and Economic Shadow.

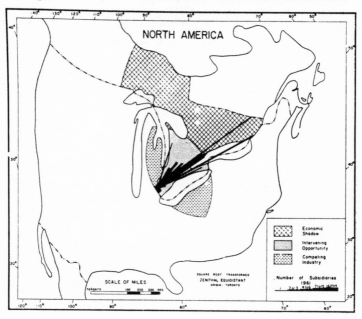

Figure 3-10. New York Subsidiaries and Economic Shadow.

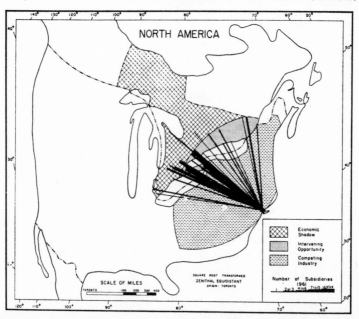

Figure 3-11. Syracuse Subsidiaries and Economic Shadow.

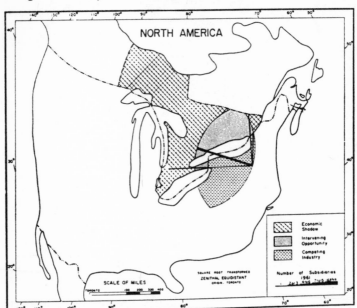

southwestern and eastern Ontario is marked: high numerical values, indicating low economic shadow, are restricted entirely to southwestern Ontario and Georgian Bay.

Compare this pattern of economic shadow with Figure 3-4. The New York concentration of large industrials reduces the economic shadow within a peripheral belt including the Niagara Peninsula and the shore of the upper St. Lawrence. This area is the intervening opportunity area for New York industrials (see Figure 3-10). A narrow wedge of moderate economic shadow extends northward from Kingston to Renfrew and reflects the proximity and intervening opportunity for Syracuse and adjacent industrial centres (see Figure 3-11). Elsewhere in eastern Ontario, economic shadow remains high.

Economic shadow is generally low in southwestern Ontario because of its proximity to the concentration of Midwest industrials. The ellipses demarcating the area of intervening opportunity for the industrial centres from Detroit (Figure 3-9) to Minneapolis-St. Paul (Figure 3-7), exclude increasingly larger areas of the Niagara Peninsula, which is the only area of high economic shadow in southwestern Ontario.

Figure 3-12. Economic Shadow in Southern Ontario.

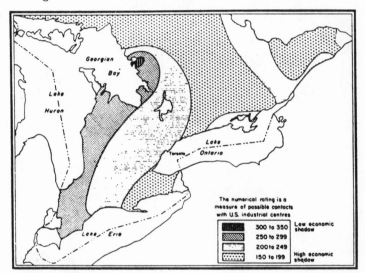

The failure of eastern Ontario to attract manufacturing industry has stunted the area's urban growth and restricted, with a few notable exceptions, their economic base to central place functions. Only Ottawa, the national capital, and Cornwall, a manufacturing centre on the St. Lawrence Seaway, have grown substantially in population since 1900. In the eastern Ontario counties of Russell, Prescott, Stormont, Glengarry, and Dundas, the population has remained stable in numbers, and predominantly French Canadian. The final section of this paper examines the central place hierarchy in part of eastern Ontario and the relationship of urban size to central functions and functional region.

Figure 3-13. Eastern Ontario: Population Distribution.

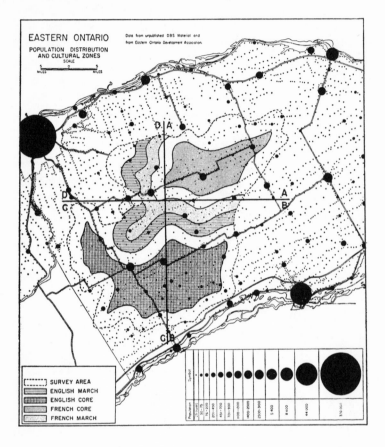

Central Place Functions

In 1964, a spatially-stratified sample of householders were asked to state their first and second choice preferences and their manner and frequency of shopping for a list of consumer goods and services (see Figure 3-14). Mother tongue was recorded in order to determine cultural differences in consumer travel behaviour.[64] The first choice shopping patterns for rural farm families have been mapped by drawing desire lines from place of residence direct to the place providing each service. These maps are ordered from hamlet level to regional capital level services to stress the relationship between level of service and size of functional region.

Food Services: *Figure 3-15*. Food services are a hamlet level function offered by all central places. A symmetry in the desire line pattern emerges from consistent consumer travel to the closest centre. The few exceptional cases where consumers ignore an intervening opportunity are explained by multipurpose travel behaviour, or by cultural differences, with some French Canadian farmers preferring a French Canadian central place to a closer English centre. The perimeters of the desire lines delimit the functional regions and their length reveals the range of the good. The range of the good for food purchases is under three miles, and the maximum profit area that can be commanded by a centre for this service is very small. In a few cases, such as Limoges and Embrun, and St-Rose-de-Prescott and St-Isidore-de-Prescott, a small functional region forms an enclave within a larger area. These smaller centres are candidates for early drop-out in the inter-urban competition to provide central functions.

Auto Repair Services: *Figure 3-16*. Note the similarity between pattern of functional regions for food and auto repair services. This service is also considered hamlet level, although half the hamlets fail to offer it and have their entire region absorbed by the closest larger central place. Such failures generally reflect proximity to a larger centre. For example, Inkerman fails to offer auto repair services and its region is absorbed by Winchester. The Limoges region is, however,

---

[64] Robert A. Murdie, "Cultural Differences in Consumer Travel", *Economic Geography*, Vol. 41, July 1965, pp. 211-233. Murdie finds significant differences in the consumer travel behaviour between Old Order Mennonites and "modern" Canadians in Waterloo and Wellington Counties of southwestern Ontario for traditional goods (auto and harness repair, food, clothing, yard goods and shoes).

Figure 3-14. Eastern Ontario: Ethnic Origin of Interviewees.

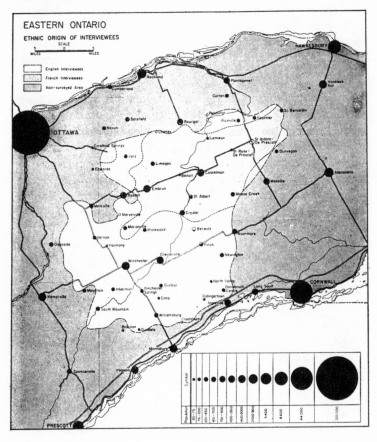

Figure 3-15. Eastern Ontario: Food Services.

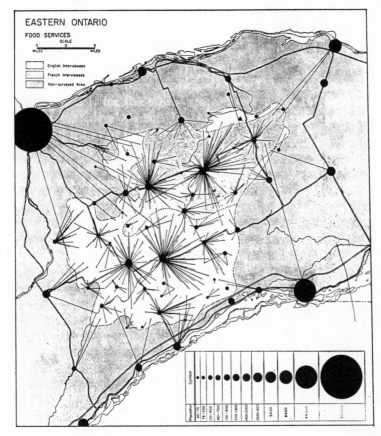

Figure 3-16. Eastern Ontario: Auto Repair Services.

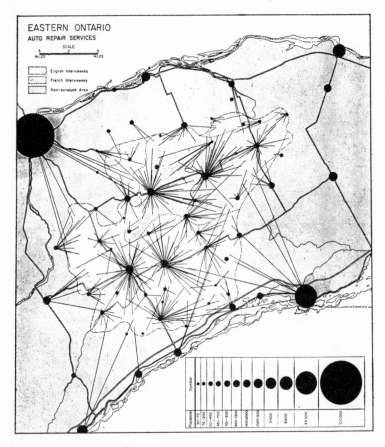

served by Lemieux for auto repair, the only service provided by Lemieux. For all other services, Limoges forms a part of the Embrun region.

In a few exceptional cases, services may survive in a central place despite proximity to a competing centre. Winchester and Chesterville both offer food and auto repair services even though their proximity truncates their functional regions. This conflict between the two centres becomes more obvious for higher order services and provides an example of "dispersed-city phenomenon".[65]

Figure 3-17. Eastern Ontario: Banking Services.

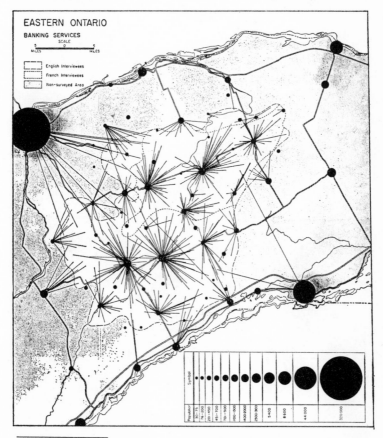

[65] Ian Burton, "A Restatement of the Dispersed City Hypothesis", *Annals of the Association of American Geographers*, Vol. 53, September 1963, pp. 285-289. Burton defines a dispersed city as a number of discrete urban centres in close proximity to each other and functionally interrelated, although usually separated by tracts of non-urban land. Dispersed cities replace a single regional capital by capturing some of the functions of such a centre and surrendering the remainder to more distant regional capitals.

Figure 3-18. Eastern Ontario: Medical Services.

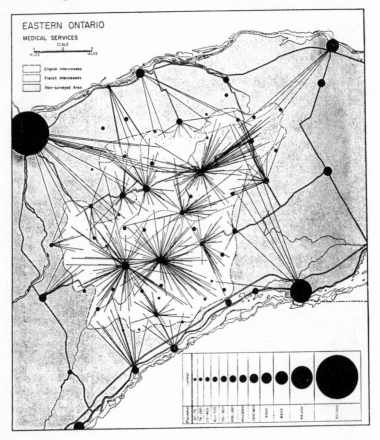

Figure 3-19. Eastern Ontario: Legal Services.

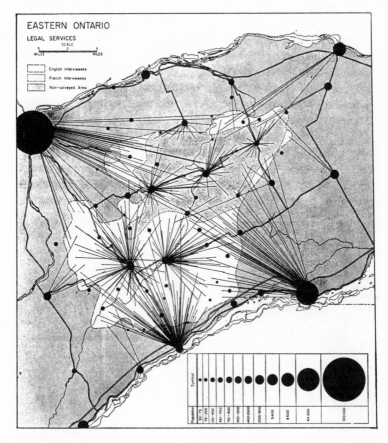

Banking Services: Figure 3-17. Banking services are a village level function and are offered in only half of the centres providing food services. The two travel patterns appear similar because the drop-outs form enclave regions at the hamlet service level and do not cause realignments at the village level. The hamlets of Winchester Springs, Dunbar and Elma, for example, are served by Winchester, Chesterville and Williamsburg respectively. No cultural preferences are apparent. French Canadians living closer to Russell than to Embrun use

Figure 3-20. Eastern Ontario: Dental Services.

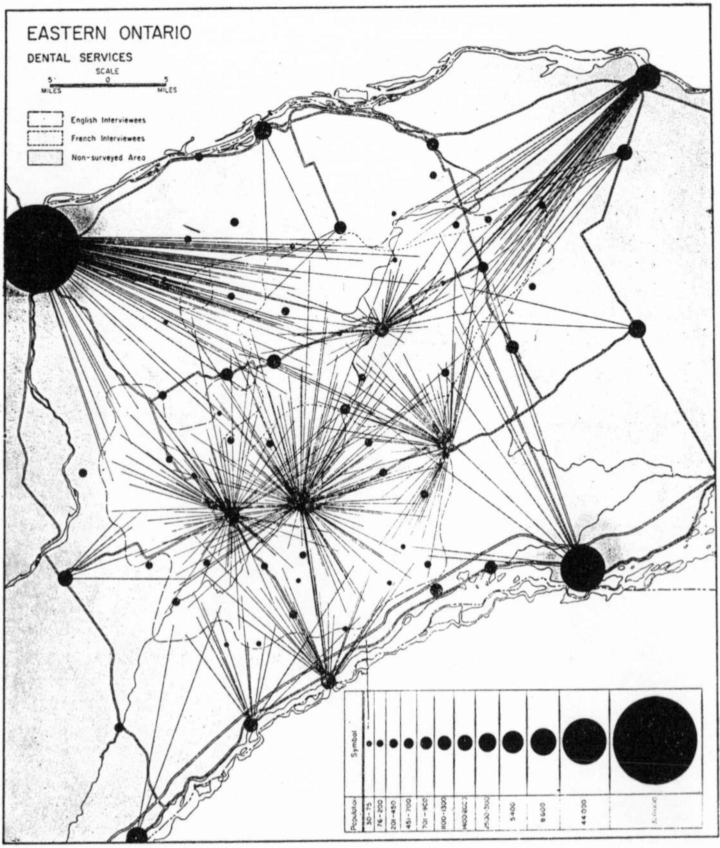

the Bank of Nova Scotia at Russell rather than the Caisse Populaire at Embrun, for example.

Medical and Legal Services: Figures 3-18 and *3-19*. Medical and legal services are town level services; the village of South Mountain and its region, for example, are served by Winchester. Higher order services are used less frequently than low order services and consumer decisions are consciously weighted rather than random or habitual, as is the case with

Figure 3-21. Eastern Ontario: Optical Services.

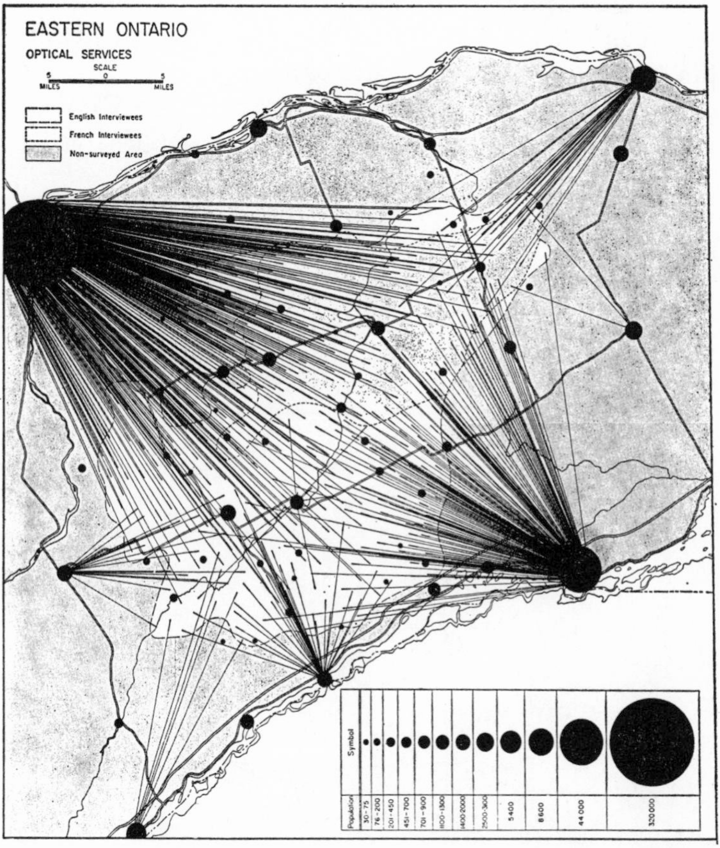

lower order centres. Quality of service can outweigh proximity and, consequently, consumer desire lines cross each other to produce more complex patterns. Cultural differences too play a more obvious role. The northern limit of Chesterville's medical services region follows the ethnic boundary (see Figure 3-18). Crysler's banking region is bisected, and its medical clientele exclusively French Canadian. Similarly, the French doctor at Embrun serves French patients beyond Vars, while English patients at Vars travel to the English doctor at Russell.

The map of consumer travel for legal services also reveals important ethnic differences (see Figure 3-19). Legal services, provided by a *notaire* are lower order than medical services and restrict Ottawa's penetration into the French Canadian area. Legal services are of higher order than medical in the

Figure 3-22. Range and Threshold Graph for
Eastern Ontario.

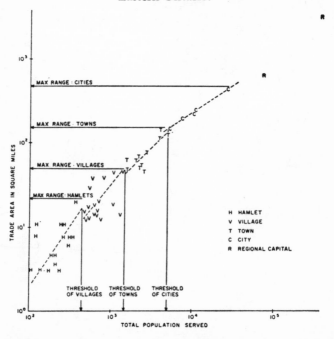

Figure 3-23. Increase in Central Place Population in
Eastern Ontario with Increase in Number of
Central Functions Performed.

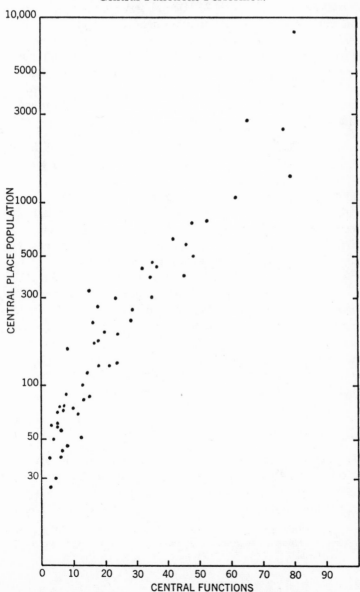

English Canadian area and Russell, Metcalfe, Osgoode, Williamsburg, and Finch all have physicians but no lawyers.

Dental Services: *Figure 3-20*. Dental services are a city level function. In the French Canadian area, Casselman alone has dental services; this is provided in the public school by the Hawkesbury dentist. Winchester and Chesterville both have larger functional regions which extend into the French ethnic area. Casselman, Winchester and Chesterville are about equidistant from their competing centres, Ottawa and Cornwall, and just beyond the range of their effective competition.

Optical Services: *Figure 3-21*. The Ottawa and Cornwall functional regions meet for optical services which are a regional capital function. The functional regions of Casselman, Winchester and Chesterville fall entirely within the Ottawa region. The pattern of areal functional organization is fully nested so that the region served by the regional capital subdivides into city, town, village and hamlet subregions in turn.[66] This nesting agrees with other empirical work.

The increase in maximum ranges and thresholds for each level of the eastern Ontario central place system is shown in Figure 3-22. French and English centres are randomly intermingled within the system and cultural differences do not appear to affect the size and spacing of central places. The increase in central place population that occurs with increase in number of central functions performed is indicated in Figure 3-23.

Conclusion

"Human activities are distributed over the national territory in certain rhythms and patterns which are neither arbitrary nor the workings of chance. They result rather from the interdependencies that give form to economic space."[67] This paper

---

[66] A. K. Philbrick, "Principles of Areal Functional Organization in Regional Human Geography", *Economic Geography*, Vol. 33, 1957, pp. 306-336.

has traced the interdependencies between geographic location, urban functions, functional regions and urban growth. It shows that one area, eastern Ontario, has been unable to attract United States manufacturing subsidiaries because it is in the area of high economic shadow cast by Toronto, even though its geographic location, as measured by market potential, is otherwise favourable. The central places in the eastern Ontario study area generally have been unable to supplement their basic central place functions with manufacturing and other national and sub-national market area activities. Their growth has become stunted at the population levels that can be supported by the equilibrium between population served and the functions acquired. This equilibrium assumes spatial expression in the size and the spacing of the central places.

---

[67] Friedmann and Alonso, *op. cit.*, p. 2.

4 Urban Land Use: An Economic-Geographic Concept

N. H. Lithwick
Gilles Paquet

Introduction

Students of methodology in the social sciences repeatedly complain that important problems do not always conform to the boundaries of the various academic disciplines. Since crossing these boundaries opens a Pandora's box of complex difficulties, these problems remain unsolved. One critical factor inhibiting cross-disciplinary analysis is the lack of adequate concepts. All too often the concepts derived from any single discipline are single-purpose instruments shaped by the presumptions of their place of birth and incapable of any extension beyond their original vocation. For example, to the architect, blight refers to an aesthetic appearance, while to the economist it means functional obsolescence. The concept is used to shed light on those specific aspects of reality with which each discipline is dealing. Once we attempt to discuss the eradication of blight through urban renewal — which spans economics and architecture, and many other areas as well — the specificity of the usage deters effective communication. It is therefore necessary to develop broader concepts extending beyond these narrow views of the specific disciplines.[1] This chapter is an experiment along these lines.

---

[1] F. Perroux, "La méthode de l'économie géneralisée et l'économie de l'Homme", *Economie et Civilisation*, Tome II, Ch. 5, Paris, 1958. Some interesting attempts to construct these generalized concepts have already been made. F. Perroux, *Economie et Société*, Paris, 1960; also A. K. Cairncross, "Programmes as Instruments of Coordination", *Scottish Journal of Political Economy*, June 1961.

It would be impossible to develop here the whole arsenal of concepts necessary to conduct a complete analysis at the cross-disciplinary level. The many combinations of disciplines necessary to approach meaningfully the diverse aspects of the urban phenomenon are beyond even a simple enumeration here. Moreover, some phenomena, such as urban renewal mentioned above, require that three or four of the standard disciplines be brought to bear on the problem before any helpful analysis can be generated. However, since we are interested not so much in a compendium of two-discipline or three-discipline concepts as in the process of developing generalized concepts in order to approach a real problem more usefully, it will be sufficient to use a few examples of such concepts.

Given the structure of this section of the book in which economics and geography are brought to bear in turn on the problem of the relationships between city and region, we have chosen to concentrate our attention on one of these notions at the cross-roads of economics and geography which can be regarded as a generalized concept — urban land use.

A generalized concept is one which is being broadened. What is of interest then is not simply the state of development of the concept but rather the process through which it is being generalized. This can be studied most effectively by examining the genealogy of the concept and by classifying its uses. We must emphasize that we are not dealing as yet with a general concept — that is, one which has crystallized into its final form. General concepts can best be analyzed through the construction of an ideal-type demonstrating how it embodies components borrowed from the different disciplines. It is the very nature of the concept currently being generalized which has led us to follow the approach suggested above. This approach better reveals the possibilities of the concept by examining it at work, so to speak, in the various studies which have used it.

In this process we shall encounter necessarily many other ambivalent notions which could be usefully anatomized in the same fashion. For instance, we shall deal with the notion of density; and although we shall not analyze it here, hopefully it will provide some insight into other "generalizable" concepts over the span of other disciplines. The process leading to generalization is much more crucial here than the outcome of any such process. Consequently we have not attempted an exhaustive review of the diverse contexts in which the concept of land use is employed; the items presented have been selected for their illustrative usefulness.

The choice of this particular concept for our demonstration is amply justified by its importance both in economics and geography. Land use is the geographical image of the results of the operations of the urban land market; it is also inversely the dimension of geographical space inserted into the market place. Whether one deals with *types* of land use, or with the intensity or density of land use (this is the link between land use and density concepts), one is clearly within this area that some call economic geography and others geographical or spatial economics. This concept of land use permeates both disciplines and is mentioned in at least two thirds of this book. Moreover, in a venture of this sort, it is preferable to start with the intersection of economics and geography since their respective property-spaces[2] are more closely related than those of any other pair of disciplines. Finally, if one were to develop the density of land use concept, one would quickly spill over into the domain of the ecologist and the sociologist. Therefore, land use is not only an easier but also a more fruitful point of departure.

The Context of Urban Land Use Analysis

In order to trace the genealogy of the concept of urban land use and to better evaluate the uses made of this concept, it is helpful to classify the various contributions according to a simple grid which we can then prospect systematically. This

---

2 On the notion of property-space, see A. H. Barton, "The Concept of Property-Space in Social Research" in P. F. Lazarsfeld and M. Rosenberg (eds.), *The Language of Social Research*, Free Press, Glencoe, Ill., 1955.

grid has to recognize the peculiar partitioning of the *literature*, of the *approach* and of the *subject matter*.

(a) The studies on urban land use are varied; they span studies of *single concepts*, examinations of *simple relationships* between two variables, and even complete *models* which attempt to provide a simplified (yet complete for the purpose at hand) picture of a hierarchy of variables.

(b) Concepts, relationships or models may deal either with highly aggregative entities (*macro-urban analysis*) or may focus on individual decision units (*micro-urban analysis*). Since this distinction is valid both for geography and economics, it is important to make sure that both sets of studies are represented in our genealogy.

(c) Finally, one of the few points of agreement between geographers and economists on the urban problem has been the distinction between *within-city* and *among-city issues*.[3]

These three variables of classification seem to identify fairly well the different areas of urbanology where work is currently being conducted. They help to summarize usefully the context of urban land use analysis. Our classificatory grid is captured in the following table.

TABLE 4-1

	Concepts or Variables	Relationships	Models
1. Within cities			
(a) Micro-analysis	A	E	I
(b) Macro-analysis	B	F	J
2. Between cities			
(a) Micro-analysis	C	G	K
(b) Macro-analysis	D	H	L

[3] See Chapter 8.

Although we shall not attempt here to deal with the 12 sub-cases suggested by the classificatory grid, we shall look at each of the three main classes of studies focusing on concepts (*ABCD*), relationships (*EFGH*) and models (*IJKL*). In each case a few well chosen studies should exemplify the way in which the concept of urban land use has evolved and is currently being generalized.

Studies of Single Concepts

Most social scientists have recognized that in studies of cities[4] social processes cannot be divorced from a spatial orientation. The initial task, then, is to forge a link between dynamic spaceless variables and relevant spatial arrangements in the urban context. We will use the expression *urban land use* to establish this necessary connection. This use of the concept follows a well established if often confused terminology.[5] We have gone beyond the difficulties generated in the literature by the shift from soil to land to space. We have progressed from the strictly physical connotations of soil to the notion of land which "connotes location in relation to cultural features, property rights and boundaries, and the whole characteristics of place relevant to the concept and operation of a firm".[6] The widespread confusion in the literature over these two concepts accounts for much of the haziness in the analysis.

More recently, almost everywhere the word *space* has come to replace the word *land*. This shift to the notion of space has been triggered by the work of geographers who have prepared the way for the use of *topology* in geography.[7] However, this word is more ambiguous than it first appears, despite the many space-indices used by planners and municipal administrators.

---

4 Allan Pred, "Industrialization, Initial Advantage, and American Metropolitan Growth", *The Geographical Review*, Vol. 55, April 1965, p. 98.

5 Land use has been defined by John Rannells as "repeated activities of individuals and establishments as they relate to the use of space at fixed locations and among these locations" in *The Core of the City*, Columbia University Press, New York, 1956, p. 11.

6 C. E. Kellogg, "Soil and Land Classification", *Journal of Farm Economics*, Vol. 33, No. 4, 1951, pp. 500-501.

7 W. Bunge, *Theoretical Geography*, Gleerup, Lund, 1962.

Its main contribution has been to shift the attention of urban students from the two-dimensional world of soil and land to the three-dimensional universe including the real structures erected on land. In this three-dimensional view, the ratio of structures to land gives an index of the intensity of land use. However, with the revival in the last quarter century of spatial economics in the Löschian sense,[8] space has become a thoroughly confused term. Moreover, the notions of abstract and property space were popularized at approximately the same time in sociology and economics[9] without either discipline attempting to discover whether these notions were parallel to topological developments in geography.

The notion of urban land use more clearly expresses the link between social processes and their spatial context in the geographical sense of the word. The dichotomy of types and density of urban land use seems to capture this economic-geographic dimension for which we are searching. And it is linked with the socio-political dimensions through an extension of the notion of density from structure/land ratios to population/land ratios.

Studies of Relationships

In the introductory section it was suggested that sociologists are identifying the problem of urbanization with the problem of the growing density of population at given locations. Much of Peter Pineo's material might be subsumed under a heading such as "The Circumstances of Densities of Population". Economists and geographers have examined this intensity dimension of urban land use at some length, at least as much as the different types of land uses. Indeed the *type* and the *intensity* of land use may be regarded as not totally unrelated. Some early attempts were made to relate this concept to certain spatial characteristics of interest to the geographer. The works of Stewart, Clark, Sherratt, Weiss and Berry-Simmons-

---

[8] A. Lösch, *The Economics of Location*, Yale University Press, New Haven, 1954.

[9] A. H. Barton, *op. cit.*; F. Perroux, "Economic Space: Theory and Applications", *Quarterly Journal of Economics*, Vol. 64, No. 1, 1950.

Tennant[10] attempt to analyze the exact relationship between urban population density and spatial pattern, and they have prepared the way for more ambitious studies in which density and its associated spatial relationships are related in a variety of interactance models. Some of these involve between-city effects[11] while others use the concept of density to "explain" a variety of characteristics associated with the spatial pattern of activities within cities.[12] Two points about these studies should be noted. The first is the exclusive stress on geographical distance, or *accessibility*, as the key concept denoting spatial density patterns; and second, the distressingly thin theoretical basis upon which the empirical work has been constructed. Only recently have some workable models been developed to give theoretical meaning to many of these early empirical regularities.[13] The role of economists has been of primary importance in implanting a soul into a rather lifeless body of facts.

We must sort out the various concepts being used in these studies of relationships. For instance, the role of population has been stressed by both geographers and sociologists, but it has acquired different meanings in the process of analysis. The original models worked with the concept of *absolute population* and were thus largely intra-city oriented. However,

---

10 J. Q. Stewart, "Empirical mathematical rules concerning the distribution and equilibrium of population", *Geographical Review*, Vol. 37, 1947, pp. 461-485; Colin Clark, "Urban population densities", *Journal of the Royal Statistical Society*, Vol. 114, 1951, series A, pp. 490-496; G. G. Sherratt, "A Model for general urban growth", *Management Science, Models and Techniques*, Vol. 2, 1960, pp. 147-159; H. K. Weiss, "The Distribution of urban population and an application to a servicing problem", *Operations Research*, Vol. 9, 1961, pp. 860-874; B. J. L. Berry, J. W. Simmons and R. J. Tennant, "Urban population densities: structure and change", *Geographical Review*, Vol. 53, 1963, pp. 389-405.

11 For example, see J. Ross MacKay, "The interactance hypothesis and boundaries in Canada: a preliminary study", *Canadian Geographer*, Vol. 2, 1950.

12 For instance, M. J. Beckman, "On the distribution of rent and residential density in cities (MIMEO)" or R. C. Schmitt, "Population densities and real property values in a metropolitan area", *Land Economics*, Vol. 35, 1959.

13 The work of William Alonso, Lowdon Wingo, Jr. and Richard F. Muth will be examined in this connection below.

attention soon shifted to a *relative concept*, density, in order to standardize for size. More recently stress has been placed on *population growth* as the crucial measure of the role of population in comparing cities and segments within cities.[14]

As for the second important variable in these studies of relationships, namely *accessibility*, economists have been able to do no more than work this well defined geographical concept into their models. Many measures exist and they may differ, but not fundamentally. Fortunately there has been little confusion over this concept, and it has proved most satisfactory in locational models.

In evaluating these studies of relationships, we should like to point out two shortcomings that economists have attempted to remedy. The first is the inadequate integration of a fundamental concept into these relationships. We are referring to a second "input" into a site (besides accessibility) which Berry calls land,[15] but which we (in the style of Rannells)[16] call *availability*. As economists, we are concerned with land as a commodity which is supplied and demanded in particular *quantities*. This emphasizes the specific interest of the economist and the difference between his view of the commodity, land, and that of the geographer concerned with central place theory. The difference might be usefully illustrated by contrasting the notion of "range of a good" of central place theory, which is primarily concerned with accessibility, with the notion of "degree of publicness of a good" of modern public finance theory, which is dealing with notions of availability.[17]

---

14 For these three meanings see Clark, *op. cit.*, Stewart, *op. cit.*, and E. N. Thomas, "Areal associations between population growth and selected factors in the Chicago urbanized area", *Economic Geography*, Vol. 36, 1960.

15 B. J. L. Berry, *et al.*, *op. cit.*, p. 391.

16 J. Rannells, *op. cit.*, p. 150.

17 One might compare B. J. L. Berry and W. L. Garrison, "A note on central place theory and the range of a good", *Economic Geography*, No. 34, 1958, with A. Breton, "A theory of government grants", *Canadian Journal of Economics and Political Science*, Vol. 21, No. 2, 1965. Some attempt to integrate those two concepts would be in order and it would illuminate some of the problems of integration of economics and geography.

A second problem that has long troubled economists is embodied in Stewart's plea for "measurement without theory".[18] In his own words, "the final rational interpretation of such empirical rules (referring to certain empirical regularities which had been observed) cannot come until after the rules themselves are established". He felt that a whole range of these rules should be tested and specified.[19] In the same vein in 1951, Colin Clark suggested a new rule which he contended was "true for all times and all places studied".[20] Apparently the time had not yet come for the rationale, as none was proposed. However, these rules were not without use. Operations research quickly discovered that they could be used very profitably. Sherratt demonstrated that a slightly altered version of a Clark-type within-city model applied to Sydney, Australia could be used to improve dramatically the efficiency of distribution of gas and other municipal services affected by urban population densities. In effect, he was suggesting that these rules could be used to determine the location of factories and business premises.[21] More recently Weiss has shown that a combination of the Zipf "rank-size rule" explaining between-city density and the Clark rule could be applied to determine the optimal location of city-serving units.[22]

As a result, for *normative* purposes, the reliance on these rules has been necessary. But we must not lose sight of their lack of a rationale. In a recent paper, Berry *et al.* have attempted to show that the theory of urban land use as it has been developed by economists has provided the rationale for Clark's rule.[23] This has been confirmed partly by Lowenstein's

---

[18] J. Q. Stewart, *op. cit.*, p. 461.

[19] *Ibid*. Four rules were suggested by Stewart:
    (1) The rank-size rule
    (2) The urban fraction rule
    (3) The potential rule
    (4) The rural density rule.

[20] C. Clark, *op. cit.*, p. 490.

[21] G. G. Sherratt, *op. cit.*, p. 158.

[22] H. K. Weiss, *op. cit.*

[23] Berry *et. al.*, *op. cit.*, pp. 391-396.

findings,[24] which appear to substantiate the usefulness of the economic theory of land use in providing a theoretical foundation for these rules.

Before indicating how economics has incorporated these rules into theoretical models, we should note that these early two-variable relationships have been expanded to incorporate some of the wider dimensions of the urban unit, and further that these broader relationships have undergone some interesting empirical verification. Weiss, in his attempt to apply these empirical rules, linked within-city rules to between-city rules. This is of particular interest because the degree of consistency between these components provides at least a weak test of the usefulness of the regularities as explanatory devices. Another approach has been to relate not two rules to each other but one rule to some other problem, so that the empirical regularity might be used to explain some standard social, economic or geographic issue. One such application relates Clark's b-parameter to the efficiency of intra-urban transportation systems.[25] Another, proposed by Beckman, begins with the hypothesis that each family "which has chosen to live in the outer area of a city attempts, within its means, to maximize the amount of living space it can occupy".[26] From this, he has been able to relate residential density and rent to the distance from city centre. Schmitt, taking the same approach, added a most interesting study by relating densities to property values. Despite the crudity of the approach, it is an important contribution to our stock of knowledge to find, using census tracts for metropolitan Honolulu, that two measures of density (place of work and place of residence) "provided an almost complete statistical explanation of tract-by-tract variations in property values".[27] The theoretical foundations for such a relationship of population density (which is clearly a vital component of the demand for space)

[24] L. K. Lowenstein, "The Location of Urban Land Uses", *Land Economics*, Vol. 39, November 1963.

[25] Colin Clark, *op. cit.*, p. 495.

[26] J. M. Beckman, *op. cit.*, pp. 1-2.

[27] R. C. Schmitt, *op. cit.*, p. 367.

to property values are well established;[28] and whereas Schmitt's findings do not provide a valid test of this hypothesis, they are useful in suggesting the appropriate strategy for so doing.

The importance of the population density variable extends far beyond the scope of single city analysis. It has been a central variable in studies of "between cities" relationships. E. N. Thomas has found that for very large clusters of cities, this variable is once again a primary or "common" factor in explaining the spatial arrangement of many urban systems.[29] These arrangements of cities themselves (between-city spatial patterns) have been explained in terms of simple density-distance relationships. These relationships are generally called gravity or interactance models. The models explain exchange between urban units, defined by demographic or communication links, by the relationships of their respective densities to the distance between them. One could even pursue the analysis one step further by using an extended notion of distance which would fully exploit the various dimensions it might assume ranging from geographical to social to economic. This further enables us to translate particular boundaries into distance-determined concepts.

Many qualitative variables have been added to the empirical rules. Lowenstein's study of business location by type has already been mentioned. In addition, the phenomenon of ghettoing and other sociological variables are clearly important in the locational choice of individuals. In general analysis has started from the concepts of population density and/or distance from the city centre with relevant variables then plugged in. Originally we considered only those studies which were obviously relevant in developing a *general theory of land use* (and implicitly, land values) in the urban community, and of these, only the work that had undertaken some statistical verification of the hypotheses. We will now narrow our sights even further to concentrate on four works that have been pub-

28 P. F. Wendt, "Theory of Urban Land Values", *Land Economics*, Vol. 33, August 1957.
29 E. N. Thomas, *op. cit.*

lished in the past four years. They represent the best of the technical work by geographers and economists who are recognized experts in urban land studies. Judging by the cautious titles of their papers the authors do not make extravagant claims for their studies. The actual work reveals that they have not discovered the underlying mechanism; rather, they are proposing some "determinants" or "factors", "effects of" or "approaches to" the problem.[30]

In general, these studies lack a mechanism or theoretical model capable of explaining the observed relationships. Thus, it is statistical functions (whose parameters are derived by standard estimating techniques) which are represented as models. However, since the derived relationship does not result from behavioural assumptions but is given with little if any theoretical justification, we must reject this use of the word "model". Despite the infancy of the methodology of model-building, we are beyond the point where a statement can be passed off as a model.[31] To be fair to the authors we must note that except for the unfortunate use of the word model, none has claimed anything more than the establishment of an empirical *fit* at some level of statistical significance.

Three of these studies attempt to explain land values by multiple regression techniques. Although they do differ in detail, the variables are sufficiently similar to permit us to deal with them together. The general format is $V_i = f(A_i, Q_i)$,

---

[30] E. F. Brigham, "The determinants of residential land values", *Land Economics*, Vol. 41, No. 4, November 1965, pp. 325-334. C. Czamanski, "Effect of public investments on urban land values", Mimeo. M. H. Yeates, "Some factors affecting the spatial distribution of Chicago land values, 1910-1960", *Economic Geography*, Vol. 41, No. 1, January 1965, pp. 57-85. T. R. Lakshmanan, "An approach to the analysis of inter-urban location applied to the Baltimore region", *Economic Geography*, Vol. 40, No. 4, October 1964, pp. 341-370.

[31] When we test the demand theorem, we test the hypotheses that price and quantity demanded are inversely related, but the theory of demand is not contained in this relationship. The multiplicity of models that can be tested by fitting a demand curve explains our contention that curve fitting does not *per se* and automatically verify any theory.

where
   V_i is defined as unit land value;
   A_i is some index of accessibility,
         including a variety of attraction points;
   Q_i is a variety of qualitative variables,
         including amenities, age, zoning, and so forth.

Whereas Yeates examines the changing role of the variables over time, the Brigham and Czamanski studies are purely static. The latter two claim to study land use by examining different functions for different users, avoiding thereby the fundamental issue of allocating land among users.

The fourth paper by Lakshmanan also disaggregates users; but instead of trying to estimate land values, he uses them as one of the explanatory variables. He thus seeks to explain the growth of land users in the various sectors, divorcing the study completely from concern with land.

All these papers involve many independent variables, selected quite arbitrarily and fitted into a wide variety of regression-models. That some of the statistical results should be quite significant is hardly surprising.

Models of Urban Land Use

Over the past decade, a number of impressive studies have been produced which, by and large, deserve to be classified as models. We shall briefly review the more interesting of these within the framework we have proposed in Table 4-1.

The majority of work has involved intra-city issues. The most satisfactory have been the analyses carried out *at the micro-urban level*. First we have Muth's study,[32] which starts with a theory of consumer behaviour with respect to housing and a theory of the behaviour of producers of housing. From these theoretical relationships, a market for housing emerges that is fully specified in terms of its spatial impact. From this, the author is able to derive the density to distance relationship which Clark discovered empirically. His model also predicts

---

[32] Richard F. Muth, "The Spatial Structure of the Housing Market", *Papers and Proceedings of the Regional Science Association*, Vol. 7, 1961.

the impact of transport costs and income changes on this relationship. These are all tested statistically and found to be significant. This study therefore meets our requirements that the theory be derived from behaviour equations and that statistical procedures be introduced to test this theory. This example should explain our dissatisfaction with the previous studies which were largely curve fitting exercises based upon implicit theorizing.

A model, similar in many respects to Muth's, was developed almost simultaneously by Wingo.[33] He stresses the effect of transportation technology on the market price of urban land. The demand side of the market is based upon the preferences of households alone, thus limiting the scope of the model. Furthermore, no specific testing of the overall model is presented.

William Alonso has recently developed a rather more comprehensive theoretical model.[34] He considers the roles of both households and firms in arriving at a market equilibrium. In addition, his model indicates the part played by agricultural land at the periphery. However, as we shall see later, his technique for solving the system involves an iterative procedure that is highly artificial. Nevertheless, his model is perhaps the most theoretically advanced of all we have encountered.

An interesting study by Duane Knos lies somewhere between the model and the quasi-analytical approach.[35] His theory relates land use to land value, and variance analysis is used to confirm that the various uses are associated with significantly different land values. In this initial study, he sets out to explain land values alone by fitting a relationship similar to those in the studies discussed in the previous section. The author does not proceed beyond this point, but the basic tools are at hand for an interesting simulation of the system. By the

33 Lowdon Wingo, Jr., *Transportation and Urban Land*, Resources for the Future, Inc., Washington, 1961.

34 William Alonso, *Location and Land Use: Toward A General Theory of Land Rent*, Harvard, Cambridge, 1964.

35 Duane S. Knos, *Distribution of Land Values in Topeka, Kansas*, Center for Research in Business, The University of Kansas, Mimeo, May 1962.

introduction of exogenous shocks, the impact on land values can be estimated. Since land values are uniquely related to types of land use, the effect of any change on land use can be calculated. Because of the serious problems encountered in relying on purely analytical solutions, the simulation feature makes this study of some interest to us in attempting to explain the allocation of land to various users.

A substantially different approach has been taken by Wendt,[36] who deals with the profitability of locating at particular sites. While his model skirts the fundamental issues discussed by Alonso and Wingo, he does introduce the idea of a supply function for land, and more recently he has become interested in the micro-dynamics of urban land values. These issues are important when considering the longer run problems of urbanization.

Finally, we should mention a fascinating study from an entirely different perspective, that of an architect.[37] Rannells' work is an analysis of the Central Business District in terms of a variety of new and often ingenious concepts. Of particular interest are the host of linkages he recognizes between establishments, and his measures of land use. Significantly, he recognizes the three dimensions of urban activity to be accessibility, availability and linkages, which provide the "outline for describing and explaining the interplay of central district establishments".[38] The author makes no pretense of having developed a complete model of location. Indeed, he offers the present work as "a general orientation and descriptive analysis of the use of space by establishments".[39] Its originality and its very stimulating character have prompted us to mention it at this point.

[36] Paul F. Wendt, "Theory of urban land values", *Journal of Land Economics*, Vol. 33, pp. 228-240, August 1957; "Urban land value trends", *The Appraisal Journal*, Vol. 26, April 1958, pp. 254-269; "Economic growth and urban land values", *The Appraisal Journal*, Vol. 26, July 1958, pp. 427-443.

[37] John Rannells, *The Core of the City: A Pilot Study of Changing Land Uses in Central Business Districts*, Columbia University Press, New York, 1956.

[38] *Ibid.*, p. 152.

[39] *Ibid.*, p. 188.

Turning now to models dealing with *macro-units*, we will refer to two studies. The first is by now well known to most urban researchers and derives from an immense research undertaking by Chapin and Weiss.[40] This construct is based not on behavioural assumptions but rather on significant factors in land development. Land development is initially expected to follow a circular normal distribution, but use of this theoretical distribution is abandoned for simpler linear relationships. A number of multiple regressions are estimated using 13 independent variables to explain the intensity of land use in grid units. The selected key variables can then be inserted into a framework which becomes the basis for a simulation exercise to discover the impact of various policies on the intensity of land use. This is perhaps the most comprehensive use of simulation in this field, but the work has not been developed sufficiently to permit a final evaluation. What is of interest to us is their ability to focus on only one type of land use to date, namely residential. Since Knos has developed a potentially useful allocating device, also within a simulation format, integration of these two approaches might help solve the single most important block to further progress in this field, namely an effective allocation mechanism for land.

A second construct has been developed recently in France by Chaîneau.[41] This is the only fully specified effort to join the two issues of between-city and within-city effects. The model is based on demographic change in the course of economic development which creates certain attractions between an urban centre and its hinterland, and which also establishes the interdependence of urban centres themselves. The model is fundamentally a gravity-type and when tested

---

[40] F. Stuart Chapin and Shirley F. Weiss, "Land Development Patterns and Growth Alternatives", Chapter 13 in Chapin and Weiss (eds.), *Urban Growth Dynamics in a Regional Cluster of Cities*, Wiley, New York, 1962. See also subsequent progress reports in the *Urban Studies Research Monographs*, Institute for Research in Social Science, University of North Carolina, Chapel Hill, N.C.

[41] A. Chaîneau, "Une modèle d'analyse de l'espace économique français", *Revue d'Economie Politique*, Vol. 75, 1965.

yields highly significant results. The level of aggregation in this model is so great, however, as to preclude an analysis of the land use problem we are considering.

The final study to which we will refer attempts to evaluate the impact of a policy decision, zoning, on urban land values.[42] Yeates, using his earlier relationship[43] explaining land values in Chicago, attempts to discover the importance of commercial zoning on land values in adjacent areas. He finds that zoning is important, although there may be some question as to the lines of causality. In addition, his tests reveal that a different set of spatial forces operate on land values depending on the zoning category.

Our survey of models has been necessarily brief. We have found some growing understanding of the micro-urban reality, but only under highly artificial assumptions about the homogeneity of land and its users. The attempts to break through this barrier have not succeeded. At the macro-urban level, more successful results in an operational sense appear to be forthcoming, although analytical solutions are still far off.[44] Finally, an attempt has been made to show how even a simple model is invaluable for predicting and evaluating the outcome of policy measures. Without some mechanism for explaining the uses and values of urban land, our understanding of the effect of such policies must remain superficial.

Conclusion

By placing the notion of urban land use in this broader context, we hope we have shown some of the steps which have led it to become an economic-geographic concept which spins off into sociology. The notion of urban land use covers the whole range ABCD and lends itself to most useful analyses

---

42 M. H. Yeates, "The Effect of Zoning on Land Values in American Cities: A Case Study", in J. B. Whitton and P. D. Wood (eds.), *Essays in Geography for Austin Miller*, University of Reading, Reading, 1965.

43 M. H. Yeates, see footnote 30.

44 There are serious doubts in our minds at this stage about using the word "model" to describe the above-mentioned studies at the macro-urban level.

either through a partitioning in types or through an examination of the intensity of land uses. Most of the studies of relationships that we have reported have used the latter avenue, while the many models from Chapin and Weiss to Alonso have rather concentrated on the former avenue, emphasizing the types of land use rather than the intensity of use.

Clark's Type-*F* and Thomas' Type-*H* relationships exemplify the prevalence of macro-analysis at this level. The lack of theoretical underpinnings is most often correlated with a lack of micro-analysis. Such is not the case at the level of models. Alonso (*I*), Knos (*J*), Chapin and Weiss (*K*), and Chaîneau (*L*) exemplify the diversity of uses which the notion of land use spans. However, it is quite clear that the notion is much more useful for intra-city than for between-city analysis.

The notion of urban land use has come to occupy a fairly important place in urban analysis. Our sketchy genealogy of this concept has revealed that it extends very neatly over geography and economics but also that it has come to encompass both a typology of land use and measurements of degrees of intensity of land use. One would have to spend much more time to reconstruct a coherent history of the development of this concept which has now become a most useful cross-disciplinary tool of analysis. Urban land use has qualified as a general concept although one must clearly state that this notion is still in the process of being developed. Moreover, our survey has not attempted to be exhaustive. A possible extension of this systemic review would be an examination of the dynamics of land use. The rather successful exploration of land use adjustments in agriculture may hold some promise for the study of urban land use dynamics.[45]

Although such procedures may appear to be somewhat cumbersome, it would seem to be prerequisite to moving into cross-disciplinary work, for it is impossible to erect any solid construct on inadequate or shaky concepts. In fact the main

---

[45] For instance see *Dynamics of Land Use: Needed Adjustment*, Iowa State University, Center for Agricultural and Economic Adjustment, Ames, Iowa, 1961.

source of confusion in urban analysis may well be the haziness of the commonly used concepts.

We shall have to consider extending the approach to other concepts and other disciplines to capture some economic-sociological or economic-political conceptualizations. Such ideas as the difficult notions of neighbourhood or the problem of the range of public goods might be thus analyzed. At this stage in the development of urbanology, clarification of terminology might produce higher returns than the attempts to erect complex theoretical constructs on the quicksand of ill-defined and/or narrow concepts.

Part Two

Urban Analysis:
Some Case Studies

Because the first section of the book has a bibliographical and methodological vocation substantive findings appeared only incidentally. The second section of the book is directed mainly toward a demonstration of the contribution to be made by the different disciplines to an understanding of the urban phenomenon as a whole. The principal areas of concern are economics, political science and sociology. Each author has interpreted his assignment differently. This is due partly to the stage of the respective research and partly to the degree of development of the different disciplines.

Lithwick and Paquet have attempted to construct a model of the urban economy which, although somewhat formally presented, remains tentative and in some way "unsolvable" by the usual techniques. Given the nature of the construct, its broad vocation, and its stage of development, only preliminary and partial results of their work on Ottawa can be presented. Some of the results illuminate the process of locational choice for residential land users, and the activity of the municipal macro-decision-maker in the urban community. The benefits of the global model approach will not become apparent, however, until more work is done on the operations of firms in their locational choice at the intra-city level and until more is learned about the operations of dealer-speculators.

Harold Kaplan has approached the problem of the urban unit differently. By taking a functionalist approach, and by choosing to deal with the integration process within Metropolitan Toronto, Kaplan has elected to exemplify systems analysis. This represents a good illustration of the application of a set of interesting definitions and of a behavioural approach to the discussion of the strategy of integration in Metropolitan Toronto. The procedure defined, the reaction generated, the process of conflict resolution, and the selection of the adaptive process in a local political system are sketched very neatly. Kaplan has dealt with only one aspect of the politics of the urban unit, but he has selected one which stresses its dynamics and which captures the salient features of the whole as opposed to the functioning of parts.

Peter Pineo has chosen a slightly different breakdown. He has made use of the traditional society-industrial society framework to study the process of urbanization. In both his survey of the relevant literature and in the brief report he presents of his extensive work on the Hamilton area, Pineo emphasizes greatly the rural-urban dichotomy. Urbanization for him is the process which links the traditional society to the industrial universe. He has chosen to focus his attention on the process of urbanization rather than the functioning of the urban unit. His observations on Hamilton capture some of the elements of the impact of the shift from a homogeneous society based on a routine economy and technology to a heterogeneous and innovative society rooted in a stratified culture and social structure.

Although these three approaches to the urban unit as a whole come from diverse disciplines, in different ways and in connection with different urban areas in Canada, they cannot purport to exhaust the subject. They are only a few facets of a giant kaleidoscope. Fundamentally they represent different ways to approach a total social phenomenon: one feels after reading them that they capture only part of the story. Lithwick and Paquet have insisted on a global but static structural model. Kaplan has selected a functional approach to a dynamic process. Pineo has attempted to deal with an aspect of the dynamics of social change. One might have wished for a greater degree of complementarity between these case studies. However, the editors felt that the costs of such an enforced complementarity would have been too high. It is only after each discipline and each research worker has realized the limitations of his partial analytical apparatus that a global approach to the city becomes possible.

The Lithwick-Paquet paper leads into Kaplan's discussion. Although the structural model used could not be set into motion at this stage, it seems obvious that as a result of the solution obtained by simulation techniques, it becomes possible to determine the appropriate institutional arrangements for acceptable solutions. Indeed some preliminary work has been done along these lines.[1] One can therefore perceive already the common ground between these two approaches. As for Pineo's approach, his emphasis on the broad features of social change as opposed to the circumstances of the social adjustments involved in city life makes the junction with the other two papers more difficult. However, it points to some of the elements which must be inserted as data into the politico-economic models. Indeed some of the facts that Pineo examines about the persistence of traditional behaviour in an urban context may explain why the process of urbanization is not necessarily equivalent to the adoption of the city way of life. This is a factor emphasized by Elazar[2] in the United States, and to which we shall return in conclusion: the fact

[1] O. A. Davis and A. B. Whinston, "The Economics of Complex Systems: The Case of Municipal Zoning", *Kyklos*, Vol. 17, No. 3, 1964.

[2] D. J. Elazar, "Are We a Nation of Cities?", *The Public Interest*, Summer 1966.

that people have become urbanized does not necessarily mean that they have been citified. Consequently, it might be that the economic and political arrangements proposed on the assumption that urbanized people are citified will not be appropriate to the society generated by the process of urbanization.

5 The Economics of Urban Land Use[1]

N. H. Lithwick
Gilles Paquet

Introduction

In Chapter 4, we examined the genealogy of an economic-geographic concept — the notion of urban land use. Our survey revealed that although the study of urban land use has been a well recognized field since the 1920's the literature still leaves much to be desired. Many variables, not always clearly specified, have been recognized at one time or another as important in explaining the pattern of land use. These have been inserted into literally thousands of relationships with all sorts of permutations and combinations of the variables yielding statistically significant results.[2] Research workers in this field are not yet convinced that regression lines by themselves are meaningless. Nor do they realize that, by sufficient manipulation, statistically good fits but largely meaningless results can always be obtained. Since statistical analysis is designed primarily to either support or reject a theory or model, once again we are made aware of the fundamental problem in this field — the lack of a meaningful theoretical base. Without it, the remain-

[1] This paper is a by-product of a larger study conducted under grants from the Canadian Council on Urban and Regional Research and from the Central Mortgage and Housing Corporation. We would like to acknowledge the research assistance of J. P. Harkness and J. S. Parsons.

[2] For example, the 1200 regression equations of Chapin and Weiss, and the 174 equations of Czamanski.

ing structure drifts in space, contributing nothing to our comprehension of the urban reality.

Our task then is to explore the extent to which theoretical constructs can be used to explain urban land use and its corollary, urban land values. For such a device to merit the classification of model it must stem from a set of behavioural assumptions. Therefore, we must isolate at the outset the decision-makers in the urban economy who determine the use of urban land. Once the actors are defined, some elements of the plot begin to emerge. It is unrealistic to assume that the entire story will flow smoothly thereafter. On the contrary, this problem may prove to be not at all well structured — i.e., no available operational-research type methods can be expected to yield a mathematically precise solution. While we shall start with the naïve assumption that such is not the case, we are fully prepared to accept the possibility that our initial approach, based on traditional analytical methods, is inappropriate for the problem at hand and to admit that quasi-analytical techniques will have to be employed.[3]

In the next section of this chapter, we shall present the broad requirements of a model of urban land use. One of the great difficulties is the process of aggregation of the different behavioural statements into a "solvable" whole. For this reason, we shall consider at length the problem of aggregation implied by such models and methods of obtaining a solution. In the third section, we shall report briefly on the empirical work done on Ottawa to test the fruitfulness of such an approach to the urban reality. Since the project is still running, this section will constitute only a progress report. In conclusion, we shall suggest some directions for future research.

Some Theoretical Boxes

To begin, we shall deal in turn with the actors, the commodity and the behavioural assumptions used to specify a

---

[3] On these methodological issues see, H. I. Ansoff, "A quasi-analytic method for long range planning", C. W. Churchman, and M. Verhulst (eds.), *Management Sciences — Models and Techniques*, Vol. 2, Pergamon, New York, 1960.

theoretical model. At a second stage, we shall deal with the aggregation procedure and with the methods of solution of such a model.

The Decision Makers

As economists we are interested in the commodity "land" and the market for it. Thus, we must distinguish the participants in this market. One possible classification of these people is based on the Keynesian approach, which considers the nature of final demands for a commodity. These are typically segregated into consumption, investment and government. This approach is indeed satisfactory when dealing with final demand, but the demand for land is largely a *derived* demand. Therefore, it is more useful to conceive of the market participants in a micro-economic sense, where buyers and sellers have more complex roles. Thus, consumers demand land for housing and perhaps other amenities (desires for lawns, driveways and so on). Firms demand land because of the necessary complementarity between production and land. Governments also demand land because of the public component of land, which enters into the activities of government as a producer and as the agent for public consumption. We shall leave this latter issue in abeyance for the moment.

Most theoretical models focus entirely on firms and consumers. As we shall show, another group of market participants must also be considered. These are the developers and speculators. The latter act as arbitragers and thus add to the demand for land. Real estate developers have a unique function: in the short run, they demand land as an input into their production function, just as Keynesian investors demand capital goods; in the long run, when the supply of land is not fixed, their activity in transforming land from one use to another clearly affects the supply side of the market as well.

The Commodity

So far we have dealt with land as if it is analogous to any other commodity. This reduces the problem of urban land use to a purely economic issue, which is antithetical to the multidimensionality we hope to explain. We remind the reader that we are not dealing with soil but with land as defined by Kellogg.[4]

The particular complexity is introduced by urban land because it has two attributes that enter independently into its demanders' utility functions. The first of these, availability, meets the need for *quantities* of space due to the technical coefficients of consumption and production as well as the apparent desire for space in its own right. To capture this concept it is not sufficient to deal with ground area alone. The third dimension can be captured by introducing the notion of intensity of land use, measured as the ratio of total square feet of space to the square footage of supporting land.

The second attribute, accessibility, has been shown by geographers and by transportation and location economists to be a factor in the demand for urban land by all users. Consumers demand residence locations near place of work, shopping areas and schools; firms place high priority on locations near the central business district or arterial roads.

The commodity land then can be defined only by the interaction of these two attributes, accessibility and availability. This corresponds to K. J. Lancaster's new approach, which involves "breaking away from the traditional approach that goods are objects of utility and, instead, supposing that it is the properties or characteristics of the goods from which utility is derived".[5] This definition of land has implications for the concept of land use, which is now the outcome of a market process wherein urban land is allocated to the various participants in the market depending on their respective valuations of the accessibility and availability attributes of sites.

---

[4] C. E. Kellogg, "Soil and Land Classifications", *Journal of Farm Economics*, Vol. 33, No. 4, 1951.

[5] K. J. Lancaster, "A new approach to consumer theory", *Journal of Political Economy*, Vol. 74, April 1966, p. 133.

Behavioural Assumptions

In a short-run analysis, allocation will depend on the demand side of the market alone. If we consider the supply of land, and therefore its accessibility and availability attributes as being constant, the demand for land will depend on the behaviour of consumers (households), firms, dealers and speculators, and the government. What determines the behaviour of these various demanders? To explain the role of consumers and firms, we have the elaboration of Isard's work by Alonso. In this model, land and transportation (a proxy for accessibility) costs become arguments in the utility function of the household and in the production function of the firm. These functions are then maximized subject to a set of standard constraints.

FIGURE 5-1

THEORETICAL CONSUMER BEHAVIOUR

OBJECTIVE FUNCTION: $MAX \ U_i = f_i \ (L_i, \ T_i, \ C_i)$

CONSTRAINT: $\qquad\qquad Y_i = P_L L_i + P_T T_i + P_C C_i$

WHERE: $\quad$ i represents the ith individual

$\qquad\qquad L_i$ is the quantity of land used by i

$\qquad\qquad T_i$ is his transportation input

$\qquad\qquad C_i$ is a composite commodity — all commodities consumed by i excluding land and transportation

$\qquad\qquad P$ is the price of the relevant input

$\qquad\qquad f_i$ is the general representation of the utility function

$\qquad\qquad U_i$ is the ith individual's utility

$\qquad\qquad Y$ is the ith individual's income

FIGURE 5-2

THEORETICAL FIRM BEHAVIOUR

OBJECTIVE FUNCTION:
$$MAX \ \pi_j = R_j - E_j$$
$$= P_v \ V_j - (P_M \ M_j + P_L \ L_j + P_T \ T_j)$$

CONSTRAINT: $\quad V_j = h_j \ (M_j, L_j, T_j, A_j)$

WHERE: $\quad j$ represents the jth firm

π is its profit

R is its revenue

E is its expenditure

V is its output

L_j is the land used by the jth firm

T_j is the transportation input used by the jth firm

M_j is all the inputs used by the jth firm excluding land and transportation

P is the price of the relevant variable

A_j is the state of technology of the jth firm

h_j is the general representation of the production function.

There is little point in stating the large number of postulates required to make this machinery viable. It is evident that these participants can deal with land *economically*. The result will be an optimal solution for the allocation of land. Before examining the implication of this result, however, we should consider the role of the all-important dealer-speculator. His specialty is capitalizing on imperfections in the market. He will have a net demand for land, which may be negative or positive. As a result of this intermediary role, his actions might be the major determinant of the price of land in the short-run. This is due to the relatively small exchange of land in the short-run and the resulting volatility in the price of traded land. While it would be easiest to deal with a pure speculator, he is too rare to demand our attention. We must focus rather on the speculator-developer, for whom land not only is a pure exchange commodity, but also has a convenience yield. He will present his demand for land in advance of actual transformation time if the potential gain in having the land ripe for transformation outweighs the market rate of interest.[6]

Conceptualizing the speculator-dealer's behaviour is not as simple as it is for the other actors. However, in the light of some recent developments in economic theory, one can now fit this third actor into suitable models.[7]

We assume that the speculator-dealer is holding land at time t but that he is trying to maximize realized profits. These profits are derived from buying and selling land over a given period. P_t and H_t are vectors representing a set of prices and a set of holdings of different types of land at time t. Profit is measured by summing over the change in holding in a specified period given the relevant prices. From this one must deduct the cost of holding land. This component consists of many items including the direct cost and the risk charge. However, since our speculator is also a dealer — a user of land in other phases of his operations — it is essential to recognize that the availability of land at a given time has a convenience yield for him. We have simplified the model by assuming that initial holdings are equal to zero. However, the model could be very easily adjusted to include initial stocks, non-land properties, and even differences between initial and final stocks of land. In this case we would relax the need to deal only with realized profit; the basis of the model would remain the same.

This speculator-dealer (in both the short and the long run) is an important feature of the equilibrating mechanism.

6 See Stigler's short-run market adjustment in G. J. Stigler, *The Theory of Prices*, Macmillan, New York, 1952, Ch. 9.

7 As a sample of this literature, see M. J. Brennan, "The supply of storage", *American Economic Review*, Vol. 48, March 1958; H. Working, "A theory of anticipatory prices", *American Economic Review*, Vol. 52, June 1962; and L. G. Telser, "A theory of speculation relating to profitability and stability", *Review of Economics and Statistics*, Vol. 41, August 1959.

Indeed it is possible to consider equilibrium in the land market as being determined by the fact that the algebraic sum of the changes in holdings of speculators-dealers and of all other actors in the land market is zero. In the short-run, one might regard speculators and non-speculators as engaged

FIGURE 5-3

THEORETICAL SPECULATOR-DEALER BEHAVIOUR

OBJECTIVE FUNCTION:

$$MAX \ \pi_w = \int_{t=O}^{v} P_L^t \ L'_w \ dt - \int_{t=O}^{v} N'_w$$

CONSTRAINTS:

(1) $L_w = O$

(2) $\sum_{t=O}^{v} L'_w = O$

(3) $N' = Z' + X' - B'$

WHERE: w represents the wth speculator-dealer

t represents time, so that $t = O$ is the initial time period and $t = v$ is the final time period

π_w is the profit of the wth speculator-dealer

P is the price of the relevant variable

N' is the cost of holding land for a unit time period

L_w is the amount of land held by w

L'_w is the change in the quantity of land held by w during a unit time period

Z' is the direct cost of holding land during period t

X' is the risk charge for holding land during period t

B' is the convenience yield from holding land during period t

in some sort of zero-sum game, although obviously in the long-run this need not be the case. Although we would have to be more careful about this, it may even be possible to relate the operations of the speculator-dealer and his profits to the degree of price instability as measured by price variations for a given type of land. On this point however much more research is needed.

It is interesting to note that with the inclusion of the speculator-dealer there are two broad sets of forces acting on the value of land: the forces based on the use-value of land for the consumers and the firms; and the forces based on the strict market behaviour expectations operating through the speculator. However, since our speculator-dealer is a hybrid character, he will embody some of the impact of both sets.[8]

One specific issue dampens our enthusiasm for this typical economic solution. This concerns the constraints imposed by the government on the market participants, which determine this frame of reference. Decision-making by the government can take two forms: first, it may make structural decisions which affect only the rules of the game (for example, zoning or taxation decisions); or it may also decide to participate directly in the marketplace (for example, urban renewal). In the latter case, the government becomes a marketeer also and an analysis of its behaviour must come within our purview. The decision-making process of government at the urban level is, however, difficult to deal with. Many would no doubt be tempted to characterize it as a purely heuristic process. Economic theory has given a relatively realistic explanation for public expenditures by borrowing to some extent from sociology and organization theory.[9] This theory enables us to handle both the structural decision-making and the market behaviour of government, and especially the latter because the theory is

---

[8] Those interested in parallels might have already noticed that our treatment of land has come very close to the analytical framework used to study the stock market and capital markets. On this point see W. J. Baumol, *The Stock Market and Economic Efficiency*, Fordham University Press, New York, 1965.

[9] See M. Olson, Jr., *The Logic of Collective Action*, Harvard University Press, Cambridge, Mass., 1965.

concerned with public goods which are produced, consumed and/or financed to some extent publicly. While the assumption of a structural decision-making role for government at an early stage of our analysis might be acceptable, it cannot be carried too far. Furthermore, since we cannot count on political science to provide us with a behaviour model of municipal government, the introduction of this marketeer role will also be most difficult. It might be possible to deal with it by following a Tinbergen or Theil approach. The Tinbergen approach, based on the specification of a group of targets and a set of policies designed to make their joint attainment feasible, is much closer to the real world than the Theil approach, which is based on defining a specific preference function for the macro-decision-maker. But neither of these approaches is sufficiently operational to serve our present purpose.[10]

Aggregating Behaviour

We have taken a very strong stand regarding the appropriate procedure for developing a land market mechanism. We have suggested who the appropriate participants are, particularly the speculator-dealer, and what their behaviour is. We have stressed that the problem is inordinately complex, partly because we have to consider the derived demands of multi-role actors and partly because the government's role is difficult to specify. Still, this does not prevent us from posing questions and attempting to answer them. On the contrary, to deal with the problem as a set of well structured partial issues presents a very strong temptation. However, this would amount to a rejection of a "total phenomenon" conception of the problem and that is precisely what we are trying to avoid.

Thus to solve the allocation problem we must deal with these participants in an interrelated fashion. As a first step, we

10 For a comparison of these, see, B. G. Hickman (ed.), *Quantitative Planning of Economic Policy*, Brookings Institution, Washington, D.C., 1965 (introduction).

could try to aggregate by means of a linear programming model that would maximize "land use" subject to certain constraints on the actors. The "dual" of this problem is of particular interest since it would provide shadow prices for the various inputs into land use. Many subcases of this general formulation have been examined but none seems to satisfy our basic requirements for an operational and illuminating model. For example, we have tried to define land as a commodity with two inputs, availability and accessibility, and then to allocate it among users so as to maximize some weighted index of available quantity and accessibility. This is an operations research type of formulation, and into it we could insert any other input which interests us (say, taxation) and evaluate its impact on land use and land value simultaneously. But constructing the "land use" variable requires too much qualitative information, which is readily recognized by political scientists and sociologists as crucial, but which is non-quantifiable.

A less ambitious use of linear programming techniques permits an alternative approach. If we consider the short run only, we may take the structural framework of the problem as given. Thus, our problem is to aggregate the three types of demanders into a market demand. This is possible if we linearize all functional relationships in our behavioural equations and formulate the land use problem of cities in a fashion similar to Henderson's for agricultural land use.[11] This approach has been taken by Herbert and Stevens[12] for a segment of the land market. There are many limitations on this type of mechanism, and a critical one centres on the difficulties of aggregation. In the *Journal of Farm Economics* of November, 1963, Richard Day[13] examined the difficulties of aggregation in linear programming models. While these

11 J. M. Henderson, "The Utilization of Agricultural Land", *Review of Economics and Statistics*, Vol. 41, 1959.

12 J. D. Herbert and B. H. Stevens, "A Model for the Distribution of Residential Activities in Urban Areas", *Journal of Regional Science*, Vol. 2, Fall 1960.

13 R. H. Day, "On Aggregating Linear Programming Models of Production", *Journal of Farm Economics*, Vol. 45, 1963.

are sufficient to discourage us from ultimately relying on linear programming it is a useful point of departure, both because it is well organized and integrated, and because it suggests the intimate relationship between land use and land value. The chief difficulties arise when we try to expand the role of the government, to deal with the badly behaved nature of the problem, and to add the supply side of the land market in the longer run context. To our knowledge, none of these issues has been properly handled as yet.

Over the long run allowance must be made for the behaviour of the actors to change. A simple model then becomes too restrictive. Consumers' tastes change, technological change twists production functions, and the speculator-dealer begins to operate on both sides of the market. In addition, a new actor, the subdivider, enters the picture on the supply side. No model has been constructed to explain his behaviour. Finally, the government enters to alter the framework of the market place and to participate in that market. Thus, in the long run, we are faced with a stock of land having associated uses within an equilibrium position, with flows subject to the behaviour of marketeers and to shocks on the market, and with manipulative activity by complex local government.

Alonso's Approach

A third possible approach might be to consider Alonso's asymmetric procedure for integrating the behaviour of the various marketeers. He has presented perhaps the most sophisticated theoretical models to explain the behaviour of consumers and producers. He has not, however, considered either government or speculator-developers. Nevertheless, his technique of combining his two groups of actors might provide us with our badly needed integrating mechanism.

At the outset he recognized our problem. To quote him, "at equilibrium, supply and demand quantities as well as prices must be equal. However, in the land market there are two goods (land and distance) but only one transaction and one price (that of land); therefore, the simple requirement of the equation of supply and demand prices and quantities becomes much more complicated".[14]

As long as quantity of land is not specified, he is able to allocate location between users in a rather straightforward manner. The moment that he shifts to quantity, the analysis becomes questionable. He starts by locating the highest bidder for land at the centre. The distance of the next user from the centre depends on the closest location after the wants of the first user are satisfied. Given the price at the centre, the quantity of land the first user will use can be determined by his demand curve for land. Knowing this, we obtain the second feasible location, the price of which will depend on the marginal price-location of the first user. Knowing this price allows him to solve for the quantity of land demanded by the second user and so on. Thus the price of land at any location can be found by solving the chain of equilibrium and marginal price-locations.

Note that the whole solution depends on the assumption as to the price at the centre. This assumption might not yield an accurate estimate of the price of land at the edge of settlement. As a result, a number of iterations based on different assumptions about this central price must be followed to finally yield an accurate estimate.

While the author favours the elegance and neatness of simultaneous equation solutions to his iterative solution, his simultaneous equations approach presupposes that an approximation to the solution has already been found by the iteration model discussed above. Thus, it is not a substitute for the model but rather a short-cut for further approximation to a numerical solution in place of repeated iterations.

Alonso's approach "works" only for a highly artificial situation. He cannot distinguish between users, and his technique does not really solve the problem of allocating both location and quantity of land. This asymmetric approach, however, might be the key to a meaningful solution, as we shall see.

---

[14] W. Alonso, *Location and Land Use*, Harvard University Press, Cambridge, Mass., 1964, p. 76.

Two Avenues

We have explained in previous sections how the different proposed modes of aggregation fail to provide both a well-structured conception of the land market and an analytical solution to our problem of urban land use. In this section we will suggest the elements of an aggregation procedure we think is more satisfactory. We will shift the emphasis from the problem of aggregation over relationships because it does not provide satisfactory procedures for complex market systems such as ours, nor does it permit us to examine the shift of land between uses, which is our major concern. We are forced to deal with the problem of land use shifts at a certain level of disaggregation. Since Alonso's dead-end has forced research workers to undertake exploratory work in other directions, we will proceed to a "synthesis through dynamic coupling".[15] We will contend that such a synthesis may be the only satisfactory way of integrating the different components of a behavioural model of urban land use. In the next paragraphs, we will describe briefly this technique, originally developed by R. M. Goodwin, and will show how it provides a fruitful alternative to the Alonso-type of integration.

One of the distinct impressions that the reader gets from Alonso is that he is "faking" the market equilibrium solution. Both in the text and in the appendix, the reader has some difficulty in perceiving how a solution is obtained. We feel that Alonso used the wrong technique but that the underlying strategy, which seems to be the rationale for such an approach, is fundamentally correct. Goodwin at the beginning of his 1947 paper[16] undertook to state the problem of interdependence in economics and suggested, as a broad strategy, that one should remember that "there is a pervasive asymmetry in economic interdependence, which is of fundamental impor-

---

15 R. H. Day, "Dynamic coupling, optimizing and regional interdependence", *Journal of Farm Economics*, Vol. 46, No. 2, May 1964, p. 446.

16 R. M. Goodwin, "Dynamic couplings with especial reference to markets having production lags", *Econometrica*, Vol. 15, No. 3, July 1947.

tance in reducing the difficulties of analysis".[17] The problem then boils down to a choice of explicit assumptions: either one is willing to assume asymmetry or one has to assume that there is no asymmetry but then one has to formulate clearly the nature of the feedback mechanism.[18] The first approach leads to some set of possible asymmetries (iteration of the Alonso type), while the second leads to the use of simulation techniques which provide some estimate of the "average behaviour" of a system via experiments involving artificial samples.

In the following section we shall explore the first approach but we have not closed the door to the simulation procedure; we will explore it systematically in a later section. The prototype to be presented in connection with the first approach represents only one of many interesting types of asymmetry which might be exploited in an attempt to solve the urban land use problem. This specific subcase was chosen because of our interest in the flow of land through uses in the process of urbanization.

A Recursive Approach

Dynamic coupling analysis refers to the partitioning of an economic reality into segments which are related asymmetrically so that given a partition of reality in three subsets, A, B, C, it may be said that A influences B (without being influenced by it), B influences C (without being influenced in turn by it). One could re-formulate the problem in cybernetic terms and simply state that the economic universe is partitionable into a series of relatively isolated systems.[19] Furthermore, if lags and time horizons are properly used, an economic universe

---

[17] R. M. Goodwin, op. cit., p. 181.

[18] In the first case, a solution is obtained by partitioning the system in such a way that unilateral coupling is assured between sectors. In the second case, a solution is obtained by a sequential analysis of the structure-performance interaction.

[19] The notion of relatively isolated system has been developed by H. Greniewski, Cybernetics Without Mathematics, Pergamon, New York, 1960.

can be partitioned so as to make a two-sector model satisfy the conditions for unilateral coupling. Our contention is that in the short run, we may assume the supply of urban space to be a given stock and may therefore tack onto it a marketing model for this existing space. The assumption of a fixed stock of land could be removed while preserving the conditions for unilateral coupling by assuming a one-year lag in construction and/or in subdivision activity. We would then have a complete short-run universe defined as a unilaterally coupled pair of models.

Now how can one adjust this technique to arrive at a solution to the urban land use problem? We could assume that in the urbanization process land is flowing from the rural market and that there is a one-year lag in the process of subdivision of land — that a year is required for the passage from non-subdivided to subdivided land. Therefore, at time t we will be faced with a set of subdivision decisions based on parameters of $t-1$. On the other hand the consumption of land by consumers and producers of non-land commodities will be taken as that at time t on the basis of parameters at this point in time. One might then be able to adapt this universe to a simple unilateral coupling problem. Even our dealer-speculator might be inserted in this system as a clearing-the-market entity, the holdings of the speculator being equal to the difference between the consumption and production of the commodity called land. This would obviously represent a way to synthesize the production and consumption of the land market. However, we would not be satisfied with this sort of simplification. Our consumption side is too complicated to be assumed as a unique element. Moreover, if we attempt to disaggregate the demand side, we find that we are falling into the interdependence trap again.

A more useful partitioning of the urban universe so as to permit the unilateral coupling of its components may, however, be proposed. It derives from the linkages between markets although we shall at this early stage concentrate on the labour side only.

We begin our model by assuming a firm that, by virtue of its growth performance and/or productivity, may be taken to be a "growth pole".[20] As it serves a national or international market, the demand curve for its product is price-elastic. Thus, the first unilateral coupling is achieved.

This firm has a production function $V_j = h_j (S_j, K_j, L_j, A_j)$ where (V) output is some function of (S) labour, (K) capital, (L) land and (A) technology. We assume in the simplest case that the use of land is dependent on some resource content. This extreme assumption may be readily modified to include, for instance, the industry's choice of a particular site for its activities. Thus, this firm's land-use decision is given.

The size of the labour force and its income is determined by the production function. This provides us with our second coupling. The behaviour of these workers in terms of location of residence may then be determined. Alonso's model of consumer behaviour seems to be an appropriate mechanism at this point. The accessibility variable for them will relate, however, solely to the place of work.

With the labour force of the growth pole now located, the third coupling emerges. It is based on the demand of this group for goods and services which will be met by servicing industries that again have their own production function $V_k = h_k (S_k, K_k, L_k, A_k)$. The scale of initial income will determine the composition of these servicing industries. Thus, for small-scale growth poles, the services will be largely importing and distributing. As the scale expands, manufacturing for the domestic market becomes feasible so that the industrial structure may change within our model.

The production function enables us to derive these industries' demand function for land by Alonso's method. The key variable is accessibility to consumers. Thereafter, the fourth coupling emerges. For the labour force in the service industries must proceed to find residential sites and, once again, we turn to the Alonso demand function.

[20] F. Perroux, "Les industries motrices et la croissance d'une économie nationale", in F. Perroux et al., Problèmes de Planification, Les Presses des Hautes Etudes Commerciales, Montréal, 1964.

The end result of this first iteration is a set of equilibrium prices, locations and land quantities for all participants. In the process of achieving this equilibrium, our speculator-dealer, recognizing gaps between equilibrium and actual prices at any point, begins to operate in the land market arbitraging these differentials away or, if a dealer, affecting the supply to meet anticipated demands.

The entry of a new growth pole sets off a parallel chain of reactions. There will be repercussions on the first constellation, and the new equilibrium relationships must recognize interaction between the two poles; but we foresee no insurmountable problems resulting. We must recalculate the locational distribution of the labour force, and then of the service industries and finally their workers. But the markets remain unilaterally coupled and the same functions will serve to allocate variables of different magnitudes.

This particular approach endeavours to remove the point-oriented urban base theory from its essentially sterile view of urban activity. Using a similar concept of economic linkages this approach makes allocation of land an integral part of the process of urban dynamics, so that urban growth, urban development and urban land use mesh into a unified model.

A Simulation Approach

In the previous section we presented a sketch of an integrated model synthesizing some of the most important economic and geographic features of the urban phenomenon. This synthesis was based on assumptions establishing a structure of markets unilaterally coupled. However, such a model has some serious limitations, for one might not be able to partition the economy or to disaggregate it very much without running into serious interdependence. At that point the dynamical coupling theory would, of course, collapse. This suggests that one may have to resort to both alternatives discussed in the previous section: built-in asymmetry, and simulation. To resort at last to simulation is to admit that the problem tackled was ill-defined.[21] However, the use of simulation need not be an admission of defeat; it may be the only appropriate way to tackle ill-structured or ill-defined problems. Such problems are process-oriented rather than outcome-oriented and they can be approached only by quasi-analytic techniques. Simulation is one of those techniques. Simulation provides in effect an empirical and an artificial way of generating some notion of the "average behaviour of the system" which, for some purposes, might be regarded as an approximation to a solution of this particular system.

Some work has already been done in this direction by economists and geographers[22] who have realized that current techniques do not suit their ill-defined problems. They have discovered that most of the work being done either dealt with well structured ones or attempted to squeeze ill-defined problems into existing slots. In this section we introduce the concept of simulation to suggest how this technique might be used to solve our urban land use problem.

In a fascinating paper, C. W. Churchman has presented an analysis of the concept of simulation attempting "to make explicit what body of scientific effort is to be included under the concept".[23] He has proposed there that X may be said to simulate Y if

X is a system and Y is a system
X enables us to predict Y within certain limits
Y describes reality
the rules of validity in X are sampling rules

Each of these necessary conditions is clear enough except perhaps the last one which refers to the mode of inference

---

21 W. R. Reitman, "Heuristic decision procedures, open constraints and the structure of ill-defined problems", in M. W. Shelly and G. L. Bryan, *Human Judgments and Optimality*, Wiley, New York, 1964.

22 "Simulation: A Symposium", *American Economic Review*, Vol. 50, No. 5, December 1960; W. L. Garrison, "Toward simulation models of urban growth and development", in K. Norborg (ed.), *Proceedings of the IGU Symposium in Urban Geography, LUND 1960*, Lund, 1962.

23 C. W. Churchman, "An analysis of the concept of simulation", Working Paper No. 34, Management Science Research Center, Berkeley, July 1961, (Mimeo), pp. 9-18.

implied by the simulation procedures. When sampling techniques rather than direct inferences are used to derive consequences from assumptions, the techniques are said to be "non-analytic". Churchman posits that the sampling procedure becomes an integral part of the inference process:

> . . . if the domain of X is sampled in a certain manner and whenever $p(x)$ is true, $q(x)$ is also true, then one can make the inference that "$p(x)$ implies $q(x)$" with a certain degree of confidence.

This definition of simulation is in a sense puzzling since it presents the relationship "X simulates Y" as meaning that X is an approximation of Y. This might lead some to confuse it with other approximations referred to as model or theory. But as Churchman puts it, the specificity of simulation is that it is a kind of system in which "the rules of validation require sampling of the relevant entities".

The same point is made by Garrison as he warns the research worker of the limitations of such an approach.

> The simulation process is the study of simple systems with the complexity of the model not being built in but being due to the stochastic properties of the real situation and the interlocking of simple systems.[24]

The research worker typically turns to simulation when unable to "achieve results with alternate tools".[25] He must then resist the temptation of "producing a complex model and reproducing the system which he wished to study in the first place" for then he would "fall into the trap of reproducing his own ignorance".[26] The difficulty is to find the right balance between intractable complexity and trivial simplicity.

J. Harling has pointed out that a simulation approach may be divided into three stages:[27]

---

[24] Garrison, *op. cit.*

[25] *Ibid.*

[26] *Ibid.*

[27] J. Harling, "Simulation techniques in operations Research", *Operations Research*, Vol. 6, 1958.

raw data in appropriate form
model construction
operation of the model

This might serve as a useful way to organize our approach to the study of urban reality via simulation models.

A certain number of studies which we will not attempt to present have already made use of the simulation approach. These models all have a large dose of specificity, and an important heuristic content characterizes most of them. As an illustration we might refer the reader to a recent study of the factors affecting land use by Chapin and Weiss.[28]

In the case of specific cities, there would be advantages in beginning with several interesting subroutines which might be able to capture some of the features of the sectors which we have identified above. For instance it would appear rather simple to apply the findings of standard transportation studies to the definition of the normal preference area of the workers. One might be able, using the method suggested by W. Goldner,[29] to generate some preference profile to serve as the basic stochastic device. From there it would be possible to examine the "average behaviour" of workers under a well defined set of constraints through a large-scale experiment using simulation techniques based on this stochastic process. Similar approaches could possibly be stages for the different segments of the population.

Other partial studies are possible along the lines suggested by Mary Rawson to examine the distribution of the burden of taxation.[30] One can easily see how such an approach could be extended to the allocational side. However, these subroutines would only prepare the way for a more pretentious model which would attempt to push the use of the non-analytic technique as fully as possible without falling into the

28 F. Stuart Chapin Jr. and Shirley F. Weiss, *Factors Influencing Land Development*, University of North Carolina, Chapel Hill, N.C., 1962.

29 W. Goldner, "Spatial and locational aspects of metropolitan labour markets", *American Economic Review*, Vol. 45, March 1955.

30 Mary Rawson, *Property Taxation and Urban Development*, Urban Land Institute, Washington, 1961.

"ignorance trap". This approach would enable us to consider the qualitative dimensions of the urban land use problem more efficiently than does the recursive approach. It might also serve, although only at an ulterior stage, to control its results.

These two avenues represent, however, crude attempts to estimate the characteristics of the urban total phenomenon. They only set the stage for the more extensive section of our own research which involves tests of some hypotheses, given this estimate of the urban system. Such work will tell us if we are warranted to push on until finally this estimate becomes the basis for the study of instrumental variables and other sources of shocks in the system.

Filling the Boxes

In order to fill these theoretical boxes, we have constructed a data bank for a major segment of the territory of the City of Ottawa. Since most of the data necessary were scattered over many city departments, it was essential to elaborate this integrated form of the data before any analysis could be initiated. Our final sample of lots contains some 8,000 elements and constitutes some 11.4 per cent of the total Ottawa lots. The composition of the sample and a few interesting characteristics of some of these components are presented in Table 5-1.

Since this sample includes 11.4 per cent of the total number of lots, one might expect a total tax assessment of some $920 million for the whole city if the sample was truly representative. (The total tax assessment for the sample is $105.4 million.) In fact, according to the Annual Report of the Assessment Department (June 23, 1966) the total assessment was about $948 million. At first glance, therefore, our sample would appear to be in the right ball park.

Our data bank contains information necessary to analyze the behaviour of all the relevant actors on the urban scene except perhaps the speculator-dealer. Since he does not operate as clearly in the open as the others, we have experienced diffi-

TABLE 5-1
Sample Data (Ottawa, 1965)

Use	No. of lots	Area in use (million sq. ft.)	Percentage of total area	Total Assessment (millions of dollars)	Assessment per sq. foot
Unimproved residential	244	2.1	3	1.0	0.48
Single residential	5288	50.1	72	57.3	1.14
Double residential	533	2.9	4	4.5	1.57
Duplex and triplex residential	975	5.1	7	7.0	1.38
Row residential	145	1.4	2	2.6	1.89
Apartment	307	3.9	6	15.9	4.06
Unimproved commercial	35	.3	1	.4	1.28
Improved commercial	168	1.5	2	4.7	3.19
Offices, etc.	75	.5	1	5.8	10.92
Total	8011	69.6	100	105.4	1.52

culty in obtaining data on positions taken at different times by the six to ten major land dealers in the areas. We have therefore postponed this section of our work to a later stage. However, for all the other actors, we are already in a position to establish an order of magnitude for some fairly important parameters. To illustrate the results available at this point we shall discuss briefly a few elements relating to these actors in turn. We shall do little, however, to integrate these components into a whole. Such aggregation will have to await a more complete and a more satisfactory sketch of the system. Moreover, we shall not delve into the details of the analysis or of the subsystem which has guided our work in this short paper. These explanations will be available in the monographs resulting from the studies.

The Pattern of Residential Land Use

At an early stage we explored the impact of the transportation input in the locational choice of households. We felt that we should be able to measure the impact of these transportation factors on the concentration of residential land uses in a given area. Accordingly, we have attempted to explain the relative importance of single residential, double residential, duplex and triplex residential, row residential, and apartment land uses as a function of distance downtown, to transit lines, to shopping centres and to schools, these being amenities attractive to diverse members of households. Some results are presented in the following table for analysis conducted at the census tract level.

These preliminary explorations emphasize what Chapin and Weiss have aptly named "activity-related factors",[31] as opposed to property-related factors or to the conditions of the site. The only important element omitted from this preliminary exploration of activity-related factors is the journey to work component. Part of it is captured by the time distance downtown, but given the multiplicity of poles of work-

---

[31] F. Stuart Chapin Jr. and Shirley F. Weiss, *op. cit.*, p. 42.

TABLE 5-2

Transportation Factors in the pattern of residential land use (selective results)

	DT	DSS	DSC	DSCS	TDT
Single[1]	−.02106	−.00771	.00545	.00209	.02961
t	(−.3136)	(−.4990)	(.2485)	(.1899)	(3.6743)
Double	.0038	−.00282	−.00277	−.00411	−.00069
t	(.1956)	(−.7541)	(−.5112)	(−1.5369)	(−.3530)
Duplex and Triplex	.00815	−.00449	−.00604	−.00349	−.00585
t	(.2867)	(−.6878)	(−.6373)	(−.7482)	(−1.7170)
Row	−.00963	−.00729	−.00219	−.00376	−.00124
t	(−.5718)	(−1.8814)	(−.3900)	(−1.3597)	(−.6133)
Apartment	−.01344	.00190	−.00243	.00172	−.00674
t	(.5387)	(.3322)	(−.2926)	(.4197)	(−2.2515)
Residential	−.00591	−.02042	−.00799	−.00756	.01508
t	(−.1128)	(−1.6932)	(−.4572)	(−.8772)	(2.3975)

The dependent variable is the proportion of land in a particular use in a given census tract as a proportion of the total amount of land of this census tract in our sample. The five independent variables are: distance from transit line (DT), distance to shopping centre (DSS), distance to public school (DSC), distance to separate school (DSCS), and time distance downtown (TDT).

1 Regression equation significant at the 5 per cent level using an F test.

ing places in Ottawa, this is a rather poor proxy for such a variable.

However limited these preliminary results are, they indicate rather strongly that it is impossible to deal with the residential sector as a whole. We must disaggregate at least to the point where the different components identified in Table 5-2 are clearly separated. The activity-related factors which are relevant to some types of residences are not all the ones which are relevant in other cases. In particular the difference between single and apartment, on the one hand, and double, duplex-triplex and row, on the other, in the seemingly important distance to downtown variable raises some interesting questions which must be explored in greater depth.

Any result obtained at the level of census tracts may or may not hold for a further disaggregation. In fact, the partitioning of the city into such components is obviously not the only possible one and any result we obtain may very well be very sensitive to the choice of a principle of classification. Moreover, the fact that we have chosen to exclude at this first stage many of the property-oriented factors which could have been included might produce distorted results. Indeed it is interesting to note that very few generalizations about the factors affecting residential location choices hold for cities of different sizes and even for cities of the same size. Some of the divergences in the few examples examined by Chapin and Weiss are illuminating in this context.

The Pattern of Non-Residential Land Use

The same type of analysis of the non-residential sector reveals that, as one might suspect, an altogether different set of factors is relevant. However, we have retained two of the indicators of activity-oriented factors: distance to transit line, and time distance downtown. To these we have added two indicators of density — the area of the census tract and the density of surrounding census tracts — hoping to capture a market-size effect. It appears that these factors perform fairly well as predictors of land use concentration at least for commercial

TABLE 5-3

Some factors affecting the pattern of non-residential land use:
Ottawa (Selective results)

	SQF	DN	DT	TDT
Commercial Unimproved[1]	−.00000000	.00000042	−.00047131	.00008296
t	−1.0314	2.2229	−.2626	.3539
Retail[2]	−.00000000	.00000163	−.01050915	.00027016
t	−1.0181	1.2947	.8714	−.1725
Retail (Owner-occupied)	−.00000000	.00000075	−.00417437	−.00032233
t	−.6614	1.4677	−.8588	−.5107
Services[2]	−.00000000	.00000054	−.01874364	−.00398863
t	(−.3474)	(.2427)	(−.8762)	(−1.4361)
Manufacturing	−.00000000	.00000029	−.00299588	−.00077697
t	(.5348)	(−.7677)	(−.8195)	(1.6369)

The dependent variable is the proportion of land in a particular use in a given census tract as a proportion of the total amount of land of this census tract in our sample. The four independent variables are: the area of the census tract (SQF), the density of the surrounding census tracts (DN), the distance to transit line (DT), and the time distance downtown (TDT).

[1] Significant at the 5 per cent level.
[2] Significant at the 10 per cent level.

land use. However, our studies show that these variables are not useful for the prediction of industrial land use.

Some results of our non-residential land use analysis are presented in Table 5-3. Such specifications of the relationships defining the factors affecting urban land use and the loadings of these factors are strictly illustrative of the convergence process which will define the final product. For instance there is little hope, it seems to us, of understanding commercial land use without understanding better the clustering of services in cities. There are complementary relationships which have hardly been explored yet but which are essential components of the decision-making process of firms attempting to maximize profit. As for the location of factories, they may be limited to a great extent by the availability of land zoned for the appropriate purpose. Any attempt, therefore, to deal with any of the actors in isolation may be more conducive to uncertainties and errors than to a good perception of the network of relationships defining the land market. Moreover industries may still be influenced by such outmoded considerations as the labour market, proximity to railroad lines or to the main waterways which were the dominant features of industrial location in previous decades. The reasons for industrial locational choices have a greater permanence and durability than those for household choices.

We would like to make two points in the light of these results. First, it seems that our crude relations are much more useful for the commercial sector than for the residential sector; and second, although our sample is fairly representative of the multiplicity of land uses, some of the weak results may reflect biases in the selection. Since our dependent variables are based on the proportion of land in various uses from our sample, the probability of sampling errors for this proportion makes it a severe test for our hypotheses about the relative concentration of land uses. At a more disaggregated level, it should be possible to achieve greater accuracy. In a way, this has to do with the choice of the partitioning and its impact on the parameters — a problem which has received little attention in the literature.

The Public Sector: Taxation and Expenditures

The decisions made by the public sector may pertain to the definition of the rules of the game or may involve simply intervening as yet another actor in the land market. For instance, zoning decisions will definitively affect land values but more dramatically will segregate the uses of land so as to insure the "highest and best" use of each plot of land. The public sector can also affect the allocation of land among uses and the distribution of the municipal fiscal residuum by its taxation and expenditures policies. It is not clear that any instrument used by the municipal government is univocal. Indeed, the municipal government's intervention on the supply side, on the demand side or on market operations regarding any land use affects not only the allocation of land but also the distribution of the tax-expenditure burden, and may even be an important instrument of community planning.[32]

Over the last fifteen years, shifting the burden of providing municipal services more and more from the city to the developer and the builder has had dramatic effects on the size of the average developer-builder's operations. This has resulted in a peculiar oligopoly which for all practical purposes defines the pattern of expectations for future development. Moreover the city's zoning policy has been at best erratic, and it is only under the pressures of this oligopoly that "eminently desirable" changes (that is, very beneficial to the group) have been brought about. For instance, only recently have changes in the zoning of the central business district permitted a much more intensive use of land.

We are in the process of preparing monographs on the impact of taxation and public expenditures on urban land use and land values. Such works will involve rather elaborate testing procedures. Therefore, we shall simply report here on

---

[32] For instance, "Municipal Real Estate Taxation as an Instrument for Community Planning", *Yale Law Journal*, Vol. 57, 1947, pp. 219-242; M. S. Wehrly and J. R. McKeever, *Urban Land Use and Property Taxation*, Urban Land Institute, Technical Bulletin No. 18, May 1952.

the nature of that work and on some of our provisional conclusions.

This study involves an examination of the different components of the tax function and the factors affecting them. Also studied is the impact of changes in these components on the allocation of land among the diverse uses and on the distribution of the tax burden among the different groups of land uses. We have found no significant bias by use; nor does there appear to be any bias for any of the concentric zones corresponding to the different stages of the city's development in the assessment to sales value ratio. This seems to imply that the assessment procedure is fairly equitable in these two dimensions. Since the tax rate (tax bill/assessed value) is given, it means that the effective tax rate (tax bill/ sales value) is fairly homogeneous across the use and the concentric bands defining the city. Our results here vary with some obtained in the United States where the assessment procedure was often found to be severely biased.

On the expenditures side, the great problem is the apportioning of the benefits from different types of public expenditures among the different groups of land uses. At this stage some preliminary computations have been made to allocate the benefits from expenditures on the police department, the fire department, the road and traffic department, and the recreation and parks department. Moreover, a study on the urban renewal schemes developed in the City of Ottawa is under way. These studies will culminate in the allocation of benefits among the different portions of the city. Obviously certain services are population-oriented, while others are property-oriented and accordingly the apportioning has been done among the census tracts on the basis of population quotas, or on the basis of land area in certain uses.

The partial results available at this stage are of no interest. However, a rough study of fiscal incidence of the municipality's operations becomes possible when these data have been constructed and distributed on a census tract basis. We will then be able, for example, to determine the thresholds defining the ranges of certain variables for the different land uses such as the fiscal residuum. We may then understand the distributive impact of alternative tax arrangements and expenditures patterns. Furthermore, if some semi-stable characteristics of the different land uses are uncovered, we will be able to demonstrate the allocative function of the land among these diverse uses through the channel of fiscal operations of the municipality. This would extend Mary Rawson's study from the distribution to the allocation side.[33]

Our study of urban renewal schemes should enable us to raise some questions about the goals of the different municipal governments' renewal schemes: is it a cheap way to assemble land for the business community, or a way to increase the tax base of the municipality; or do other motives underlie this clumsy method of removing low quality housing in an economic system where poverty seems to create a demand for such accommodation?[34]

Conclusion

These elements constitute only partial views of a broader problem. It is clear that we shall have to explore in greater detail the operations of households, firms, speculator-dealers and the public sectors before we can hope to provide an answer to the problem of allocating land to its highest and best use. In particular we shall have to examine more carefully some industries like the housing industry which is obviously one of the crucial determinants of land use. It is only at this stage that the aggregation procedures suggested above will come into the picture. The filling of these boxes will be our priority for some time to come.

---

[33] Mary Rawson, *op. cit.*
[34] R. F. Muth, "Slums and Poverty" in A. A. Nevitt (ed.), *The Economic Problems of Housing*, Macmillan, London, 1967.

6 The Integration of Metropolitan Federations: the Interaction of Political Theory and Urban Phenomena

Harold Kaplan

Introduction

The purpose of this essay is threefold: to indicate briefly how political scientists have studied urban phenomena, to suggest the areas of research that should have priority in the future, and to present — as an example of one approach — an excerpt from my own research.

Political Science and Urban Phenomena

Throughout the twentieth century, the political scientists' interest in urban phenomena has been largely confined to the study of urban government. At first, the institutional and reform approaches prevailed. Political scientists were primarily concerned with describing the formal institutions of local government and with making proposals for improving that structure. In the universities, local government was usually taught in conjunction with public administration and public finance. In the 1920's when political scientists first turned their attention to the metropolitan area, their basic purpose was to demonstrate that regional government would be an improvement over the existing state of things.

The so-called behavioural approach to urban government, largely a product of American political science, involved a greater interest in political processes — in decision making, conflict, elections and the activities of interest groups — than in the formal institutions of government. This approach also emphasized value-free rather than reform-oriented analysis, the development of more sophisticated research techniques and greater concern with general methodological problems. Particular studies in this vein may have had additional goals, but the above characteristics seem to be the *sine qua non* of the behavioural approach. The preponderance of current literature on urban government is in the institutional and reform traditions. With a few exceptions, the behavioural approach has been confined to the study of United States cities.[1]

One may also identify two camps within the behavioural bloc: those political scientists who study urban phenomena in order to contribute to general, empirically based political theory; and those who study urban phenomena as ends in themselves. The former group use urban areas as a convenient laboratory for the testing of certain propositions. Two recent books in the behavioural tradition illustrate this distinction. Banfield and Wilson's *City Politics* and Dahl's *Who Governs?* share the basic characteristics of the behavioural approach.

---

[1] The transition from institutional and reform approaches to behavioural approaches is described in Wallace Sayre and Nelson Polsby, "Political Science and the Study of Urbanism", mimeo, Committee on Urbanization, Social Science Research Council, 1961. For examples of the earlier approaches see William Robson (ed.), *Great Cities of the World*, revised edition, Macmillan, New York, 1957; or most of the textbooks on local government. Among those studies pursuing a behavioural approach are: James Wilson, *Negro Politics*, The Free Press, New York, 1960; Wallace Sayre and Herbert Kaufman, *Governing New York City*, Russell Sage Foundation, New York, 1960; Robert Dahl, *Who Governs?*, Yale University Press, New Haven, 1961; Edward Banfield and James Wilson, *City Politics*, Harvard and MIT Press, Cambridge, Massachusetts, 1963; Oliver Williams and Charles Adrian, *Four Cities*, University of Pennsylvania Press, Philadelphia, 1963; and Robert Agger, *et al.*, *The Rulers and the Ruled*, Wiley, New York, 1964. The two classics in Canadian urban government fall largely in the institutional and reform category. See K. G. Crawford, *Canadian Municipal Government*, University of Toronto Press, Toronto, 1954; and Donald Rowat, *Your Local Government*, Macmillan, Toronto, 1955.

However, Banfield and Wilson appear mainly interested in urban politics *per se*, while Dahl studied New Haven in order to better understand the operation of democratic systems.

More recently urban political scientists have broadened their perspectives and have abandoned their almost exclusive emphasis on urban government. Recent studies examine decision making at the higher levels of government on policy matters directly affecting urban areas;[2] the political consequences of rapid urbanization, particularly in developing areas;[3] and the "decentralization of powers" as a problem of national political systems.[4] At the same time attempts have been made to develop the comparative study of local political systems.[5] On these topics one may also distinguish between institutional and reform approaches and the behavioural approach. Within the behavioural camp, moreover, one may further distinguish between the systematic theorists and the political scientists who give first priority to the substantive problem being studied.

Research Priorities

Decisions on future research priorities will depend on the answer to two questions. Should the urban political scientist give greater weight to neutral analysis or reform-oriented studies? And if the behavioural or value-free type of research is to be pursued, should urban phenomena be studied for

---

2 For example, Michael Danielson, *Federal-Metropolitan Politics and the Commuter Crisis*, Columbia University Press, New York, 1965.

3 The political consequences have received somewhat more attention from sociologists than from political scientists. See Bert Hoselitz, *The Sociological Aspects of Economic Growth*, The Free Press, New York, 1964; Bruce Russett *et al.*, *World Handbook of Political and Social Indicators*, Yale University Press, New Haven, 1964.

4 For example, James Fesler, "Approaches to the Understanding of Decentralization", *Journal of Politics*, Vol. 27, August 1965, pp. 536-566.

5 See, for example, Fred Burke, *Local Government and Politics in Uganda*, Syracuse University Press, Syracuse, 1964, particularly pp. 239-246.

their intrinsic interest or for their relevance to more general questions in political theory?

The answers to these questions appear to depend on personal tastes or on one's basic values. There seems to be no way to demonstrate that one approach is better than the other. Even the value-free analyst must resort to non-empirical or non-testable value statements in explaining why he pursues this approach and not the reform-oriented one.

But not all matters need be left to personal taste. A good case can be made for paying greater attention in the years ahead to value-free, as opposed to reform-oriented, research. The reform-oriented approach has prevailed for many years, at the cost of our adequately understanding the nature of existing practices. This fact is particularly true in Canada. One may urge greater attention to neutral analysis of existing patterns primarily in order to achieve some balance in approaches. Furthermore, without insight into the current operation of urban government and politics, reform ideologies become a set of stale clichés. For the sake of intelligent reform, there must be continuous value-free research into the existing state of things.

There is another matter which, in my view, should not be left to personal taste. Whatever his preferences, it is incumbent on the political scientist to separate his descriptive analysis from his reform proposals more clearly than many urban political scientists now do. In the typical text book on urban government, important value judgements merge imperceptibly with neutral description, and crucial value assumptions are hidden in the middle of largely descriptive paragraphs. Further, those urban political scientists who *do* choose the road of neutral analysis are no longer justified in confining their description to formal institutions. Adequate description requires a discussion of the social context of politics and all the broader forces that are subsumed in the phrase "political process".

If the basic premises of the behavioural movement are accepted, one must also consider whether urban phenomena are to be studied in their own right or merely as convenient laboratories to develop and test more general political propositions. Should we try to fill gaps in theory or gaps in our understanding of the politics of urban and metropolitan areas? Some studies happily may do both; but often a choice between the two approaches must be made.

If the goal of urban political science is to explore all those political decisions relevant to the development and future of metropolitan areas, the heavy emphasis on local-governmental studies is misplaced. The senior levels play an important part in determining the future of metropolitan areas and will undoubtedly increase their role in the next few decades. However, if we are interested in contributing to recent theory on the operation of political systems, then the political scientists' focus on local politics makes good sense. For, as Dahl and others have pointed out, focusing on local politics permits one to study entire political systems at less expense than is possible at the national level.

The author's inclinations are to treat the urban world as a laboratory for the exploration of certain general theoretical notions. This approach is explored in the following pages by an attempt to demonstrate the relevance of general theory to the study of the Metropolitan Toronto government.

References to general political theory in the preceding pages should not be interpreted to mean that there is theoretical consensus in the political science profession. On the contrary, there are many theoretical interests and orientations, any one of which could be pursued at the urban level. Perhaps the most significant development in political theory in recent years is the political scientists' growing interest in "general systems" theory.[6] Some political scientists have attempted to employ and modify concepts developed by the functionalist school of

---

[6] Indications of the political scientists' interest in general systems theory can be seen in Morton Kaplan, *System and Process in International Politics*, Wiley, New York, 1957; David Easton, *A Systems Analysis of Political Life*, Wiley, New York, 1965; and Karl Deutsch, *The Nerves of Government*, The Free Press, New York, 1963.

sociology.[7] From these theoretical frameworks, I have selected one concept — integration — for examination in this essay. The concept will be discussed as it applies to the author's studies on Metropolitan Toronto.[8]

Before we proceed, one further general question must be considered. The following discussion emphasizes the relevance of general theory for the analysis of a particular case in urban politics. But what, we may ask, is the contribution of urban political analysis to general theory? The belief that such analysis *can* make a contribution to theory rests on the assumption that there are generalizations which apply to all systems so that insights gained at one level will hold true at other levels. At the moment this assumption is more a matter of faith than demonstration, although I find the idea sufficiently promising to be worth further exploration. If a general systems theory does exist, the results of studies on urban political systems can be applied easily to entire political systems at the national or international level.

At the same time great care must be taken to delineate the distinctive features of each level of analysis and to know the limits of transferability of generalizations. In short, urban political systems should be studied, not only because they are similar to other types of systems; they should be studied because they are different and because an understanding of these urban systems is necessary to round out our typology of systems. Many urban political systems in the United States and Canada, for example, operate without benefit of political parties. This fact in itself should justify research on such

---

[7] The functionalist approach has been carefully defined by Robert Merton and Talcott Parsons. See Merton, *Social Theory and Social Structure*, revised edition, The Free Press, New York, 1951. The political theorist most clearly influenced by functionalist notions is Gabriel Almond. For a recent formulation of his views, see G. Almond, "A Developmental Approach to Political Systems", *World Politics*, Vol. 18, November 1965, pp. 183, 214.

[8] The discussion of Metro that follows is drawn from a larger study: Harold Kaplan, *Urban Political Systems — A Functional Analysis of Metro Toronto*, Copp Clark, Toronto, 1968. The research has been supported financially by the Canadian Council on Urban and Regional Research and the Central Mortgage and Housing Corporation.

systems. Similarly, because of their distinctive features, the Metro case and others like it may contribute to a general theory of integration in federal systems. At the local and regional level, but not at the national or international level, there is a higher authority (the province or state) which makes all final decisions about the future of local or regional systems. Thus, discussion of integration in metropolitan federations presents an additional complexity: there are vertical relations (provincial-municipal) as well as horizontal relations (municipal-municipal). Provincial-municipal relations, moreover, are a field for exploration into interesting problems about systems within systems.

Thus, one must be wary of justifying the study of urban political systems solely on the grounds that such systems are microcosms of larger systems. For this reason it appears that Dahl and others pursuing his tack have led us into a blind alley. If one is interested in the functioning and future of democratic systems in the modern world, the obvious course is to study France, Ghana or Mexico — not New Haven, "Oretown", or some other community. The study of urban politics is better justified by the special theoretical problems these systems raise, than by the dubious universality of the theoretical problems encountered at the urban level.[9]

The Concept of Integration

Central to the functional approach is the notion of "functional requisites" or "functional imperatives" — that is, certain problems or needs which every system must meet in order to survive. Most of the imperatives discussed in the literature may be subsumed under two broad types: external or adaptive functions; and internal or integrative functions. Adaptation is the process by which a system meets the demands made by

---

[9] Most of the behaviourist studies cited in footnote 1 stress the similarity between urban systems and larger systems. There seems to have been no careful attempt to state the distinctive features of local political systems. Some preliminary suggestions along these lines are offered in *Urban Political Systems, ibid.*

its physical and social environment; integration is the process by which a system secures and maintains the support of its members. In the following discussion, I shall be mainly concerned with how the Metro system met its integrative problems, although the impact of its integrative performance on its adaptive abilities will also be noted.

In the theories of Talcott Parsons, the most influential of the sociological functionalists, integration is the means by which systems bring individual behaviour into line with the collective goals and values of the system.[10] The key integrative mechanism is institutionalization — the establishment, transmission and enforcement of values, norms and role expectations. In a sense, the individual's behaviour is governed by these norms and expectations. The product of the integrative process is solidarity or morale. A system is said to be well integrated, therefore, when the members have internalized the norms and role expectations of the system and see the system as legitimate, self-evident and perhaps even sacred. Institutionalization, or what we shall call normative integration, is Parsons' answer to the basic Hobbesian problem of how anarchy is averted and society made possible.

The political scientists' use of the concept of integration stemmed largely from an interest in the process by which new institutions take root. How does a nation emerge from a welter of tribes or clans? How can democratic institutions succeed in a society totally unfamiliar with such institutions?

---

[10] For functional imperatives and the Parsonian definition of integration, see T. Parsons and N. Smelser, *Economy and Society*, The Free Press, New York, 1956, pp. 46-84. Parsons' imperatives are more elaborate than the two listed here. Parsons divides the internal and external functions, so that his final list consists of four functions. Our use of two rather than four imperatives follows Robert Bales. See R. Bales, "The Equilibrium Problem in Small Groups", in Talcott Parsons, *et al.*, *Working Papers in the Theory of Action*, The Free Press, New York, 1953, pp. 111-161; and R. Bales and P. Slater, "Role Differentiation in Small Decision-Making Groups", in Talcott Parsons, *et al.*, *Family, Socialization, and Interaction Process*, The Free Press, New York, 1955, pp. 295-306. See also George Homan's distinction between external and internal functions in *The Human Group*, Harcourt, Brace, New York, 1950, Ch. 4-6.

How do international organizations survive in a world of sovereign nations? In attempting to answer these questions, political scientists have viewed integration more as a process than a state of being. The integrating process has been defined as one in which individuals shift their loyalties to new institutions or new systems. A state of integration exists when the members accept the system and its institutions as legitimate, exhibit a sense of community or self-awareness, resolve their differences in order to preserve the unity of the system, and commit personal resources to the pursuance of certain collective goals.[11]

Political scientists do not concur on the use of the word "integration". Some political scientists see it as a frame of mind among the system members; others equate integration with the objective indicators of integration. The former group stresses subjective variables; the latter examines rates of interaction or transaction. Moreover, some political scientists have described certain systems as integrated when their structures were sufficiently developed to achieve their functions. In this view, integration equals successful performance.[12]

As a working definition integration can be treated as the securing of support for a system and its institutions among the system's members or potential members. The Parsonian type of integration will be called normative integration. The hallmark of normative integration is the presence of values, norms, role expectations, socialization procedures, social control mechanisms, a sense of identity and solidarity, and a

---

[11] For the political scientists' use of the term "integration" see Karl Deutsch, et al., *Political Community and the North Atlantic Area*, Princeton University Press, Princeton, 1957; Ernest Haas, *The Uniting of Europe*, Stanford University Press, Stanford, 1958; James Toscano and Philip Jacob (eds.), *The Integration of Political Communities*, Lippincott, New York and Philadelphia, 1963; Karl Deutsch and William Folz, *Nation-Building*, Atherton, New York, 1963; David Apter, *Ghana in Transition*, Atheneum, New York, 1963; Ernest Haas, *Beyond the Nation State*, Stanford University Press, Stanford, 1964.

[12] Haas reviews the various definitions by political scientists, of "integration" in *Beyond the Nation State*, ibid., pp. 26-29.

feeling that the system is legitimate. But members may support a system because it is convenient or fulfils some limited purpose for them. A system may win internal support and minimize internal conflict by skillfully manipulating payoffs. Thus, some degree of support may be secured for a system without the members' developing emotional or affective ties to the system and without the membership behaviour being subordinated to normative control. If the system is limited in scope, or exists within a larger system, it may survive despite the absence of either a normative or a non-normative (or calculative) basis. The distinction between normative and non-normative integration is similar to the distinction between association and community (*gemeinschaft* and *gesellschaft*). In the discussion of complex organizations, moreover, some sociologists have distinguished between normative and utilitarian organizations.[13]

Normative integration may be viewed as a higher level of integration. A decline in the members' careful calculation of advantages and disadvantages and a growth in generalized support for the system would increase the problem-solving capacity of the system, at the same time reducing the incidence of overt internal conflict. In the presence of diffuse support, balances need not be struck in each particular policy decision. The system would have some "credit" to draw upon. Those members displeased with a particular policy decision would continue to support the system with the same intensity; their level of commitment would change only if the number of objectionable decisions continued and eventually surpassed a certain threshold. The elaboration of normative control settles the integration problem and permits the members to focus more directly on problem solving or adaptation. Thus, the

---

[13] The distinction between community and association has become a central part of the main sociological tradition. See for example Talcott Parsons, *The Social System*, Free Press, Glencoe, Illinois, 1951, Ch. 3. The distinction between normative and utilitarian organizations is made in Amitai Etzioni, *A Comparative Analysis of Complex Organizations*, The Free Press, New York, 1961, p. 10 and passim.

transition from non-normative to normative integration is an important breakthrough for a political system.[14]

A Case Study: Metropolitan Toronto

Bill 80

The Municipality of Metropolitan Toronto, created by the Province of Ontario in 1953, is an example of the metropolitan federation plan. The Metro case therefore may be treated as a case study in the integrative problems of such systems.

The Metro Act, or Bill 80, brought the City of Toronto and twelve suburban municipalities under the umbrella of one regional government organized along federal lines. The boundaries and internal governmental structures of the municipalities were left unchanged. One municipal program was shifted entirely to the Metro level, many programs were left at the municipal level, but a majority of the municipal programs were made matters of joint Metro-municipal responsibility. Metro was made dominant in the fields of public transit, property assessment, capital borrowing, and in the construction of water supply and sewer facilities, subways, highways and schools. The municipalities retained all or most of their powers in the fields of zoning, police, fire, licensing, traffic control, public health and libraries. (In 1956, police and licensing powers were shifted to the Metro level.)

Decisions at the Metro level were to be made by a 24 member Metro Council, presided over by a Metro chairman. The Metro Council consisted of 12 suburban reeves or mayors, one from each municipality, and 12 members of the Toronto City Council. All 24 members served *ex officio*; there were

---

14 The transition from non-normative to normative integration is described by many political scientists as "the emergence of a political community". See Karl Deutsch, *et al.*, *Political Community in the North Atlantic Area*, *op. cit.* The notion of "levels of integration" is discussed by S. N. Eisenstadt in "Bureaucracy and Political Development", in Joseph LaPalombara (ed.), *Bureaucracy and Political Development*, Princeton University Press, Princeton, 1963, pp. 96-119; and Paul Diesing, *Reason in Society*, University of Illinois Press, Urbana, 1962, Ch. 3.

no direct elections to the Metro Council. The Council annually elected a Metro chairman who was to serve and vote on
all committees and preside over Council meetings, but to vote
in Council only in case of a tie. The chairman need not be
a member of the Council prior to his selection by the Council.
It was not made clear whether, if he were a member of
Council, he had to resign his seat upon being elected chairman. Frederick Gardiner, a former reeve of Forest Hill and
an influential member of the Conservative Party, was named
by the province as chairman in 1953 and was annually re-
elected by the Council until his retirement in December 1961.
Gardiner was succeeded by William Allen, a former City of
Toronto Alderman and Controller.

A federal structure also prevailed in education. The Metro
School Board was to help finance education at the local level
and to reduce some of the variations in educational quality
and tax rates existing within the area. The 22 member Board
consisted of 10 members named by and from the suburban
boards, 10 members named by and from the City Board of
Education, and two members named by and from the Separate
(Catholic) School Board. There were only 10 suburban school
boards because three smaller suburbs maintained a single
school district. The trustees of the local boards were popularly
elected.

This federal plan bore little resemblance to the initial
demands of the municipalities in the area. In 1949, several
suburbs had petitioned the province for permission to form
a joint service area; the city had countered with a bid to
annex the inlying suburbs. The province rejected both applications and enacted the federal plan. Because no one at the
municipal level had urged this plan and because the province
did not seek the consent of the public or the municipal
officials before enacting it, one may say that the federal plan
was imposed on the area. This fact is crucial to the following
discussion of Metro's integrative problems.

Metropolitan federations in North America have pursued
differing integrative strategies. The political base of metro-

politan government in the Winnipeg and Miami metropolitan areas has been the "good-government" interest groups that had initially joined forces to urge metropolitan reform. Metro Nashville, although still in its early stages, seems to be following this pattern. In all three cases the metro legislators are directly elected and the municipal officials have no institutionalized role to play at the metropolitan level. The excluded municipal officials have remained the system's major critics. Only strong support from the reform groups and the metro legislators have saved Metro Miami and Metro Winnipeg from political extinction.[15]

This type of integrative strategy was not available to leaders of the Metro Toronto system. Metro Toronto was not the product of an indigenous reform movement that could have provided support for the system after its creation. Moreover, interest groups were too weakly involved in Metro politics to serve as a support for the Metro system. Nor could the municipal officials be excluded as they were in other federations. Without the support of municipal officials sitting on Metro Council, no items of policy could be approved. Recruiting Metro legislators from the municipal councils avoided conflict between directly elected Metro councillors and municipal officials, conflict that has sometimes immobilized the Winnipeg metropolitan system. The weakness of the Metro Toronto plan was that support had to be secured from officials who remained

---

15 The origins and early years of Metro Miami and Metro Nashville are described in Edward Sofen, *The Miami Metropolitan Experiment*, Indiana University Press, Bloomington, 1963; T. J. Wood, "Dade County, Unbossed and Erratically Led", *The Annals of the American Academy of Social and Political Science*, Vol. 135, May 1964, pp. 64-71; Daniel Grant, "Urban and Suburban Nashville: A Case Study in Metropolitanism", *Journal of Politics*, Vol. 17, February 1955, pp. 82-99; Daniel Grant, "Metropolitics and Professional Political Leadership: The Case of Nashville", *The Annals of the American Academy of Social and Political Science*, Vol. 135, May 1964, pp. 72-83; Daniel Grant, "A Comparison of Predictions and Experiences with Nashville 'Metro' ", *Urban Affairs Quarterly*, Vol. 1, September 1965, pp. 35-54. The remarks on Metro Winnipeg are based on primary sources, mainly the *Winnipeg Free Press* and *Winnipeg Tribune*.

committed to their municipalities and indifferent to the future of the Metro system.

The integrative problems of the Metro Toronto system resembled those of a new international federation. In both cases the key political actors at the federal level continued to represent pre-existing governmental units. The essence of the integrative problem was to secure some transfer of political loyalties from the constituent units to the new federal government.[16]

But Metro Toronto differed from international federations in one crucial respect. Federation in the Toronto case was imposed by a higher authority and was maintained through the constraint applied by that authority. Provincial compulsion, therefore, provided some of the necessary integration. The province's position guaranteed that the system would not collapse through the secession of one or more of its members.

Provincial constraint did not entirely remove the need for Metro to secure internal support. Although the municipal officials could not secede, they could obstruct Metro Council procedures or refuse to vote funds for the Metro administration. Having municipal officials sit on Metro Council made it more likely that the integrative battles of the Metro Toronto system would be fought out in the provincial legislature, but there was nothing to prevent the losers from appealing Council decisions to the courts. Litigation has been a recurrent feature of the Metro Miami and Metro Winnipeg experiments. Finally, municipal officials could maintain their steady attacks on the Metro system and thus persuade the province to abandon or alter the plan.

To use terms developed by Karl Deutsch and others in their discussion of international federations, Metro Toronto represented an "amalgamaged political structure" created in the absence of a metropolitan "political community". Provincial officials were willing to create the formal structure first and gamble that a community would eventually follow. In the 1950's, a Metro government existed, but "Metro mindedness"

---

16 See the works by Deutsch and Haas cited in footnote 11.

(to use Gardiner's term) did not. Like such federations as the "European community", Metro lacked — and never acquired — an emotional overlay. No one on the Council, aside from the two Metro chairmen, advocated submerging municipal interests in order to promote regional unity and the metropolitan idea.

The First Thirteen Years

The Metro system, in 1953 and succeeding years, lacked norms, socialization, social control mechanisms and a sense of solidarity. Most of the system's important actors wished to see the system replaced with something else. More support for Metro came from without the system than from within. Only the two Metro chairmen were eager to see it succeed and were willing to try constructing a political base for it.

From the outset Metro councillors saw themselves as municipal spokesmen attending an intergovernmental conference. They were municipal officials first and Metro councillors second. (In fact the term "Metro councillor" was one that Gardiner and the newspapers coined, but one which the members of Council never used to describe themselves.) Basically, the municipal official sat on Council to protect his municipality from unwelcome intrusions by the Metro giant and to see that favouritism was not shown to other area municipalities.

Some reasons for this hostility to Metro and this continued defense of municipal interests have already been implied: the novelty of the Metro plan, the lack of indigenous support for the plan and the recruitment of Metro councillors from the ranks of the municipal councils. Furthermore, Metro councillors thought that the system would not last. Metro appeared to be a clever political compromise rather than a final solution to the area's problems. Provincial promises that the system would someday be reviewed and revised — promises made to soften initial municipal opposition to the federal plan — only strengthened local views about Metro's transient nature.

The strategy of municipal officials sitting on Council was to overstate their mistreatment at the hands of Metro in order to improve their bargaining position when the time came for provincial review. Statements of municipal opposition and provincial promises of review interacted in a cyclical fashion during the first thirteen years. When the municipalities stepped up their criticisms of Metro in order to provoke a provincial review, the province would try to appease these municipal officials by indicating that a review was under consideration. Such a provincial statement would encourage municipalities to increase their level of attack on Metro. Impressed by these new criticisms, Ontario officials would then order a review. The 1957 review proposed, and the province agreed, that no changes be made in the Metro system. This provincial statement temporarily quelled municipal opposition to Metro; but after 1960 the upward phase of the cycle reasserted itself. The result of the renewed criticisms was a Royal Commission in 1963.

Paradoxically, a strong statement of provincial support for the existing Metro system would have substantially reduced municipal opposition to Metro; but the existence of municipal opposition made the province unwilling to issue such a statement. Indications from the Ontario cabinet that Metro Toronto was just an experiment impeded integration at the Metro level.

A transfer of loyalties from the municipalities to Metro did not occur, but neither did a municipal rebellion. Contrary to fears voiced in 1953, no officials tried to boycott Metro Council meetings or obstruct Council business. Only three decisions taken by the Council between 1953 and 1965 were appealed to the courts by the losing side.

A minimal degree of non-normative integration emerged. Metro councillors would tolerate the system and cooperate in its proceedings as long as Metro provided tangible payoffs to the municipalities in the form of improved services and dramatic public works. Moreover, the councillors thought that benefits, particularly construction projects, should be distributed in an "equitable" manner. Equity, or what I call "regional parity", required that each municipality receive benefits roughly in line with its tax contribution to Metro and that no one municipality benefit more from the Metro system than the other municipalities making a similar tax contribution. Members of the Council were particularly sensitive to the balance of capital expenditures between Toronto and the 12 suburbs. But the suburbanites also insisted on some balance among the northern, western and eastern portions of the suburban area. Thus, Metro had to provide specific and tangible payoffs, and had to do so in a manner that the municipal officials considered "fair".

This calculative attitude can be traced partly to the debate that preceded institution of the Metro system — particularly to the province's promises that Metro would yield immediate and tangible returns to the constituent municipalities. Gardiner, who thought that the provision of quick and observable results would be the best way of building municipal support for Metro, encouraged the emergence of these calculative attitudes. The emphasis on regional parity, moreover, added some flexibility to Council politics. As long as a councillor was satisfied with the overall distribution of capital expenditures, he would support particular projects in other municipalities and would give the chairman and cabinet large amounts of discretion in project planning. Thus, it is incorrect to see Council's attitudes as the stimulus and Gardiner's integrative strategies as the response. The two factors formed a circular chain of causation.

In attempting to build support for the metropolitan system, Gardiner had no weapon at his command but the manipulation of Metro's policy output. Providing payoffs to the municipalities would gain only grudging acceptance for Metro in the short run; but Gardiner apparently hoped that in the long run this tolerance would evolve into diffuse support for the system itself. If integration were first achieved on a calculative basis, normative integration might follow. At some point in Metro's history, then, the system might become the object of emotional or affective loyalties. With the appearance of diffuse, non-calculative support for the system, policy decisions would be liberated, at least in part, from integrative considerations. Metro officials could then take for granted the overall stability of the system, thrust integrative considerations into the background, and focus more clearly on environmental problems.

Until that day arrived, the chairman's strategic choices were restricted. The core of Gardiner's integrative strategy was to emphasize his floor-leading role over the mustering of non-legislative support, to base his legislative effectiveness on informal persuasion rather than on the authority of office, to build legislative majorities on an *ad hoc* shifting basis, and to use substantive policies as a means of making payoffs to municipalities and building majorities. In its general terms, Gardiner's strategy seems to have been the most effective response to Metro's integrative problem. Whatever degree of integration Metro attained during its first 13 years was largely attributable to the skillful leadership of Gardiner and Allen.

Gardiner's detailed procedural strategy as floor leader may be summed up in the following terms. He felt that Metro Council could stand the strain of only one major controversial issue per annual legislative session. Resolution of such an issue should be followed by a breathing spell in which no issue of great import was brought forward. The breathing spell was an opportunity for tempers to cool and grudges to be partially forgotten. The tenuous unity of the Metro Council would be reasserted in preparation for the next divisive issue.[17]

His strategy also prevented controversial issues from accumulating. A divisive issue would not be brought forward until earlier controversies on other issues had been settled. Taking the big issues one at a time kept the temperature of Council politics below the boiling point.

The chairman did not press for Council approval on an emotionally-charged issue unless he was certain of an overwhelming, as opposed to a bare, majority. Wherever possible, Gardiner wanted a majority of both the suburban and City

---

[17] Gardiner's use of breathing spells resembles the vacillation between instrumental and affective requirements noted in small groups. See R. F. Bales, "The Equilibrium Problem in Small Groups", in Parsons, *Working Papers in the Theory of Action, op. cit.*, pp. 111-161.

blocs behind the move. He feared excessive reliance on 13-11 or 14-10 majorities would convince some municipalities that issues were being rammed down their throats. The chairman's insistence on consensual majorities is one reason why so few decisions of Council were appealed to the courts. Gardiner was not always able to obtain this large majority and sometimes proceeded to a final vote without it; but the bipartisan majority on controversial issues remained his ideal.

Some controversial issues, particularly those relating to the organization of the Metro federal system itself, were kept out of Council. In a sense, the price of achievement on substantive issues was to accept Metro's basic structure without question.

The chairman's decision about when to proceed with a controversial issue depended on his interpretation of Council's mood, particularly as it related to regional parity. If one bloc were dissatisfied, a proposal unfavourable to that bloc could not be pressed. Gardiner's view seemed to be that, given time, the correct moment to introduce almost any policy proposal would be found.

Much of Gardiner's legislative strategy, therefore, involved regulating the *pace* of Council's problem-solving. Gardiner's role was that of a "gatekeeper".[18] He usually did not define the issues himself, but he did select those issues that would be brought to Council and did decide when they would be presented. Most problem-oriented (or adaptive-oriented) actors in the Metro system found Gardiner's pace too slow. But, as the chairman realized, an increase in pace would have strained the already shaky municipal tolerance of Metro. Only if there had been diffuse support for the system could the rate of problem-solving have been substantially accelerated.

When Gardiner pressed for approval of an issue that divided the Council along factional (or city-suburban) lines, he generally relied upon the support of the bloc favouring the proposal and tried to split off enough "rebels" from the other bloc to muster a substantial majority. However, Gardiner thought it

---

[18] The notion of "gatekeeper" is developed by David Easton in *A Systems Analysis of Political Life, op. cit.*, pp. 87-99.

essential that the chairman be seen as a middleman affiliated with neither bloc. While he often based his majorities on one of the blocs, he was careful to alternate between reliance on the city and suburban blocs. His purpose was to prevent either bloc from becoming a permanent opposition and to prevent the chairman from becoming a factional leader. Gardiner's response to factional divisions in the Council was not to split the difference in the demands of the two blocs but to keep shifting the basis of his majorities.[19]

Given the basic attitudes of the Metro councillors, it is difficult to see how Gardiner, or any other Metro chairman, could have pursued substantially different tactics.

The absence of stable factions in the Council made reliance on *ad hoc* majorities a necessity. There were no parties, factions or alliances in the Metro area's municipal elections. Unstructured electoral politics produced unstructured legislatures. Since the city and suburban blocs often took differing stands on issues, Metro Council resembled a two-party legislature. In that respect Metro Council was more structured than municipal councils in the area. But Metro Council's "parties" were far too loosely organized and incoherent to provide a chairman with stable majorities. Moreover, neither bloc controlled more than half the seats. Except on those rare occasions when absenteeism was a crucial factor, majorities had to include members of both parties.

Even assuming that reliance upon one bloc had been a workable strategy, such a course of action would probably have produced a boycott or filibuster by the opposition bloc and subsequent intervention by the Province. The integration of the system was not strong enough to permit a majority party and a loyal opposition. Regardless of feasibility, both Gardiner and the province thought that Metro integration ought to be

---

19 Haas lists three ways that conflicts are resolved in international organizations: splitting the difference, finding the least common denominator and upgrading the common interest. To this list might be added Gardiner's alternating between two blocs. See Ernst Haas, "International Integration. The European and Universal Process", *International Organization*, Vol. 15, Autumn 1961, particularly pp. 367-368.

based on the support of all the municipalities, rather than on the support of just one faction.

Gardiner's attempts to build certain rituals and ceremonies into the Metro Council proceedings probably were designed to promote Metro integration on a non-calculative basis. It might be said that the chairman tried to construct a sense of solidarity in the Metro Council and facilitate his majority-building efforts through the elaboration of emotional symbolism.[20] Gardiner initiated the practice of making Metro Council's opening meetings, which took place in January following each municipal election, a ritualistic occasion. He also instituted the practice of having the chairman deliver a "speech from the throne," outlining his program for the coming legislative session. To some extent these opening meetings became characterized by the statements of goodwill and camaraderie that mark the opening days of federal and provincial parliamentary sessions.

However, there were clear limits to how much diffuse support could be generated through the manipulation of "affect". These rituals had only minimal impact on the councillor's view of Metro. Moreover, the press sometimes ridiculed attempts to introduce solemnity into Metro government. Symbolism and ritual were viewed as appropriate at the national level but somewhat ludicrous at the local level.

Gardiner rarely went beyond a floor-leading role in his attempt to secure Metro integration. For the most part he took the status of public, press, and interest-group opinion as given and did not attempt to build grass roots support for the system or grass roots pressure on the councillors to support the Metro idea.

Could Gardiner have secured greater Metro integration by taking his case outside the legislature and building stable relations with private groups and local newspapers? In Metro Winnipeg the first Metro Chairman increasingly resorted to the mobilization of interest group support in order to counter-

---

20 Parsons considers "expressive symbolism" in *The Social System, op. cit.,* Ch. 9.

act criticisms voiced by municipal officials. In the Metro Toronto area, however, such a strategy would have produced marginal gains. Interest groups were not intensely involved in Metro Toronto politics. Whether attempts at education and interest articulation would have activated these groups and provided a supportive coalition for the Metro system is debatable. An attempt to create widespread public support for Metro, in the hope that this support would lead to the election of more "Metro-minded" municipal officials, also would have been a dubious strategy. More important, such strategies would not have been tolerated by the Metro Councillors. Members of Council were willing to accept a leading role for the chairman, but they strongly opposed his becoming a popular figure. The councillors were prepared — indeed, pleased — to have Gardiner deal directly with private groups when the result was settlement of a particular controversial issue; but they opposed his going outside Council to seek grass roots support for the metropolitan system. In the Winnipeg area, it might be noted, the directly elected metropolitan councillors generally shared the chairman's enthusiasm for the Metro system and joined in his public relations efforts.

From the foregoing account of Council's calculative attitudes, one might conclude that the councillors were constantly at loggerheads and that the chairman's majority-building task was a near impossible one. In fact, Council rarely experienced intense conflict.[21] Council's hostile and calculative attitudes toward the metropolitan system created a potential for intense conflict but Council's attitudes on participation depressed the incidence of conflict.

Metro councillors were not aggressively interested in most Metro issues. These councillors remained far more committed to their roles at the municipal level and far more immersed in municipal business. The chairman often prevailed because he was the only Council member who had had the time and incentive to fully acquaint himself with the facts of the case

---

21 I present evidence in the larger study to support my argument about the lack of intense conflict.

and because he felt more strongly about the issue than did any of the councillors. The orientations of the Metro councillors were calculative but not intense. Weak commitment to the Metro system on the part of Council members meant not only weak support of the system but also weak interest and involvement in the resolution of Metro issues.[22]

The areas of strong legislative interest centred on questions of regional parity and questions affecting the structure and continuance of the metropolitan federal system. In policy areas unrelated to regional parity or Metro's future, the legislative situation was fluid, slack, and amenable to the chairman's persuasive efforts.

In Parsonian analysis the normative integration of a system is viewed as a means of managing the tensions and conflicts that could tear the system apart. Thus, integration and conflict are often treated as reverse sides of the coin. Even the calculative or non-normative integration defined above might make the system's members more willing to smother or settle their controversies in order to preserve the system.

It does not follow, however, that the alternative to integration, either normative or non-normative, is intense conflict among the members of a system. Similarly, the absence of sharp conflict in a system cannot be taken as evidence of a system's integration.

Perhaps it is more accurate to see political integration as the centre of a spectrum, with intense conflict at one pole and withdrawal and apathy at the other. Weak commitment to a system may mean that individuals press their particular demands without regard to the survival of the system and without recognizing any legitimate limits to their tactical behaviour. But weak commitment may also lead to a reduction in involvement and a transfer of loyalties and interest to other systems. The Metro Toronto system, for example, developed in the direction of apathy rather than anarchy — that is, in the direction of limited involvement rather than

---

22 One major argument offered by Easton in *A Systems Analysis of Political Life* is that the level of demand-inputs is often on a par with the level of support-inputs.

intense conflict. In such poorly integrated, low-involvement systems, an increase in membership commitment probably would expand the incidence of conflict over the short run, as members showed more interest in the system's policy output and raised the level of their demands. In the long run increased commitment might produce more elaborate normative controls on behaviour and greater membership support for mechanisms that control conflict.[23]

The Effect of Integration on Policy

In terms of substantive policy, Gardiner's integrative strategy accorded first priority to construction or public works programs and lesser priority to welfare, regulatory, service and structural reform issues. Within the Council there was strong, generalized support for construction programs. No other type of program could provide such tangible and dramatic demonstrations of Metro's utility to the municipalities. No other program would win municipal support or tolerance for the Metro system so quickly. In the public works field the problem was simple — a lack of roads, schools, and similar facilities. The solution was just as simple — build the necessary structures. By comparison problems in the non-construction programs seemed more subtle, and the solutions more elusive. In addition, such "soft" programs provided intangible benefits, aided a special clientele within the general public, and generated more controversy in Council. Quick returns were ruled out in such "welfare" programs as public housing by the laborious nature of intergovernmental negotiations.

Also, there was a minimum amount of conflict between the adaptive and integrative needs of the metropolitan system in

---

23 This argument owes a good deal to David Apter's discussion of "institutional transfer" in *Ghana in Transition*. Apter treats anarchy and apathy as two alternative consequences of unsuccessful transfer. Apathy might be more likely to result in segmental systems where members may always increase their involvement in some other segmental system. The segmental system is one in which the scope of controlled behaviour is small and the level of integration low; see Merton, *Social Theory and Social Structure*, revised edition, p. 311.

the area of public works. The technical and political personnel agreed that the metropolitan area needed extensive public construction. As long as parity considerations were met, the politicians on Council left the detailed planning of projects to the administrators. As a result there was little conflict between the long-range planning of projects and the operation of democratic politics. Political demands, mainly relating to the geographic distribution of capital budgets, could be met without damaging the integrity of the long-range plan.[24]

Adaptive and integrative considerations came into sharpest conflict over the question of increasing Metro's powers. The cabinet saw additional transfers of power as essential to the solution of regional problems. Gardiner, although personally agreeing with the cabinet on most transfers, insisted on deferring to Council opinion. In this policy area Gardiner subordinated his personal views to tactical considerations. Structural reform was the area of Gardiner's smallest achievements.

William Allen was more committed than his predecessor had been to expanding Metro's role in the non-construction areas. He tried, without substantial success, to increase Metro's achievements in public transit service, off-street parking facilities, urban renewal and redevelopment, and public assistance. Among the reasons for his limited success was the Council's weaker support for these "soft" programs, in comparison to the dramatic construction projects. In addition, the low degree of integration set a limit to the Metro system's problem solving or adaptive capacity. By the early 1960's, Metro could explore few new areas of policy without adding to its formal powers, mainly at the expense of the municipalities. But few

---

[24] The clash between planning and democratic politics in the American context is emphasized in Marver Bernstein, *Regulating Business by Independent Commission*, Princeton University Press, Princeton, 1955; and Alan Altshuler, *The City Planning Process*, Cornell University Press, Ithaca, 1966, Ch. 7. Myron Weiner, in examining the Indian experience, notes that the compatibility of planning and democratic politics depends largely on the nature of the demand-inputs in the particular political system. See Myron Weiner, *The Politics of Scarcity*, University of Chicago Press, Chicago, 1962, p. 234.

members of the Metro Council wished to see the metropolitan system strengthened. If, for example, urban renewal and public assistance had been Metro responsibilities in 1961, Council probably would have moved ahead with problem solving in these areas. But because these policy areas were municipal responsibilities, substantive problems in these areas became enmeshed with structural or federal questions.

By 1965 the Metro system appeared to have reached an impasse. In terms of policy outputs, it had gone as far as it could within the confines of non-normative integration. Adaptive or problem-oriented actors were becoming increasingly restive. The Council, though willing to continue and expand construction programs, was unwilling to explore new policy areas.

Gardiner's integrative strategy and his image of future development were analagous to the position taken by "gradualists" on questions of international organization. Gardiner, like the gradualists, believed that an "international" organization could be strengthened by degrees, if the non-controversial issues were dealt with first and the divisive issues put off. The satisfactory resolution of the easy issues and the obvious achievements of the system would increase member loyalties and would subsequently make the controversial issues easier to resolve. In time all the issues that Gardiner deferred could be settled by Metro Council; but it was first necessary to build up a reservoir of goodwill. The effect that Gardiner hoped to produce is often referred to as "spillover".[25]

Spillover did not occur in the Metro system. The ease with

---

[25] The "gradualists" are also referred to as "functionalists," but I have refrained from using the latter phrase in this context. The gradualist position is defended by Amitai Etzioni in: "The Dialectics of Supra-national Unification," *American Political Science Review*, Vol. 56, December 1962, pp. 927-935; "The Epigenesis of Political Community at the International Level", *American Journal of Sociology*, Vol. 68, January 1963, pp. 407-421; and "European Unification. A Strategy for Change", *World Politics*, Vol. 16, October 1963, pp. 32-51. A careful and more skeptical appraisal of the gradualist approach is contained in Ernst Haas, *Beyond the Nation State*, Stanford University Press, Stanford, 1964. For "spillover" see Haas, *Beyond the Nation State*, pp. 407-414 and passim.

which construction programs were implemented did not make the non-construction issues any more tractable. Metro's achievements in public works helped produce municipal tolerance for the system, and this tolerance helped create a spillover effect within the construction field. Satisfaction with one's share of the capital budget made one inclined to go along with construction projects located in other municipalities. But because Council attitudes on "soft" programs differed significantly from Council attitudes on works programs, there was no spillover of goodwill from the construction field to the non-construction fields. Moreover, the fact that most "soft" programs could not be pursued unless Metro's official powers were first expanded also set clearcut limits to the operation of spillover. Negative spillover was more likely to occur. The bitterness engendered by an emotional debate might impede issue resolution for the remainder of Council's annual session. In general terms, and despite specific successes on the floor, Gardiner's gradualist strategy was a failure.

Reform of Metro after 1963

In 1963, the provincial cabinet, prompted mainly by the City's renewed campaign for total amalgamation, appointed a Royal Commission on Metro Toronto. This process of review culminated in a reorganization of the metropolitan system, approved by the Ontario legislature as Bill 81 in May 1966. Rather than speculate on all the possible structural reforms that might have broken Metro's functional impasse, the following discussion will deal only with reforms that were seriously considered during the 1963-1966 period.

Obviously, the integration problem could have been largely solved by abolishing Metro and creating one unified city for the area. But the province quickly rejected this possibility, for the same reasons that had prevailed in 1953. "Total amalgamation" would stir strong resentment elsewhere in the province, create a government rivalling the province in size and importance, and possibly lay the groundwork for the emergence of a unified city bloc in the provincial legislature. Amalgamation would certainly be denounced by the twelve suburbs and might weaken Conservative Party strength in that area. There is an obvious paradox in the provincial concern over suburban opposition. If the metropolitan system had secured more integration and had created the "metropolitan spirit" of which Gardiner often spoke, abolition of the system would have been more seriously considered by the provincial politicians. Metro's failure to attain a greater degree of integration ensured the survival of that system!

Of all those proposals urging revisions in the federal structure, three received major attention before being rejected: a proposal to have the Metro councillors directly elected, a proposal to have the Metro chairman elected in the area at large, and a proposal to transfer several important powers from the municipal to the Metro level. The Royal Commission accepted the first but rejected the second and third. The province rejected all three. Although the question is an academic one, one might ask what effect these reforms would have had on the Metro deadlock.

The transfer of powers to the Metro level, in all likelihood, would have greatly facilitated problem solving. Certain substantive problems would have been separated from structural or federal issues.

The direct election of Metro councillors might have made the councillors more inclined to seek re-election on the basis of their record at the Metro level, to support the metropolitan system at least as much as they supported the municipal unit, and to devote most of their political time to Metro business. Direct election appears to have these effects in the Metro Winnipeg system. But the Royal Commission's proposals differed from the Winnipeg plan in two respects. First, none of the newly created Metro Council constituencies would cross municipal boundaries. Second, in order to avoid conflict between the two levels of government, the Commission proposed that Metro councillors also hold seats on their respective municipal councils. Thus, the Metro councillors would continue to interact on a regular basis with municipal officials and might continue to see the municipality as their crucial reference group. The Metro councillor's decisions about reference groups would also hinge on his career aspirations. If he looked to a career in provincial or federal politics, he would be more "Metro-minded" than if he hoped to become the mayor of his municipality. On the whole, however, a directly elected councillor would probably assign somewhat more loyalty and time to the Metro system than a councillor recruited from the municipal councils.

Thus, the direct election of Metro councillors would probably increase the level of both integration and adaptation within the Metro Council. But the support given to Metro by a Metro councillor, and the resulting expansion in the system, would be sharply criticized by municipal officials. Greater integration within the Council would be secured only at the price of increased municipal dissatisfaction with the system's performance. These municipal officials could no longer disrupt Council proceedings or bring Metro's policy making process to a standstill, but they could press their attack at the provincial level and perhaps force another Metro reorganization. On the other hand, direct elections would also expand the size of the Metro system's relevant public. The municipal officials, though still important, could no longer claim to be the only actors who spoke for the electorate. The net effect of direct elections on Metro's long-range integrative problem would depend on how much weight the province gave to the opinion of municipal officials and to the opinion of Metro councillors.

Having councillors directly elected, though expanding Metro's developmental capacity over the long run, might increase the incidence of Council conflict over the short run. More demands would be made of the chairman by Metro legislators. The councillors probably would be more involved in Metro business and less willing to "go along".

A higher level of commitment among the councillors might produce a greater incidence of legislative conflict and perhaps stalemate. But this increased commitment could have the

opposite effect if the chairman's ability to coordinate legislative behaviour were increased accordingly. The direct election of the chairman and some expansion in his formal powers
might enhance his ability to build majorities. In other words,
Gardiner's reliance on informal powers and purely intra-
legislative influence was effective in a low-pressure, low-
involvement Council. Increasing the level of commitment
without also increasing the means of coordination would probably lead to a reduction in Metro's policy output. Increasing
both commitment and coordination would permit Metro to
expand its policy output significantly.

In 1965 several adaptive-oriented actors, eager to see Metro
expand, nevertheless opposed the direct election of Metro
councillors unless the province also agreed to provide for a
stronger popularly elected Metro chairman. These people,
though unhappy with the *status quo*, implied that they would
rather see a perpetuation of low-pressure Council politics than
the appearance of a more intense — but also uncoordinated
and unpredictable — brand of Council politics.

The provincial cabinet seemed convinced that the direct
election of Metro councillors and the Metro chairman would
encourage open partisan intervention in Metro area politics.
The large size of the Metro constituencies would probably
encourage candidates to seek more extensive party assistance.
Most cabinet officials opposed partisan local politics in principle and feared that party intervention in the Metro area
might set a precedent for other Ontario cities. In addition,
some cabinet members apparently feared that one of the
opposition parties would capture control of the Metro Council.
Even if the Conservative Party were to capture control, Conservative Metro councillors might become a pressure group
within the party, embarrassing the provincial leadership with
their demands on Metro's behalf. A popularly elected Metro
chairman, openly affiliated with one of the political parties,
could not help but be a source of irritation and embarrass-
ment to the Premier. If the chairman were a Liberal or New

Democrat, he would be a regular critic of the Premier. If the chairman were a Conservative, he could become the head of a Metro bloc within the party.

No official at the provincial or local level favoured an increase in the formal powers the chairman unless provision were also made for his popular election. Thus, once the province had decided against popular election of the chairman, an increase in formal powers was necessarily ruled out. The chairman, of course, could continue to exert his *de facto* leadership, but officially vesting these powers in a non-elective official was seen as inappropriate. Moreover, to provide statutory recognition of the chairman's chief-administrator and floor-leader roles would mean challenging Ontario's weak-mayor tradition. The cabinet was not intensely committed to that tradition but, at the same time, was reluctant to create a strong-mayor precedent for other Ontario cities. Finally, a popularly elected Metro chairman with the formal powers of a strong mayor and with control over a bureaucracy larger than those of most Canadian provinces would become the second most important politician in Ontario. Such a strong chairman would force the Premier to share the political spotlight and the attention of the news media.

As for the proposal to transfer major municipal programs to the Metro level, the province could not have accepted this reform without destroying the rationale for a federal system. If the municipalities were to be stripped of every significant power, the obvious question was why retain the municipal units at all.

In view of the these considerations, it is not surprising that the 1966 reorganization provided for minimal changes in the system. Retained were the federal form of government, the recruitment of Metro councillors from the municipal councils, the appointment by Council of a chairman with no significant formal powers, and most other features of Bill 80. The number of municipalities was reduced from thirteen to six, the size of the Council was expanded, and the basis of municipal representation on Metro council was altered.

The 1966 Act decreed only one change in the distribution of powers between the Metro and municipal levels. Welfare, or public assistance, was transferred to the Metro level.

Finally, a dramatic change was enacted in the field of education. The federal structure was retained, but the Metro School Board was given power to levy one school tax rate for the entire area and to assume virtually complete control over the fiscal decisions of the local boards. The Metro Board, then was given the means to realize its "equalization" task. The number of local boards was reduced to six, and the basis of municipal representation was changed accordingly. Here, as in Metro Council, the City's representation fell below the 50 per cent mark. Although the province added its assurance that local boards would continue to control policy, most school officials doubted whether this local autonomy could coexist with centralized control of expenditures. Amalgamation behind a facade of federalism seemed likely to emerge in the educational sphere.

Aside from the areas of education and public assistance where breakthroughs will undoubtedly occur, the reforms seem unlikely to solve Metro's impasse. The Metro councillor's basic orientation to the system, and his hostility to future development remain intact. The same integrative or "political" leaders, who found the original reform satisfactory were equally satisfied with the 1966 reorganization. The adaptive leaders, far less satisfied prior to reform, found more to criticize than praise in the 1966 reorganization. Bill 81, therefore, did little to eliminate or lessen the gap between adaptive and integrative leaders. The adaptive leaders will continue to advocate an expanded rate of problem solving; the integrative leaders will continue to oppose any venture into new policy areas.

This impasse will be broken only by the appearance of new actors and new issues or by the construction of a Council majority behind some multi-faceted package plan. In an indirect fashion, the 1966 reforms may improve the Metro chairman's ability to achieve a breakthrough in Council. The mere fact that reform was completed and is not likely to be considered again for at least five years may encourage the Metro councillors to temporarily lay aside their grievances and cooperate with the chairman. Metro, in 1966, was entering the first phase — the most harmonious phase — of the five-year cycle described earlier. Further, the 1966 reforms may convince City officials that amalgamation will never be imposed by provincial statute. In the early 1960's City officials had insisted that Metro be abolished not expanded. After 1966, the City may return to its earlier view that steady expansions in Metro's power will introduce total amalgamation through the back door.

7 Social Consequences of Urbanization

Peter C. Pineo

Introduction[1]

Throughout this century urbanization and the frequently accompanying process of industrialization have been problems of major interest to sociologists. This paper will present a selection from the work done by sociologists using two different approaches. The first section will consider the basic set of assumptions pervading much of the work of sociologists concerned with urbanization. The rest of the paper will deal with three more restricted topics — the impact of urbanization upon ethnic relations, social stratification and primary relationships. This final section will also include descriptive material from the author's recent study of a neighbourhood in Hamilton, Ontario.

The Significance of Urbanization to Sociology

Consensus is rare among sociologists, yet probably most would agree that the movement of population from the countryside to the city is one of the major historical trends of the past century in the United States, Canada and related societies.

[1] Analysis of the empirical data here presented was made possible by a grant from the Canadian Council on Urban and Regional Research.

Statements to this effect appear early in the literature. In 1938, Louis Wirth wrote:

> The growth of cities and the urbanization of the world is one of the most impressive facts of modern times.[2]

And the statements continue. A recent introductory textbook includes the following:

> Population growth and the increasing percentage of the population living in urban areas has been and continues to be a major trend in the United States. . . . Aided and abetted by the automobile and mass communications, not to speak of the demands of industrial and commercial activities themselves, the urbanization trend shows no let-up. And certainly it is basic to many of the other institutional changes occurring in our society.[3]

In the United States the proportion living in urban areas changed from 6 per cent in 1800 to 15 per cent in 1850, and 40 per cent in 1900 to 59 per cent in 1950.[4] In 150 years American society changed from principally rural to principally urban. The trend was closely parallelled in Canada. But the mere occurrence of a trend does not make it important. The impressiveness of the change lies in the sociologists' assumption that urbanization was transforming the attitudes and behaviour of individuals and the structure of the society.

The list of social changes which sociologists felt to be caused at least partly by urbanization would be very long. Within the field of family relations, for example, the changes included higher rates of family dissolution, lower birth rates, greater equalitarianism between husband and wife, and more permissive child training. Within the field of deviance, not only crime rates but also mental illness and suicide rates appeared higher in the cities. Sociologists thought people were becoming less devout in their religious life and also that a Protestant

---

2 Louis Wirth, "Urbanism as a Way of Life", *American Journal of Sociology*, Vol. 44, July 1938, pp. 1-24 and especially p. 2.

3 Robert L. Sutherland, Julian L. Woodward and Milton A. Maxwell, *Introductory Sociology*, 6th ed., Lippincott, Chicago, 1961, p. 376.

4 William Peterson, *Population*, Macmillan, New York, 1961, p. 20. An urban area is defined as a community of at least 2,500 population.

theme was developing within Catholicism. The amount of social mobility — that is, movement to better or worse jobs, either between the generations or within a single life span — was felt to have increased. And the behaviour of people toward one another was said to have moved toward greater anonymity, superficiality, impersonality and freedom.

These changes were assumed to be irreversible. As the society became predominantly urban the new patterns would replace the earlier rural patterns of behaviour and become the expected and normal modes of behaviour in the society.

For a variety of reasons all these changes must be considered as much *assumed* as proven by sociologists. Clear proof was not possible, essentially because the effect of extraneous factors could not be assessed.

A major difficulty in taking inventory of the social consequences of urbanization lies in determining which of the accompanying changes in the society are caused by urbanization and which are somewhat or completely independent. The feminist movement, for example, occurred during this period. One might work out a plausible rationale for a causal connection between urbanism and feminism, but the counter claim that feminism was a wholly independent development in the culture cannot be disproven. Even the observation that the movement began in the cities is not conclusive proof because this might be only a comment on the pattern of diffusion of new ideas which can develop in an urbanized society.

Of all the accompanying changes, the trend to industrialization provides the greatest problem. Urbanization and industrialization have largely occurred together in recent history so that disentangling the effects of the two trends is virtually impossible. The sociological literature reflects this difficulty. However, there is a difference in the sort of social changes that are typically discussed by those sociologists who emphasize industrialization and those who emphasize urbanization.

When urbanization is emphasized, sociologists concentrate on the consequences of greater population density and larger communities. If the anonymity of the large city frees individuals from constraints which produce the higher deviance rates, then deviance is more a consequence of urbanization than of industrialization. Similarly, if reduction in family size is mainly a reaction to insufficient house space, then this also is a product of urbanization. The three topics forming the final sections of this paper are three of the more important areas which clearly show the effects of density and the greater size of communities, although the influence of industrialization is also evident.

Sociologists who emphasize industrialization are concerned with the changes resulting from the differences between agricultural and non-agricultural occupations. For example, the farm family was a unit of production as well as of consumption. Orders necessarily flowed from the male head to the wife and children because they were not simply fellow family members but also co-workers. Only as work became separated from family life could marital equalitarianism and permissiveness toward children develop.

While in some cases it can be plausibly argued that either urbanization or industrialization is the important causal factor, some recent writings avoid the issue by combining both trends under the term "modernity".

A second difficulty in conducting sociological studies of urbanization is the separation of the lasting effects of urbanization from the short-run effects. The effect of living in a city can be confused with the effect of moving to a city. Some of the reports of greater anonymity and individualism in the city may be the product of dislocations of conventional social arrangements among migrants. When an individual moves to the city he necessarily leaves behind some friends and relatives. But in subsequent generations, when people are born and die in the city, a cohesion more like that reported for the rural areas may develop.

A third difficulty lies in the fact that, in some sense, the societies which have recently urbanized and industrialized were the first ever to do so. It has been argued that there were distinctive elements in Calvinistic theology which were conducive to industrialization.[5] This "Protestant ethic" — including an individualism of initiative and responsibility — may have motivated people to take the special risks involved in the development of industrialization. But the risks are smaller now that the system has been invented and the goal is in view, so that this requirement may no longer hold. Similarly, special demands may have been placed on individuals during the period when urban life was developing and these may no longer exist. In general, one must not assume that all the concomitants of urbanization and industrialization found in Western European and North American experiences will necessarily be found in societies elsewhere in the world undergoing the process.

A final and major difficulty with these studies is that the pre-urban society against which urban society is being compared has been inadequately described. While the urban family is said to be more equalitarian, there is really no adequate description of rural family life which would enable one to prove this. It has been suggested, in fact, that some aspects of the "dating complex" are a long standing tradition in northern Europe.[6] Similarly, differences in accuracy of reporting may account for urban deviance rates appearing higher. The difficulties are even more intense when one speaks of a growing impersonality or superficiality of interaction in the city. Not only are there no firm historical data, but even contemporary measurement techniques would have trouble with qualities as elusive as these.

The difficulties outlined here have not received the serious consideration they deserve by the majority of sociologists. For this reason the picture of the massive social consequences of

---

[5] Max Weber, *The Protestant Ethic and the Spirit of Capitalism*, Scribner, New York, 1958.

[6] William J. Goode, "The Theoretical Importance of Love", *American Sociological Review*, Vol. 24, No. 1, February 1959, pp. 38-47, especially p. 45.

urbanization should be accepted with caution. Perhaps the difficulties have been glossed over because those discussing urbanization have been partially motivated by ideological rather than scientific considerations. The shift to the cities was met with ambivalence by the intellectuals of the time.[7] To many, reared in Jeffersonian ideology, the city was the villainous source of all evil. They noted the negative characteristics of cities, such as higher crime rates. Others romanticized the city; they thought all elements of the American dream were realizable in the city. For a period of time American scholars, particularly sociologists, debated the nature of the ideal society while appearing to discuss the consequences of urbanization. In the course of this debate, the empirical issue of actual differences between city and countryside became hopelessly clouded and remains so even today.

More careful observation of countries in Africa and Asia now urbanizing may help to distinguish the essential from the accidental concomitants of urbanization. Even this will not provide a perfect test, however, because certain customs, (for example, the hoola-hoop or rock-and-roll) appear in other countries simply because of diffusion. And also, there is the possibility of the self-fulfilling prophecy. The assumption that urbanization requires an American-like or European-like society has been taught around the world. The elite of new Africa are outlawing witchcraft because they believe this will hurry the pace of industrialization. If we find that witchcraft becomes less frequent as societies urbanize, we still will have no clear proof of causality.

However, in some ways the recent changes in Quebec seem to confirm the majority viewpoint. The birthrate is falling, as the theory says it should. Secularism is reported to be greater. Demands for greater democratization are being made, and research shows the urban French Canadians to be most involved in these demands. Yet, in concluding a recent study of urbanization in Japan, Thomas O. Wilkinson wrote:

---

[7] Ely Chinoy, *Society: An Introduction to Sociology*, Random House, New York, 1961, pp. 209, 212.

> The unique ways in which a Japanese urban system
> evolved, utilizing modified elements from its traditional
> social organization, underscore the theoretical contention
> that there exists a wide range of alternatives to the patterns
> of adaptation present in Western urban systems.[8]

Similarly, the usual account of the impact of industrialization upon the American family has recently been called "exaggerated" by an American sociologist.[9]

Implicit in this prediction is the assumption that not only will these new societies necessarily undergo the changes, such as the falling birth rates, which occurred in the West, but also that certain features found in the pre-urban West will necessarily develop elsewhere. The custom of monogamous marriage may be given as an example. It may be argued that because the West was monogamous in its pre-urban era it was able to industrialize and urbanize while others were not. Thus monogamy also is assumed to be a necessary concomitant of urbanization. Or one might argue that because the West never had cross-cousin marriage or unilineal descent groups, these are inconsistent with the urban-industrial complex and will disappear with urbanization and industrialization. These assumptions imply that everything in the Western way of life is necessary for the urban-industrial complex. This extreme viewpoint is unacceptable.

One thing we have learned from social science is that people tend to exaggerate the importance of their own historical epoch and to treat as natural their own society. It is unusual for men to look upon their own social customs as merely arbitrary. Rather they legitimize them, stating that without this custom all else that is known and cherished would disappear. Sociologists are a product of their culture. It is not surprising that they see as imperatives such quaint customs as monogamy. (Only 20 per cent of the societies in Murdock's

---

[8] Thomas O. Wilkinson, *The Urbanization of Japanese Labor; 1868-1955*, University of Massachusetts Press, Amherst, 1965, p. 208.

[9] Frank F. Furstenberg, "Industrialization and the American Family", *American Sociological Review*, Vol. 31, No. 3, June 1966, pp. 326-337, especially p. 337.

World Ethnographic Sample were strictly monogamous before Christianization.)[10] Nor is it surprising that they see a recent transition in their own society — from rural to urban — as a major historical event. Because this is a recurring fallacy one should attempt to correct it. Try to imagine an industrialized and urbanized society with polygyny, for example, or matrilineal inheritance. In general, the extent to which urbanization will homogenize the world is questionable.

There will be no breakthrough in the solution of this problem. Research is difficult because amid all the discussion, as has been pointed out, the actual description of pre-urban United States or Canada was poorly done. Comparing Time One and Time Two is extremely difficult when Time One can be seen only through a glass darkly. The societies now urbanizing are imperfect tests because of diffusion effects. All sociologists who study urban life are nibbling away at this problem. The answer is unlikely to be all-or-nothing; probably some changes will be found to be necessary concomitants of urbanization while others will not. A slow and laborious classification of practices is necessary. Describing urban life, although a slow and largely unrewarding process, will produce eventually a description of the whole society. Not only does the majority in a country like Canada live in urban communities but also recent research suggests that a feed-back effect has occurred. Our remaining rural population increasingly resembles its urban counterpart. Differentials in crime, in birth rates, in marriage dissolution rates, and so on are disappearing. The changes are brought about mainly by rural areas adopting urban customs.[11]

The author's own work on this problem has been a detailed survey of a single working class neighbourhood in the north end of Hamilton, Ontario. The neighbourhood is a single census tract. It was selected principally because it was slated for urban renewal, but it had other interesting characteristics

10 William N. Stephens, *The Family in Cross-Cultural Perspective*, Holt, Rinehart and Winston, New York, 1963, p. 33.

11 Alvin L. Bertrand (ed.), *Rural Society*, McGraw-Hill, New York, 1958, p. 430.

as well. It was, for example, the frontier of the Italian community. A random sample of households in the tract was selected from the City Directory, and 327 interviews averaging ninety minutes each were conducted by trained student interviewers. Eighty-five per cent of those in the sample were successfully interviewed. Because much of our basic information in sociology is founded on United States research there is a need in Canada for descriptive studies to test quickly if the Canadian situation is similar to the American. This study was designed to cover many topics quickly in order to help achieve this result. Three of the basic topics covered in the study will be discussed. These are also three of the current problems of interest to sociologists who study the city. They are ethnic relations, social stratification and primary relationship.

The Impact of Urbanization

Ethnic Relations

The neighbourhood we studied showed the characteristic pattern of ethnic segregation found throughout North America. It is well known that cities in the United States have almost all their negro population in spontaneously produced ghettos. Nearly 80 per cent of the Chicago negro population would have to move to different census tracts to achieve complete residential desegregation in that city.[12]

Similarly, it is well known that cities can have Jewish ghettos. One is aware that Montreal has an area in which most of the Jewish community resides. It is perhaps less well known that other ethnic groups such as the Poles and the Italians are also found to be living more or less in ghettos. In the west end of Boston, for example, the present population is over 40 per cent Italian.[13] The Italians are mainly

---

[12] Otis Dudley Duncan and Beverly Duncan, *Chicago's Negro Population*, Chicago Community Inventory, Chicago, 1956, p. 82.

[13] Hebert J. Gans, *The Urban Villagers*, The Free Press of Glencoe, New York, 1962, p. 8.

second generation; the ghetto is not just a short term effect of immigration, although a few more decades will probably make considerable difference.

The Boston example brings up a derivative point. Not only are American cities broken into ethnic enclaves, but there is a continuous process of reshuffling. The west end of Boston is now Italian and Polish. Formerly it was as much as 75 per cent Jewish. Before that it was Irish.[14] Sociologists have used the analogy to plant and animal life in describing this phenomenon. They speak of invasion and succession, and ecological dominance.

The situation in Canada, of course, is similar; one need only glance at a tract book for any Canadian city to see the pattern. The neighbourhood studied in Hamilton included a corner of one of the city's two Italian communities. The balance of the inhabitants consisted of Canadians born in Hamilton, Canadians born elsewhere in Canada, some older north country English, and a small group of eastern Europeans mainly from Poland and Hungary. Some residents remembered when it had been largely an Irish neighbourhood.

Sociologists are interested in explaining why this well known pattern of ethnic segregation occurs. It is a great oversimplification to find its cause simply in discrimination. A large number of factors operate. The Italians were probably drawn to that particular area in Hamilton partly because it had large inexpensive houses. Their "invasion" appeared to reach its limit (if it has) when they reached a zone containing only small houses. The north country English were drawn to the area by the work provided in the cotton mills in an earlier period.

But there are social attitudes which help to produce the segregation. We asked all but the Italians how they would feel about living in an Italian neighbourhood. Fifty per cent expressed opposition to the idea. In similar questions, 40 per cent were opposed to living in a French Canadian neighbour-

---

14 *Ibid*, pp. 6-7.

hood, 29 per cent in a Polish neighbourhood and 20 per cent in a Ukrainian one.

A principal reason for rejecting the idea of living in a neighbourhood with a concentration of some non-English nationality was the language problem. Respondents said such things as:

> Well, I'm not prejudiced against them as long as they can speak the English language.

> I have nothing against race, colour or creed — just the language barrier.

> I think it is the language problem that bothers me most because if I could understand them it would make a world of difference.

People quite naturally wish to live near others with whom they share a language. We found also that in a few people conversation in a language they do not understand provokes a near paranoid response:

> . . . you think they are talking about you because they talk in their own language.

While many referred to the language problem others had complaints which we have called "complaints about neighbourhood behaviour". Examples of these are given below, with the Italians being the group discussed in each case:

> They talk too loud. I wouldn't like them as neighbours. They are nervy.

> . . . they stand in the way when I'm pushing the baby buggy.

> The children think they own everything and they can do what they feel like.

> . . . they shout across the street.

> Italians are mostly noisy. They talk so loud you think they're fighting.

> I don't like the way they hang around (on the street). Sometimes they seem to be quite arrogant and sometimes pass remarks about the girls and women.

A total of 21 per cent gave complaints about the neighbourhood habits of the Italians.

Studies in the United States have shown that people who are prejudiced against one group are likely to be prejudiced against many.[15] In the Hamilton neighbourhood, those who were opposed to living with Italians also tended to be opposed to living with any of the other three groups we suggested. Among those opposed to living with Italians the proportions opposed to living with French Canadians was .57, with Poles .53 and with Ukrainians .44. In contrast, the proportions opposed to other groups among those favourable or neutral to Italians were .30, .13 and .03 respectively. One must discount specific complaints given of specific groups because in many cases they are probably rationalizations of a prior attitude. Many respondents actually preferred to discuss nationality as a general factor rather than specific groups:

> I prefer my own kind — English speaking, and that would go for any other nationality unless they are English.

> I don't care what nationality people are. I feel God loves them all and He makes them the way He wants them to be. God plants flower seeds and they all come up different colours and it don't matter what colour they are. They're all nice.

Is ethnic hostility peculiarly an urban phenomenon? I think most sociologists would say no. Is it more intense in urban areas? Possibly. A variety of factors may bring about an intensification. If prejudice derives from personal frustration, as has been suggested,[16] it will be more intense where frustration is greater. But we do not know that urban life is more difficult than rural life.

It might be argued that urban life forces differing people into closer contact with one another, either producing hostility or making it more overt. While it is possible that the

---

15 Else Frenkel-Brunswick, *et al.*, "The Anti-Democratic Personality", in Eleanor E. Maccoby, *et al.* (eds.), *Readings in Social Psychology*, Holt, Rinehart and Winston, New York, 1958, pp. 636-646, especially p. 640.

16 See, for example, S. Stanfeld Sargent and Robert C. Williamson, *Social Psychology*, Ronald Press, New York, 1958, pp. 588-589.

urbanite wards off intimacy so that physical density does not produce social density, contact can hardly be as infrequent as in the areas of widely spaced farmhouses produced by our peculiar homestead system of settling North America. Also, even if contact is greater in the cities, there are data which suggest that greater contact under certain specialized conditions may reduce rather than increase prejudice.[17] The results of any test of the effects of contact upon prejudice in the Hamilton data are far from definitive. Rejection of the Italians is greater than of the other four suggested groups, but it cannot be concluded that greater exposure to Italians causes this. Also, cultural differences are sharp here because this Italian community consists of very recent immigrants. More of those who live in the predominantly Italian parts of the neighbourhood complain about neighbourhood behaviour and the related topics of moral behaviour and house care than do those who live in the part with few or no Italians. The proportions which complained were 31 and 23 per cent respectively; the difference is not statistically significant. The overall rejection rate among those in the Italian area is no higher (48 per cent) than in the balance of the neighbourhood (52 per cent). It appears that those who are in the Italian area have found the language problem not so great as they had anticipated but they develop other complaints and, therefore, remain at the same level of prejudice. The factor of out-migration of the prejudiced was not taken into account, however, so the data can only suggest, not demonstrate, this conclusion.

One influence of urbanization upon ethnic relations is clear. Only in larger communities is the number of people involved sufficient to produce large and relatively stable ethnic ghettos. What in a small community would be only a small cluster of houses becomes in a large city an area of many blocks. For both the scientist and the resident, ethnic segregation is considerably more obvious in larger centres.

[17] Morton Deutsch and Mary Evans Collins, "The Effects of Public Policy in Housing Projects upon Interracial Attitudes", in Maccoby, *op. cit.*, pp. 612-623, especially p. 620.

Should we expect ethnic hostility to continue indefinitely in our society? If its sources are malleable or changeable, perhaps not. Even if the sources are fixed, other targets may be found. Two French demographers have written about the fate of a single Protestant community in a wholly Catholic area of France. Greatly inbred, the Protestant villagers developed epilepsy which was shared eventually by almost all the village. The Catholics in the area gradually lost the distinction in meaning between the words for epileptic and Protestant. A religious difference became confused with a difference in physical health.[18] Just about anything can happen, and one should not underestimate the capacity of humans to form new categories to dislike. As we shall see, however, class consciousness seems a more likely ground for distinction than physical health.

Social Stratification

Contemporary sociology is extremely interested in the phenomenon of social stratification. In my opinion the source of this interest is not theoretical — a derivative of Marx — so much as empirical. We have found that a small but appreciable amount of variation in attitude or behaviour on almost all the topics in which we are interested may be explained by social stratification.[19] Some weighted average of an individual's income, education and the prestige of his occupation will give a moderately strong prediction of many of his social habits and attitudes. As income and occupation are involved in the measurement one could conceivably call this area of research the study of the social effects of our economic system.

The social attitudes accompanying the stratification system are complex. It is apparent that class consciousness in Marx's sense of the term does not exist. People in North America

18 Jean Sutter and Leon Tabah, "Les notions d'isolat et de population minimum", *Population*, Vol. 6, 1951, pp. 481-498.
19 See, for example, articles in Reinhard Bendix and Seymour Martin Lipset, *Class, Status and Power*, Free Press, Glencoe, 1953.

characteristically opt for "middle" or "working" class when given the alternatives of those two responses and "upper" and "lower" class.[20] But the answers appear to be somewhat random; an individual's self-categorization generally does not relate so strongly to other facts about him as does an index based on income, education and occupation. The reverse would be true were there actual class consciousness. While neither is statistically significant, the tendency for low family income to predict voting Liberal or New Democratic in the Hamilton neighbourhood is stronger than the tendency for the self-categorization as working class to predict left-of-centre vote.[21].

Even without a statistical example, the sorts of answers people give when asked why they chose middle or working class show a lack of confidence in the choice which suggests their answer lacks reliability. For example:

> Middle class. Well, upper class has servants and everything.

> Working class. Because all I do is work. I don't believe in class.

> Any man who works in a factory is a working class man.

> Working class. None of us drink or anything. . . .

> Middle class. I can't say upper class. Working people are all middle class as far as I'm concerned.

> Middle class. (Respondent hesitates, points to a badly kept house across the street.) Because I think the working class is over there. I think (that's) the way some of the working class live.

> I'd just say we were common ordinary people. What's the difference? They're all one kind of people. They're just people.

---

[20] See Natalie Rogoff, "Social Stratification in France and in the United States", in Bendix and Lipset, *ibid.*, pp. 577-588, especially p. 580.

[21] Further details on voting patterns in this neighbourhood are to be found in: Grace M. Anderson, "Voting Behaviour and the Ethnic-Religious Variable: A Study of a Federal Election in Hamilton, Ontario", *Canadian Journal of Economics and Political Science*, Vol. 32, No. 1, February 1966, pp. 27-37.

> Middle class. We're not upper class but not lower class. Here class makes less difference . . . than it did in Germany.

The average Canadian perceives his social position and that of others in a complex way, intermingled with a belief in equality of opportunity and in his own worth. This is a tenuous and unstable situation, and predictions of eventual change seem reasonable.

Has urbanization in any way helped produce this peculiar system of social stratification, and will further urbanization be likely to change it? Industrialization rather than urbanization has probably produced our present system. The elaborate division of labour in the work world appears to be a root cause of the system; people can rank jobs according to their prestige and the rankings show remarkable stability over time and similarity between nations.[22] In the answers to this question are found the reliability and stability of response missing from the answers to the question regarding social class. The ranking of jobs may well be the structural alternative to class consciousness.

The rural society found on this continent lacked the basis for differentiation of the sort produced by industrialization. Lipset has described the homogeneity of rural Saskatchewan. All were farmers. But more than that, all were wheat farmers. Their holdings were of roughly equivalent size. And they enjoyed good and bad years at the same time.[23] In our own recent past on this continent we may have experienced a period of relatively little class formation, to which recent writers have looked back with nostalgia. This may be one

[22] Robert W. Hodge, Paul M. Siegel, and Peter H. Rossi, "Occupational Prestige in the United States, 1925-1963", *American Journal of Sociology*, Vol. 70, No. 3, November 1964, pp. 286-302; Peter C. Pineo and John Porter, "Occupational Prestige in Canada", a paper read at the meetings of the Canadian Association of Sociology and Anthropology, Sherbrooke, Quebec, June 1966.

[23] Seymour Martin Lipset, "Social Structure and Political Activity", in B. R. Blishen, *et al.*, (eds.), *Canadian Society*, 2nd ed., Macmillan, Toronto, 1964, pp. 299-312, especially p. 302.

reason for the lack of popular understanding of the stratification system that has developed with industrialization.

The impact of urbanization upon the stratification system is seen in the formation of one-class neighbourhoods in the city. Professional men, for example, are found in small towns but not in sufficient numbers to form the sort of community-within-a-community that develops in the larger centres. While the Hamilton neighbourhood was slightly variegated in ethnic composition, it was virtually a working class ghetto. Eighty-five per cent of the household heads held blue-collar jobs. The few white collar families either had very small retail businesses or occupied a handful of larger, more expensive houses on a corner commanding an impressive view of Hamilton harbour.

All North American cities — perhaps all cities — show this tendency to form into "neutral areas" which are largely homogeneous in social class. The boundaries are rarely precise, of course. Because these areas are large, they tend to have their own school, their own churches, their own voluntary associations. Thus in the larger cities a segregation by social class is possible; a child may be raised with little contact outside his class. Possibly over the years differences in attitude and habit between the classes will become sharper.

The structure of our cities confuses the public awareness of social stratification. Because of one-class neighbourhoods, people are unaware of the true amount of variation in the society. Middleclass people perceive the society as being composed mainly of others like themselves. Largely unaware of how many are poorer, because they do not see them, they can simultaneously enjoy their advantages and feel they are living in an equalitarian society. A similar confusion develops when distinctions are made within the homogeneous group. In the Hamilton neighbourhood we asked if the people in that part of the city were "pretty much alike". Despite the almost wholly working class composition of the population the differences between people most frequently perceived by the residents were related to money and occupation (27 per cent of those reporting some difference). The existence of idiosyncratic local distinctions may prohibit the growth of any national consensus in ideology.

But the city structure also clarifies the stratification system. Insofar as people are aware of "better neighbourhoods" and "poorer neighbourhoods" social class can be discussed in this vocabulary. In the Hamilton neighbourhood people spoke of wanting to move to live "on the Mountain". A woman, who did not like the north end and called it "lower class", gave the following reply when asked if she planned to move:

> Yes, I have definite intentions to move either to the Mountain or West End — and rent. I don't like the schools here at all and I've gone down and watched the kids here in the playgrounds at the school and decided I didn't want mine going to school around here if I could help it. I want to give them a fair chance and I don't think they'd get it here.

Similar usage is found in the response of an older woman to the same question. Her children had moved away and were encouraging her to follow them:

> (I've thought of moving) many times. Many times the children get the idea that they don't like me to live in the north end. All our family is up on the mountain but I don't think it makes any difference where you live as long as you have a nice place and enjoy living there. Home is everything.

People can phrase desires to move ahead in the stratification system in highly localized and non-abstract terms using neighbourhood place names, and at the same time they can say truthfully, "I don't believe there are social classes in Canada".

At this time, ethnicity and social class are associated phenomena. This is, of course, the point behind the title of Porter's *The Vertical Mosaic*.[24] A French Canadian may complain about lack of chances for mobility by blaming "the English". What to the sociologist appears to be a statement

---

24 John Porter, *The Vertical Mosaic*, University of Toronto Press, Toronto, 1965.

about social stratification is felt by the individual to be a statement about ethnic relations. Perhaps there would be clearer awareness of the class system in a country which lacked ethnic heterogeneity to confuse the issue.

The present close relationship between the structure of our cities and the social stratification system may deteriorate in time. Even if those with higher income continue to spend it upon superior and newer houses, greater variation in housing type within city areas could produce quite a different situation. It is possible that the strong tendency for our present cities to have distinct areas of high cost and low cost housing is only the result of the first construction period. In the first cycle of construction a gradient in age of housing from the centre to the outskirts seems inevitable. In the second construction period, more variation is a definite possibility. Luxury apartments, for example, appear both in the central business district and the suburbs. The tendency for city structure to reinforce class distinctions would be reduced by such housing variations. Also the use of the names of city areas as a special local language to discuss class differences would tend to disappear.

Primary Relationships

Those who early discussed the effects of urbanization expected a sharp change in the style of interaction between ordinary people on ordinary occasions. A clear exposition of this is given in Wirth's paper, "Urbanism as a Way of Life".[25] While small rural communities were characterized by intimate, emotional and close relationships, in the city (so the argument ran) a greater proportion of acts would be formal, business-like and distant. (A clumsy presentation of the viewpoint would imply that all intimate relationships would disappear.) This exaggerated expectation was, of course, very vulnerable

---

[25] Wirth, "Urbanism as a Way of Life". Wirth's assumption that city populations are necessarily heterogeneous is important to his argument. The problem in this assumption is that people may be *taught* to perceive a situation as either heterogeneous or homogeneous.

to disproof. Philippe Garigue's work in Montreal demonstrated that urban French Canadians do retain contact with relatives.[26] Similarly there are a number of American studies of friendship, neighbouring patterns and contact with relatives. The title of one is indicative of the general theme: "Urbanism Reconsidered".[27]

While the complete disappearance of primary relationships in the city is easily disproven this was not the major contention of the sociologists making the prediction. Rather they contended that the number of such relationships had decreased, and secondly that their character had changed. Here either proof or disproof is virtually impossible because the Time One data are not adequate. We do not know if the incidence of visiting, or of intimate conversation is less in the city. Nor do we know if the present definition of friendship, for example, is the same as it was fifty or one hundred years ago. We can only describe with accuracy the way of life in our cities today so that changes from now on can be measured. Also, insights into the probable magnitude of recent change may be gained as we learn under what contemporary conditions primary relationships attenuate. Different areas within the city may be compared, or the behaviour of recent in-migrants can be contrasted to that of those born in the city. For example, 93 per cent of the Italians reported they had kin in Hamilton. Clearly migration can follow kin lines and this may reduce the inevitable social cost of migration. Finally, if we can understand what stake people have in these relationships we may be more able to assess the probability that change has occurred.

One might complain that this is hair splitting and that it is obvious that a change has occurred. In the city, or the urbanized society, the basic and important work of the society is conducted through formal mechanisms. Control of deviance

---

26 Philippe Garigue, "French Canadian Kinship and Urban Life", *American Anthropologist*, Vol. 58, No. 6, December 1956, pp. 1090-1101.
27 Scott Greer, "Urbanism Reconsidered: A Comparative Study of Local Areas in a Metropolis", *American Sociological Review*, Vol. 21, February 1956, pp. 19-25.

is an example. Putting it the other way, in the rural society crucial functions were discharged through informal and primary organization; in the city virtually all these are left to formal agencies. This argument assumes that we have identified the crucial functions of the society. We lack any formal means of curing minor mental illnesses. Can we assume then that this is not a crucial function? We tend to define informal relationships as a sort of social luxury called leisure. But this is a popular not a scientific judgment.

As I have shown in an earlier paper, the people in the Hamilton neighbourhood were involved in primary relationships; and their frequency of contact with relatives outside their own households was roughly equivalent to that found in studies in the United States or England.[28] Sixty-eight per cent reported at least weekly contact with some relative outside their own home.

These people were also in frequent contact with friends and neighbours. Their involvement with friends seemed as intense as their involvement with kin. While 68 per cent reported at least weekly contact with some relative, 63 per cent reported at least weekly contact with "their best friend in the neighbourhood". In fact, more (37 per cent) reported daily contact with the best friend than reported daily contact with some relative (21 per cent).

The basic structure of the friend and kin networks may differ. While respondents show a pattern of moderately frequent contact with a large number of relatives, they show a pattern of very frequent contact with a smaller number of friends. It may be that the contact rates with relatives represent the minimal fulfilment of a social obligation to "keep in touch", while contact with friends is the expression of a definite preference. The present data are inadequate to confirm this.

Altogether, 77 per cent of the respondents reported they visited or had visitors at least weekly. One intuitively feels

---

28 Peter C. Pineo, "The Extended Family in a Working-Class Area of Hamilton", in Blishen et al., op. cit., pp. 135-145.

that this represents a considerable degree of involvement, although some comparison is needed to make such a statement. A rough comparison may be made with other leisure activities. In a list of seventeen leisure activities "visiting" was the third most frequently reported, following only "listening to the radio" and "watching television".

In analyzing the Hamilton study one aim has been to differentiate between types of primary relationships. Contemporary sociology tends to lump them, implying that both the character of the relationships and the functions they perform are not different. One finds measures of involvement in primary relationships which sum the frequency of contact with friends, neighbours and relatives; others differentiate.[29] Greer has suggested, for example:

> In fact, kin relations may be seen as growing in importance just because of the diminished reliance placed upon neighbourhood and local community.[30]

Greer implies an inverse relationship between dependence upon kin and upon other forms of primary involvement. I have attempted to test this expectation, with negative results. Table 7-1 presents nine correlation coefficients, all of which should be negative if the relationship between kinship and friendship involvement were inverse. In fact, all are positive and five of the nine approach or achieve statistical significance in the positive direction.

Because the idea of "involvement" is vague three alternative measurements are used for each variable in Table 2-1. The kinship involvement score is the most complex measurement. All respondents were given a score which was the sum of the following:

Six points for each related family seen at least weekly.

Three points for each related family seen at least monthly.

---

[29] Aida K. Tomeh, "Informal Group Participation and Residential Patterns", *American Journal of Sociology*, Vol. 70, No. 1, July 1964, pp. 28-35.

[30] Greer, *op. cit.*, p. 25.

One point for each related family seen less than monthly but at least now and then.

It may be considered the most direct test of the hypothesis because both the number of kin and amount of contact are considered. The headings of column two and three are self-evident. However, as the measurement for kinship involvement changes, the actual nature of the hypothesis changes. Column two seeks to establish whether those who are deprived of kin through migration, death or some other external factor show unusually heavy reliance upon friends. In column three, the idea is that friends may be difficult to accumulate but more desirable, so that with the acquisition of friends, a person may begin to see his relatives less and less frequently. I have tested three slightly different forms of the hypothesis that the kin and friend networks are alternative social structures, and all have been rejected.

TABLE 7-1

Pearsonian correlations between measures of kinship and friendship involvement[1]

	Kinship Involvement Score	Number of kin in city	Percentage of kin seen weekly
Number of friends in neighbourhood	.03	.02	.10
Frequency of contact with friends	.10	.06	.13
Number of friends outside neighbourhood	.10	.04	.14

[1] The sample size was 327 and the 5 per cent level of significance is .10.

Perhaps this is simply a problem in measurement. People may be reporting some kin as friends and the reverse so that there is double counting. Or perhaps both are an expression of simple gregariousness and a differentiation between them is not theoretically or practically valid.

A second differentiation which may prove valid, and which is hinted at in the literature, is the one between the size of the primary network and the amount of energy put into it. An example of this distinction, again from the Hamilton data, is given in Table 7-2. For three age groups there is virtually no difference in the frequency of contact with kin or with friends but there is a steady increase in the percentage reporting a large number of friends in the neighbourhood. That is, the amount of energy put into primary relationships appears to be a constant through the life cycle, excluding of course the very elderly, but the size of the networks steadily increases.

TABLE 7-2

Relationship of age to contact with kin, contact with friends, and number of friends[1]

Percentages	Less than 36	Age 36-50	Over 50	Results of x^2 test
Seeing kin weekly ..	68 (90)[2]	68 (118)	68 (119)	n.s.
Seeing best friend in neighbourhood weekly	69 (90)	59 (118)	62 (119)	n.s.
Reporting four or more friends in neighbourhood[2]	41 (87)	53 (103)	67 (100)	p < .01

[1] Numbers upon which the percentages are based are given in brackets.
[2] Excludes those responding "no really good friends", "neighbours only" and no answers.

Age and number of years spent in the neighbourhood are closely related phenomena in the neighbourhood studied. A gradual accumulation of friends through neighbouring may have produced the larger friend networks among the older residents. When we asked the respondents how they made friends the largest proportion (40 per cent) said that initial contact had been made through neighbouring — they had simply run into them on the street, in the shops, through the children. This finding may show to be spurious the generally accepted proposition that the elderly will oppose relocation because they are old. It may not be the rigidities of age so much as the vested interest in years spent acquiring friends in one part of the city that motivates the opposition.

Conclusions

This paper has been an attempt to present both what appears to be the majority opinion among sociologists on the question of the social consequences of urbanization and, at the same time, the author's minority opinion. While the discipline as a whole has largely emphasized the profound and extensive effects of urbanization — or rather that package of urbanization and industrialization now frequently called "modernity" — some of the historically simultaneous events in our society may have been either accidents or the effects of diffusion of custom from the first societies to become "modern".

My own research raised questions and presented data on social stratification, ethnic relations and primary relationships in the city. While the questions raised may be somewhat more restricted in scope than those considered by others, they do suggest there are unconsidered complexities to the problem. The evidence, as far as it goes, indicates that the proposition that all urbanized societies will eventually be identical is questionable.

Part Three

Public Policy for City and Region

Despite the lack of a satisfactory and integrated corpus of theories and models of the urban economy and/or the city-region compact, many important decisions are taken by all levels of government. These decisions often have urban implications which will shape the cities and regions of tomorrow. In any case, the problems cannot wait for the ideal answers. By the time they are discovered, we will already be constrained to living in a network of extant urban settings. Therefore, given the lack of an integrated body of knowledge on the pursuit of urban goals, we must use the existing fragmentary framework to develop more rational urban and regional policy.

The need for such a policy is dramatically underlined in this section. A. N. McKay and D. W. Slater have surveyed the issues which are most pressing both within the individual urban unit and among the components of the urban system as a whole. One of their key points is the appalling lack of urban policy in the face of a most impressive catalogue of urgent problems. They trace this state of affairs to the primitiveness of urban theory and to the juggling of responsibilities between the various levels of government. This paper bridges the gap between the methodological and theoretical considerations of Part One and the problems unearthed in the case studies of Part Two.

In Chapter 9, R. T. Adamson scrutinizes one area of urban affairs where policies have been developed under the pressure of circumstances despite the lack of an appropriate frame of reference. Indeed the public might believe that Canada has a housing policy and a policy of urban renewal. The author finds, however, that the situation is far from clear and that the policies pursued often embody some internal contradiction. For instance, there may be a potential conflict between urban renewal and the avowed goal of government which is the provision of adequate accommodation for the Canadian population. This incompatibility of goals stresses the need to re-evaluate our present policy instruments. However, to do so we must be willing to monitor the present experiments more carefully than we have in the past, and we must develop some basis for program evaluation within the primitive existing frames of reference. It is here that the relevance to policy formulation of the work surveyed in the previous parts becomes apparent.

D. C. Rowat shows the way to policymakers in Chapter 10. Indeed despite the lack of appropriate models, he indicates how the existing conventional wisdom in connection with relevant public administration criteria can be used to delineate meaningful regional units in political terms, so as to more optimally distribute the responsibilities for public policy. This paper should be related to the two papers of Part One which deal with regions as economic and geographic entities. It is not certain that the political units defined by Rowat will necessarily satisfy all the requirements of functional economic and geographic regions. However, the three proposed concepts of regions may not be so different after all. Whatever the merits and demerits of the spatial partitioning for Ontario suggested by Rowat, it does constitute a meaningful basis for discussion in a field where public policy is still groping for the right issues.

8 The Scope of Urban Policy[1]

A. N. McKay
D. W. Slater

Introduction

It is a gratifying and indeed a somewhat surprising development that, within the area of urban affairs, ideas that were at the outer limits of academic research only a few years ago are now finding their way into the thinking and public statements of responsible political leaders. This new awareness, particularly at the senior levels of government, was driven home at a conference in 1965[2] where Premier Duff Roblin of Manitoba, in his analysis of the changing distribution of government functions in Canada, underlined the critical role of urban growth on this redistribution. So impressed was he with this process that it was given a key role in his forecast of things to come.

This concern with the urban unit is not, however, the result of great successes in the research field. Indeed, the volume and quality of that research is deplorably inadequate. Rather, the concern stems from the rapidly growing urban problems that increasingly afflict our society and from our failure to anticipate the magnitude of these problems when framing social policy in the postwar period. The key assumption on which postwar policy was based proved to be wrong. The population

---

[1] This chapter has been prepared by the editors from a transcript of the talk by the authors.

[2] The McGill Conference, November 1965, Montebello, Quebec.

increase in this period was in fact significantly greater than even the highest forecasts. In addition, the related calculations of the proportion of the population and its activities which would locate in the urban environment were underestimated. These errors compounded to distort all estimates of the size and dimensions of urban problems in the 1950's and 1960's. An increasing gap developed between urban needs and urban policy, the size of which has only recently begun to impress our leaders.

The Issues of Urban Policy

This paper surveys the leading issues facing policymakers at the urban level. The issues can be placed usefully in two broad divisions. The first includes the experiences, analyses and policies regarding the distribution of urban activity among various distinct urban units, which may be called "among-city" issues. The second division contains those issues concerned with the internal structure of cities, or "within-city" issues.

Included in among-city issues are such questions as the size distribution of city activities. This entails the allocation of urban functions among different types of urban units. The range of concern extends from the purely descriptive classification of activities by city type to the analysis of the allocation mechanism and the impact of various policies on this allocation of functions. Thus, the general question of similarities or discrepancies in urban development, in the level and growth rate of incomes, in relative stability, in degree of poverty and so forth is related to differences among city types. At this level, research attempts to explain these patterns and to specify policy on distribution of these activities among cities in terms of desired objectives.

The second broad class of issues, those within cities, includes — for example — homogeneity or heterogeneity in the distribution of functions among various segments of cities. In this area of inquiry such matters are examined as the density of jobs and residences and their respective patterns of development; the efficiency of particular cities as organizing units for various kinds of activity; and the effectiveness of public action within cities in encouraging development and in regulating the private sector.

These broad classifications — among-city issues and within-city issues — are not mutually exclusive but overlap at various points. This is best demonstrated in a large urban agglomeration, currently referred to as a megalopolis. In Canada the clearest example is the Toronto-Hamilton axis and in the United States, the famous Boston-Washington corridor. Although these examples appear to swallow up both our classes, the distinction we have drawn has some relevance. There are issues concerning the nature of the distribution of urban activities and their growth among the gross units within the megalopolis; and there are issues of the structure and changes in that structure within each of these gross units.

This survey will focus primarily on policy issues in the realm of within-city problems. In particular, we shall analyze several aspects of urban land development and the integration of private and public interests in that process. The analysis will begin with an appreciation of several among-city issues in order to illustrate some of the ideas and policy problems arising at that level.

Among-City Issues

The main among-cities process that we shall deal with is that of growth patterns in different types of urban units. The obvious features of growth in Canadian cities, in North America in general and indeed in much of the world, are familiar and can be covered quickly. In the last two decades rapid urban growth, however one might measure it, has occurred in all classes of urban units except in villages and towns, the smallest size classes. According to some measures, there is little distinction among the growth rates of the biggest, the medium-sized and the smallest urban units.

However, the largest metropolitan units, when appropriately designated, have been *the* major growth centres. This designation excludes those medium-sized and smaller units that are contiguous to a metropolis, together with those attached to an exceptionally dynamic resource base. Despite the preponderance of the largest units, even modest cities like Belleville and Kingston have undergone rates of growth that are extremely rapid by both standards of our own historical trends and those of other parts of the world. One striking result of this growth, together with the increasing range of functions associated with it, is the expansion of urban facilities and the increasing share of public expenditures they require.

Despite these developments, there is an almost complete absence of deliberate policy in Canada with respect to desirable patterns of urban growth. Of course, Canadian policies in such areas as transportation, taxation and industrial development do influence the pattern of urban growth. In contrast to the British situation and that in several other countries, however, Canadian policies have not been designed deliberately to influence the size of cities or the distribution of the totality of urban activity among the various city units. For example, there are no policies intended to limit the size of cities such as Montreal or Toronto, Chicago or Los Angeles, which may be past their optimal size; and none to create new urban units or to accelerate the growth of suboptimal ones.

The absence of urban policies stems in part from the awesome complexity of the process of urban growth and diffusion as well as from the failure to perceive the impact of other public policies on the urban unit. In North America the pattern of urban growth has been determined by a thoroughly *laissez-faire* approach. Even the growing recognition that this absence of urban policy has precipitated our current urban crises has not altered this attitude. Notwithstanding the immobility of our policymakers, the situation is so serious that we must begin to establish the elements of rational urban policy. The questions which must be answered include:

> What are the costs and benefits of the present allocation of activities among various kinds of urban units?

What alternatives are open to us?

How can we devise new patterns and how can we attain them?

What are the implications of such a program?

A second set of issues arises with respect to the explanations of urban growth. The theoretical foundations for the majority of these explanations are rather unsatisfactory. The predominant theory of urban growth, used both to explain past growth and to formulate policies to promote the growth of particular cities, is centred on the notion of the economic base. According to this theory some elements in the spectrum of a city's activities are basic. Therefore, one can explain the totality of the city's growth as a response to the growth of the basic activities. The policy implications are clear — if one wants to affect overall growth, the size of this base must first be augmented.

Most variants of the economic base theory of city growth are remarkably similar to the naïve staple theories of economic history or the naïve export multiplier models of Canadian economic growth. In most cases, according to this view, the basic factor in a city is the exporting of products from the city. The export performance is determined by the external demand for these products, so that analysis of growth ultimately focuses on the nature, trends and scale of this external demand.

Many economic base theories are naïve in this sense, particularly in the area of policy formation with respect to urban growth. Most such models do not adequately explain the development of a city's base; for as well as accounting for its exports, they must explain why someone purchases these exports. One city's exports are, after all, someone else's imports. Furthermore, these models usually focus on the demand for exports alone, neglecting the supply side, and especially the role of technology and capital in the process of growth. These weaknesses render this mechanism highly suspect as a comprehensive explanation of urban growth or as a tool for framing urban growth policies. The narrowness of economic base theories of urban development is best exemplified in Charles Tiebout's sophisticated study of urban development[3] which contains precisely these characteristics.

Several other approaches to among-city issues are worthy of mention. These generally are concerned with the distribution of economic activity among various urban units, the two chief types of theories being central place analysis and location theory. The former has been refined and developed by geographers; the latter, mainly by economists.

Location theory is a general approach to the determination of the location of activity. Most of the work has stressed the location of industry, primarily because of the implicit link between industrial growth and urban development. However, some recent work has extended the scope to include locational decisions of households and various other groups. Central place analysis is concerned with the interaction between market size and urban structure. Regularities between, for example, urban types and urban population, or inter-urban links, or degree of urban sprawl have been found in a variety of situations. In fact, this type of analysis has recently been used to study within-city structure. Thus, while location theory may be said to be producer oriented, including inputs into production such as workers, central place theory is consumer oriented. Location theory asks, where producers will go, given consumers; whereas central place theory explains where consumers go, given producers. This contrast stresses the limitations of the two approaches but also suggests the potential gains from integrating them, once some fundamental schisms of ideas have been overcome. The integration awaits further dialogue between economists and geographers.

Despite their weaknesses, both approaches now figure prominently in the formulation of urban policy. Thus, although Canada lacks a new towns policy, the concern with slow growth areas has led to the development of policies for accelerated growth. The possibilities for growth are often

---

[3] Charles M. Tiebout, *The Community Economic Base Study*, Supplementary Paper No. 16, Committee for Economic Development, New York, December 1962.

determined by using a central place study to examine the potential functions of an urban unit. This study might be supplemented by an evaluation of the locational advantages for new growth producing activities. All too often the logical schism in these two approaches is ignored and a hybrid policy spawned with some roots in each approach but little overall consistency. If one considers the Ontario government's regional development program, the focus of which for most regions is the urban context, it is apparent that even for broad social policies, full understanding of urban processes is essential to avoid a bewildering array of conflicting programs and policies. Thus, at the among-city level, we have a variety of interesting conceptual tools, but our whole framework is still too narrow and too piecemeal to achieve rational solutions to our problems.

In our delineation of among-city issues and the scope for urban policy at that level, it becomes clear that Canada does not yet have any specific policies regarding city size or city distribution. Nevertheless many policies do influence these factors, particularly the new concern with regional policies which has important implications for the distribution of city activities. We have shown that some elements of the theory of among-city relationships are unsatisfactory. The weaknesses may lie in the fact that work on this problem has not been done in a wide enough range of disciplines. Geographers have contributed the main theoretical developments, while economists have made more limited contributions. Much more work, particularly in other disciplines, is now needed to round out the picture.

Within-City Issues

In the discussion of within-city problems we shall analyze some features of urban land development. We shall emphasize particularly the roles of the public and private sectors in the harmonious achievement of policy decisions, together with the principles governing this harmony. Some policy implications of urban taxation will also be examined. For policy purposes, it is important to realize that unbridled *laissez-faire* in the field of urban land development is totally irrelevant. The very essence of urban life is the great interdependence of various parties' interests. In the language of economics, cities are a prime example of the existence, the operation and the importance of external economies in consumption. Furthermore, cities by their very nature depend on the existence of a set of public goods. That is, cities cannot exist without a set of goods which are provided in common and paid for in common with no alternatives available. The important relevant elements of public activity in a city simply cannot be organized and paid for on the basis of user charges related to the benefits people receive. However, the city does make possible a variety of economies of scale in providing collectively some other services which are not inherently public goods. Furthermore, in the city the duration of the effects of particular actions is very great for the community as a whole, although the horizons of the people making individual decisions at any time is short. Therefore, conflict between the long-term interests of the community as a whole and the short-term interests of many of the decision making individuals in it is inherent in the character of cities. An additional problem is the range of imperfections of markets, particularly in such complicated goods as urban land and urban building, resulting from enormous discrepancies in knowledge and almost unlimited opportunities for misrepresentation. There can be no question whatsoever about the irrelevance of an unbridled *laissez-faire* approach to the structure of cities and of economic activities within them.

The policy questions we must face, therefore, are those regarding the relationship of private and public interest, the way in which they are to be blended, and the principles that must govern the operation of the public interest. The alternatives for the exercise of public interest are well known. The public authorities, through the provision of services and by guiding those activities undertaken in the interest of the private decision maker, can create an environment that is acceptable from the public point of view. Or the public authorities can operate a regulatory framework within which private decisions must be taken. In addition, public owner-ship of urban land, or a certain proportion of urban land associated with a system of appropriately specified leaseholds might be implemented. All three of these approaches have relevance and, were it not for municipal governments' record of inefficiency in managing urban land, more public owner-ship of land might be preferable. The reasons for this will become clear shortly.

The most outstanding example of successful urban develop-ment through public ownership of urban land is modern Stockholm. Most of this city's development has taken place on land that was owned by the City of Stockholm. The city operated as the planner of the urban transportation network and of the urban periphery and thereby achieved this develop-ment.

However, it did so in cooperation with a whole series of private and semi-public bodies. The result is impressive from almost every point of view. Stockholm has achieved what is probably the most important objective in this area — an integrated pattern of urban transportation development and urban land development. By contrast, in North America urban land development proceeds as if the transportation network were a datum, and urban transportation as if urban land use were a datum. Seldom do the two developments operate in full recognition of their interdependence, and many of our urban problems today reflect this failure.

What are some of the principles that might govern public activities and the blending of public and private activities here? What might be gained from the assumption of certain very significant roles by the public authorities? The first, and perhaps the most obvious, point is that if private interest is large and long-term, private actions will more often tend to parallel public interest than when private interests are small and short-term. For example, a major land developer in his own interest has to take a long-term point of view. He must think through his whole development because what he will get ten and fifteen years hence for his land depends on his actions now. And the value of his land ten or fifteen years from now is the difference between outstanding success and failure in land development. The drawback to this situation is that a monopoly or a near-monopoly private developer wields a great deal of influence over a somewhat impecunious municipality. However, large scale, long-term private development unquestionably requires less detailed public policy to achieve urban goals than does small scale, short-term private development. The problems of monopoly can best be solved through appropriate combines legislation.

A second point is that the public authority can finance the increasing costs of urban growth by effectively diverting the gains from urban growth into the public purse. It is true that there are difficulties about techniques and administration and so forth. Nevertheless, there is a good rationale behind such policies. First of all, the growth of the city and the provision of the city functions and services are the activities which generate the increments of land value at the margins of the cities. That is, the growth of cities and city activities create increasing urban land values. These are, so far as private holders are concerned, very largely rental incomes. That is, there is a substantial element of pure rent in these, and this rent could be creamed off without making any significant difference to the availability of land for development purposes. Beyond that, a growth of cities and the provision of city services that are required in growing cities themselves impose major costs on a city. It is therefore a fundamentally sound policy to ensure that a substantial part of the increments of peripheral urban land values that are created by the growth of cities should be captured somehow by the city and used for paying for the cost of the growth of the city and the city services. A capital gains type of tax might be applicable to this problem; improved assessment procedures have brought this and other policies of collecting benefits within the realm of possibility. These are the key ideas that lay behind the

British nationalization of the development values in land in the early postwar period, a scheme that broke down because of administrative difficulties and because one cannot, in fact, very readily separate the development rights from the so-called undevelopment rights in land. Nevertheless, the fundamental idea is sound and the implications for us are clear: either we find schemes to capture the pure rents, or a substantial part of them, and turn them to general municipal purposes; or we, as cities, buy up these lands and take the benefits in the form of increments of developmental value. In other words, cities might buy the land and become the speculators, taking the difference between what is paid for the land and what it comes to be worth as the city is developed, and depositing these gains into the city's development funds. Also, if a program of compensation-betterment is to work efficiently, there should be some attempt to equate the gains from peripheral development and the possible losses from inadequate investment in central city development. There may be difficulties in administering this policy and there is no certainty that the increments that would accrue to city governments as a result will go very far in meeting their costs of development. Nevertheless, the current dilemma of private benefit and public poverty in the face of urban development will be somewhat alleviated.

Another set of issues concerns the pattern of urban land development. Present patterns give rise to serious conflicts with agriculture on the peripheries of cities. The difficulties of the so-called urban shadow are very real and important, and demand solutions. One case in point is the Niagara fruit belt. In that area, the most intensive agricultural development will require the best road, water and transportation systems. The area will have the largest rural population and the best school systems — much better than, say, the Bruce Peninsula with its poorer land. In consequence the fruit belt is enormously attractive to an urban developer, for the necessary services are already available. Thus, the creation of services to satisfy intensive agriculture serves to encourage urban development. The same conditions apply to the explicit urban shadow problem. Comparable problems exist where agricultural activity is carried out on the outskirts of cities during the ten to fifteen years when the land is passing from a potential urban development site to actually developed land. The return on holding that land invariably exceeds the return from keeping it in agriculture. It is extremely difficult to make efficient use of the land in that setting without resort to public policies.

Finally, a word about policymakers. There is a tendency to be extremely critical of the planning activity in North America, and particularly in Canada, in the last twenty years. Nevertheless, in one area considerable credit should be given to planners. Historically, premature land development led to runaway speculative booms. In the whole history of urbanization in North America, only in the last two decades has there been major urban development without fantastic booms and busts.

This leads us into several issues involved in municipal financing, primarily concerning taxation. The major tax in the hands of municipalities is the real property tax. This tax fails to meet either the benefits criterion or the ability-to-pay criterion, the two justifications for taxes in public finance theory. It appears to be used mainly because of its relative administrative ease and its historical role in raising municipal revenues. These reasons are not adequate, however, and when one considers the great arbitrariness involved in present assessment procedures, there seems to be little defence for its use at all. In addition, the current tax treatment of land in the urban fringe rewards both the speculator and the holdout by permitting them to keep land out of development in anticipation of higher rental surplus as it becomes increasingly scarce. Services must then be detoured and potentially costly additions are imposed on the city's development budget.

Despite these criticisms on the distributional or equity side, real property taxes can be an effective tool of policy. For example, the current bias in favour of slumlords could easily be removed through appropriate assessment procedures, and indeed appropriate modification of the tax on slum holdings might lead to highly desirable land use patterns. Indeed, if the property tax is based on strictly *ad valorem* assessment and levied at a uniform rate — at present not the case anywhere but nevertheless feasible — the tax will have a neutral effect on development. Many policy instruments, such as housing standards, codes and zoning regulations, now used partly to offset faulty tax policy, could then be used to pursue more positive urban goals. A popular proposal to alter the tax structure for policy purposes is the site tax, which is based on the value of the land alone. The benefits of such a tax, while superficially appealing, have not in fact been achieved. Furthermore, there are substantial grounds, both theoretical and administrative, for questioning the efficacy of a site tax.

The literature in this area is sufficiently rich to preclude our probing it in depth here.[4] The point to be emphasized is that with appropriate revisions the present tax, despite its failings, could be made an effective planning instrument.

Conclusion

Our inquiry into the scope for urban policy has revealed, first and foremost, the serious lack of any policy on this continent up to the present. This applies to both the among-city issues and the various within-city issues. Lack of planning for the former is more easily explained, though not necessarily more justifiable. In our federal structure, cities are viewed as creatures of the provinces. While this serves to explain the absence of federal policies, it does not exonerate the provinces, for there has been very little done at the intra-provincial level.

While it is pointless to criticize municipalities for failing to consider among-city problems, their propensity to disregard within-city issues cannot be justified. Their continued adher-

---

4 For example, see D. Netzer, *Economics of the Property Tax*, Brookings Institution, Washington, 1966; and F. H. Finnis, *Real Property Assessment in Canada*, Canadian Tax Foundation, Toronto, 1962.

ence to faith in optimal patterns of urban growth and urban land use through a policy (or non-policy) of *laissez-faire* flies in the face of mounting evidence to the contrary. The externalities implicit in urban activity negate efficient solutions without a substantial degree of public involvement.

If policymakers have been remiss in their approach to the urban unit, however, an important reason is the very conspicuous absence of guides to rational urban policy. This in turn may be explained by the lack of serious research and discussion at the theoretical level. Some elements of a theory of the city exist, but until much more is known about the internal dynamics and external relationships of cities, any policies will perforce be *ad hoc* and often ineffectual.

9 Housing Policy and Urban Renewal

R. T. Adamson

Introduction

Among the very complex set of issues entailed in urban renewal, none has received more attention both from policy-makers and from the public at large than the problem of residential blight. This paper is an attempt to shift the level of discussion on to a more meaningful plane through a careful analysis of the problem and of the policies being devised to deal with it.

Characteristics of Residential Blight

Virtually all cities in the world today contain extensive areas of what is described as urban blight. In its residential aspects blight means areas of housing which are occupied at a high level of congestion in terms of persons per square foot and which are generally in a state of disrepair. It means bad housing, occupied too intensively. Blighted areas may contain commercial and industrial properties as well as residential ones. Indeed they may be composed entirely of non-residential properties but in this event the sense in which they represent a defect alters. Purely non-residential blight may be considered objectionable on the grounds of its uncomely appearance and it may contain an element of human hazard to workers or clients or neighbours. But it does not carry the same implications of human suffering that are inevitably associated with residential slums.

Congestion

Slums represent nothing more nor less than a shortage of housing. The fact of shortage alone is sufficient to explain residential congestion. Since it is a matter of simple arithmetic that the number of dwellings in virtually all of our cities is less than the number of primary family units and non-family household groups, however defined, some of the families and non-family households simply have to share accommodation. This is a matter of physics, not economics, in the short run at least.

While a shortage of housing accommodation provides a sufficient explanation of residential congestion somewhere in the city, the mere provision of additional dwelling space would not eliminate overcrowding and doubling-up.

The use of dwelling space imposes two distinct kinds of costs on the occupants: the cost of access to the dwelling space; and the cost of servicing it. If there were an absolute surplus of available dwellings, the market price of adequate dwelling space would, in principle, approach zero. But the costs of servicing the space, that is to say heating it and furnishing it, paying the taxes and upkeep, and utility charges, would still represent a cost of occupancy. There are families in every city who are too poor to pay these user charges and who would still have to double-up even if the cost of access to dwelling space were close to zero.

Indeed there have been cases in which the charge for access to dwelling space not only fell to zero, but actually became negative. On occasion in the 1930's, landlords, particularly institutional landlords in possession of real estate as a result of mortgage foreclosure operations, actually paid tenants to live in houses on the grounds that occupied houses depreciated less rapidly than vacant ones, in a purely physical sense. This situation resulted, however, not from a condition of housing

surplus, but from inadequate effective demand. The phenomenon of negative shelter rents required an assumption on the
part of the property owner that the property itself had some
value, despite its immediate failure to earn any rent at all.

To get back to the main thread of argument, however, a
shortage of dwellings must inevitably — by physical, not
economic, laws — lead to congestion. But the phenomenon of
residential congestion does not sufficiently describe what we
know as urban blight. It does not explain the concentration
in particular areas, and it does not explain the general state
of disrepair and the lack of incentive to maintain the quality
of accommodation.

Concentration

Given a basic shortage of accommodation, given the inequality
of income and wealth, and given the heterogeneity in terms of
quality of the available housing stock, it follows that the poor
will occupy not only less space per person than others but
also the poorer quality space.

While the aggregate housing stock is heterogeneous in
quality, it is comparatively homogeneous over fairly large
neighbourhood areas. This feature results from the historical
process of urban growth, with different areas representing
both the social class for which the initial construction was
done and different historical epochs in construction technology
and design style. This clustered characteristic of the actual
received housing stock, together with the market selection of
housing space against the poor in terms of housing quality,
leads to a concentration of congestion.

Thus, the notion of shortage, and the facts of inequality in
incomes, heterogeneity of quality in the housing stock, and
neighbourhood homogeneity in the historical accumulation of
the housing stock can all explain the characteristics of concentration and congestion that urban blight exhibits. It
remains to discuss the characteristic of deterioration, or the
failure of the incentive to maintain the quality of accommodation.

Deterioration

Residential structures are subject to depreciation through wear and tear deriving from usage and through the mere passage of time. These sources of depreciation are inescapable and are apart altogether from technological obsolescence and extraneous events such as shifts in land uses that may affect the acceptability of a given structure as residential accommodation. This normal depreciation requires a stream of outlays, over and above user costs, to maintain the quality of dwellings. These outlays, however, need not be made since the quality of the accommodation may be allowed to deteriorate. Continued occupancy is possible at a level of expenditure far short of that which would either arrest or minimize the rate of decline of the quality of a given dwelling. There is no incentive for a property owner to maintain the quality of housing unless he is able to obtain some return on the moneys that such maintenance requires.

While housing or shelter space is a necessity, housing quality is not. And although a landlord may obtain a return on such outlays as are necessary to keep a building occupied, he may not be able to obtain a return on outlays that maintain or add to the quality of the individual unit. At the pressure of congestion and at the level of income at which the occupants of blighted areas live, the marginal rate at which people will give up space or money for housing quality is very low — too low to justify building maintenance beyond the barest minimum that the law will allow, or that continued occupancy requires. Therefore, the rate of deterioration of housing quality tends to be accelerated in congested areas.

The process is also infectious, or contagious in an environmental sense, as there are other factors at work. It is not just that there is scant prospect for returns on improvements in the quality of individual dwelling units in blighted areas. There is the additional factor that the quality of the units as dwelling space is only partly determined by the intrinsic characteristics of the dwellings themselves. The attractiveness of the units is affected by the general environmental factors over which the individual property owners have little control. Their ability to transform the quality of the accommodation they own is seriously circumscribed by the total nature of the surrounding environment. In the jargon of the economist, the economies of the process of home improvement are not all internalized at the individual property owner's level.

Further, there is the often reiterated point that property improvements are subject to real estate tax and that this tax must diminish the incentive to maintain or improve structures and amenities.

Finally, the process is further accelerated by the intensity of use of the housing stock in slum areas. The intensity of use, or congestion of occupancy, accelerates the physical process of deterioration at the same time as the defences against the process are weakened.

There is no paradox here, although there may appear to be one. The apparent paradox arises from the inference that the greater the shortage of housing, the greater the degree of congestion, and hence the weaker the forces supporting maintenance and upkeep of the existing stock of dwellings. Assuming no change in income distribution, a reduction in the available housing stock will in fact, by increasing congestion, diminish the commercial incentive to upgrade quality, or to arrest deterioration in quality. But at the same time it will support the incentive to make such minimum outlays as are essential to keep space in use. This is not a paradox. A reduction in available dwelling space represents an impoverishment in housing terms and increases the demand for inferior goods, in this case poor quality space. The price for pure space is increased, but the demand for the maintenance of its quality is reduced.

Extension

Thus far, comment has been confined to blight as a phenomenon in a given static housing shortage. But blight itself is not static. It usually has territorial ambitions and imperialistic claims. In many communities the poor are not allowed to buy inferior accommodation from the building industry. Sub-division requirements, building codes, zoning stipulations and planning sensibilities all conspire against the poor in any effort they might mount to build new areas of inferior accommodation in the growing fringes of cities. If the pressure of housing congestion increases in areas already blighted, the residents of the slums have no recourse but to extend their domain by penetration into new territories in the existing stock of housing. Increasing congestion in slum areas raises the rent per unit of space and facilitates the extension of congestion into neighbouring areas. This in turn diminishes the incentive to maintain upkeep in these areas. The results are self reinforcing through environmental effects and through the increased rate of deterioration induced by more intensive use. Thus, under pressure of congestion, blight can extend its domain by a kind of colonization and tactile infection. In the area under conquest, those who can still afford to place a high value on housing quality and a salubrious environment move out. The rest are engrossed.

Most slum areas, adjacent to the central core of cities, are themselves subject to territorial losses as the core expands and lands are acquired for purposes such as traffic interchanges and public and private buildings. These losses of living space to the lower income groups add to the pressures that they themselves can exert along the city's faltering front of respectability.

There are other pressures that increase slum congestion and that subjugate new areas to blight. Urban migration of poor people probably brings about the greatest pressure of this kind and, of course, the natural growth of population. Whatever the occasions for change, blight in a period of rapid urban growth is seldom static. There is always some outpost of decency under fire, some line of fading gentility being infiltrated. It is small wonder that we have found the modern city in many respects a rancorous and violent home. When the struggle for living space is given added emotional energy by non-economic factors such as colour, ethnic or religious differences, the hostility latent in the real conflict of interests is deepened. In severe cases, the surrogate expressions of this conflict assume the character of warfare. The line of encounter which separates the slum from the area under threat explains in part why class hostilities in urban areas are most intense, not between the rich and the poor, but between the poor and the almost poor.

Summary

The foregoing description of urban blight is purely in terms of economic concepts and observable historical facts about the housing stock. Four salient characteristics of the condition are mentioned: congestion, concentration, deterioration and extension.

Congestion arises out of the fact of housing shortage which may be taken as an almost universal urban condition but which varies of course in a very wide degree from place to place.

The concentration of congestion is the result of three conditions:

(a) the inequality of incomes;
(b) the heterogeneity of housing quality over the urban area as a whole;
(c) the comparative homogeneity of housing quality at the neighbourhood level.

Deterioration in areas of congestion is the result of three factors:

(a) the small marginal value placed on housing quality by overcrowded and poor people;
(b) the intensity of use of overcrowded stock;
(c) the externality to individual property holdings of many of the quality-determining factors.

The extension of blight stems from the loss of dwelling space to other land uses, the migration of poor people to the city and the natural growth of population.

This general description is partial, truncated, impressionistic and abstract. Because it draws nothing from the concepts of physical planning and because it depends in no way on differences between people other than differences in income, a description based solely on economic criteria is incomplete.

The Rationale for Public Renewal Policies

Not surprisingly, everybody is against blight today. It requires an abnormal sense of romanticism to plead for the preservation of slums as an indispensable refuge for some of society's more bizarre and marginal activities. The culture of poverty which develops as a response to the harshness, variety and compression of life in congested urban areas no doubt has some admirable and appealing features that are not to be found in the more indulgent, spacious and impersonalized neighbourhood environments in other parts of the city. But these expressions do not justify the deprivation and suffering from which they spring. Urban renewal, as public policy directed toward the restoration of slum areas and the prevention of the spread of blight, is advocated on three broad grounds: humanitarian, aesthetic and economic.

The extent to which renewal policies gain support, whatever the basis of the primary motivation, depends on the prevailing judgment about the cost of renewal. Particularly zealous advocates often claim that it is the slums themselves which are expensive and that their renewal will save the community money. These people, usually basing their argument on the local government point of view, point out that blighted areas provide very low contributions on a per capita basis to the municipal treasury, and that they occasion high local government outlays on social services, fire protection, police services, hospital services and education. Transformation of the areas, it is argued, would reduce their charges and increase their contributions to the local treasury, and possibly could be accomplished at some profit.

Urban renewal consists primarily of the provision and refurbishment of real estate, which can only be achieved at some cost. The services which the municipality performs, and on which the prospect of savings is based, constitute services to people who are not, it is hoped, to be removed by the process of renewal. The revenues municipalities obtain through the real estate tax on residential property depend largely on people's incomes, and the process of renewal does not fundamentally, directly or immediately impinge on income. Therefore, it is difficult to see how municipalities can make money from the business of urban renewal unless they move poor people out of the municipality and move rich people in, or unless they move people out, and industry in. And if this represents the deliberate intent of urban renewal, it is difficult to justify the participation of the Federal Government in a process which boils down to an intermunicipal game of raiding assessments and exporting the poor.

The real job, of course, is to increase and refurbish the housing available to those now quartered in blighted areas; to provide for the maintenance of the quality of these accommodations either by restoring the private incentive to maintain quality or by taking on the job publicly; and to increase, not decrease, the public services available for the people affected. Even allowing for some economies that may result from this, it is obvious that the task cannot be done at monetary profit from the point of view of municipalities collectively.

Nevertheless, the likelihood of certain economies should be recognized. It is convincing of course to argue that the reduction of congestion and the improvement of accommodations will probably reduce fire hazards, making fire protection less expensive. It is less convincing, but still plausible to argue that delinquency stems in part from bad housing conditions, as distinct from poverty, and that renewal will reduce police and other costs associated with delinquency. The same may be said about health and welfare services in general. To a degree, these problems may stem from bad housing itself, apart from other aspects of poverty. The improvement of residential conditions will do something to reduce public outlays of certain kinds. Careful study and research are necessary to separate the effects of bad housing and physical environment from those of poverty in general. Only after such study can complete cost-benefit analysis of urban renewal be carried out.

On the question of municipal revenues, urban renewal of itself has no direct and immediate effects on the income of the people who live in blighted areas. It is not apparent, there-fore, how rents could be increased to provide the basis for increased residential property taxes. As for commercial and industrial property, it is again not apparent how the mere process of renewal will increase the total demand for commer-cial and industrial plants providing a source of added revenue from non-residential property. It is likely that a certain amount of geographical shifting of both residential and com-mercial and industrial plants would result from renewal. But this would not alter municipal revenues.

Since the costs of urban renewal are very real and probably can be only partly offset, the expense must be justified on humanitarian or aesthetic grounds, and not on economic grounds.

Federal Aid to Urban Renewal

As noted at the beginning of this paper, residential urban blight originates in housing shortage and poverty, and mani-fests itself in congestion and the deterioration of housing quality. Public policy directed toward the elimination of blight should ideally be aimed at its roots: housing shortage and poverty.

Unfortunately, neither housing policy nor urban renewal policies can be counted on to free us from the problem of poverty. Better housing conditions and improved urban environments would, of course, assist in the general raising of earnings of poor people. The relief of congestion and a more salubrious environment, for health and motivational reasons alone, would strengthen the ability and readiness of people to earn more adequate incomes. But the fact remains that urban blight represents a manifestation of poverty, and the elimination of the effect will not remove the origin.

The blight itself, however, can be removed, and its removal would do away with one of the severest penalties which poverty exacts — the shortage of housing, which serves as both the source and carrier of blight.

To relieve residential congestion, it is necessary not only to provide additional accommodation, but also to make it accessible. The mere provision of additional dwellings, subject to allocation through the private market mechanism, will not of itself enable lower income people to occupy the dwellings at acceptable densities. They must still meet the occupancy costs and those current outlays necessary to maintain the quality of the housing provided. In most situations where any degree of poverty is involved, some subsidy aid to poor people will be required. Thus the provision of additional accommodation and subsidy access to it are essential features of residential urban renewal.

The National Housing Act (NHA) provides two basic techniques for the provision of subsidized accommodation. While they do not form part of the explicit urban renewal sections of the Act, their availability is crucial to the renewal process. The public housing provisions of the Act can operate, of course, apart altogether from any urban renewal application. The urban renewal provisions offer federal aids for the redevelopment, rehabilitation and conservation of defined areas in cities. The Act does not explicitly require that subsidized housing programs be conducted in cities that avail themselves of the renewal aid. But it does require that urban renewal schemes put forward by cities include an account of how people are to be rehoused if they are dispossessed or required to move as a result of the renewal program. In the majority of cases, where residential renewal is being conducted, it is impossible to devise a satisfactory program of rehousing without recourse to subsidies. Urban renewal does not offer an alternative to subsidized housing. On the contrary, it increases the need for it.

Subsidized Housing

The two broad methods by which the federal government provides aid for subsidized housing may be described as the partnership and loan techniques.

The partnership technique has been in effect since 1949. At that time provisions were made which permitted the federal government, through the Central Mortgage and Housing Corporation (CMHC), to form partnerships with provinces for the construction of housing projects. Capital costs were to be shared 75 per cent by the federal partner and 25 per cent by the province, the latter being free to obtain any part of its 25 per cent share from the local government in the area affected. Operating losses as well as capital costs were to be shared on the same three to one federal-provincial basis. The explicit provisions for meeting losses made it possible to build subsidized housing for families unable to afford the rent of decent private accommodation.

The federal-provincial partnership arrangements originally confined the assistance to new housing. Amendments in 1964 made it possible to use the partnership device to acquire existing housing as well. Prior to 1964 the legislation confined activity for the most part to dwelling units suitable for self contained family accommodation. The 1964 amendments widened this to include hostels and dormitory types of accommodation suitable for single people, with the needs of old people particularly in view.

The other technique for aiding public housing projects, the loan technique, was also introduced in the 1964 amendments. It provided for federal loans to provinces or their designates for the purpose of building or acquiring housing for the use of lower income people. The loans may be as high as 90 per cent of the project cost; they are to be amortized over fifty years; and they are to bear an interest rate in keeping with the cost to the federal government of long-term borrowing. The legislation also provided for federal subsidies to the provinces or their designates for the purpose of meeting 50 per cent of the losses incurred in the operation of such projects.

In principle, either of these techniques is capable of providing housing at whatever rent is necessary to make it accessible to low-income people. This capability is crucial to the successful renewal of blighted residential areas in cities.

Urban Renewal Aids Proper

The federal urban renewal aids proper are contained in another part of the statute and are sometimes discussed in isolation from the low rental housing provisions. The urban renewal aids are intended to support a complex process of real property improvement. They provide federal financial aid, in both loan and grant form, to local governments which are conducting actual renewal programs in a specified manner.

In order to qualify for aid, a local government must prepare a scheme for the renewal of a specific blighted or substandard area. The Act provides that CMHC will pay half the costs of the preparation of the scheme. The scheme itself is to contain at least five elements:

(1) A plan designating the properties that are to be acquired and cleared. This must also include an indication of the provisions to be made for rehousing the people dispossessed by the clearance process.

(2) A plan designating the proposed changes in public services and land uses in the whole area under the scheme.

(3) A description of the methods to be used by the local government for the control of land use and zoning and for the enforcement of building standards and occupancy conditions in the area.

(4) A description of the methods planned for the improvement of private properties in the area, and the techniques for the continued enforcement of building and occupancy standards.

(5) An estimate of the cost of the scheme.

The scheme must have provincial consent. Federal agreement to the scheme makes available the following financial aids from the Central Mortgage and Housing Corporation:

(1) Grants to the municipality representing 50 per cent of the net cost of property acquisition, clearance and disposal.

(2) Grants to the municipality representing 50 per cent of the cost of new or improved municipal service installations, excluding buildings.

(3) Grants to the municipality for 50 per cent of the costs of employing personnel specifically for tasks arising from implementation of the scheme.

(4) Loans to the municipality for two thirds of the municipal share of those costs for which the 50 per cent grants are available. These loans may be for a term as long as fifteen years and are to bear interest at a rate close to the cost of long-term borrowing by the federal government.

(5) For the owners of private residential properties in the area, insured mortgage loans, otherwise allowed only for new housing construction, are available on existing properties, in order to facilitate the process of property improvement and transfer that the urban renewal process will entail. These loans are similar to those available on new property except that the maximum loan ratio, 85 per cent is less than that available on new housing, and of course the property standards are lower.

Legislation, of course, cannot eliminate blight automatically. It requires intelligent application at both the local government level and the federal level. The legislation was passed too recently for there to have been any activity beyond the stage of scheme preparation. The following comments, therefore, are offered as preliminary speculations and not as historical judgments.

The tendency of blight to concentrate lends it to treatment by the selection of discrete areas and facilitates the preparation of a city-wide program in definite particulate stages, in keeping with the area scheme approach inherent in the legislation. This is a small and perhaps minor point but a task which is composed of parts, each more or less intelligible in itself, is somehow less forbidding than a continuous and seemingly endless undertaking. The entire task of urban renewal is very large, but it offers occasions for fairly immediate satisfactions and feelings of achievement.

The more fundamental problem of congestion among low-income people can be solved by the provision of subsidized housing, federal aids to which are available as described earlier. There is no other way by which congestion among low-income people can be relieved.

The rigid enforcement of occupancy by-laws or by the acquisition and demolition of overcrowded buildings will not relieve congestion. Both of these techniques are contemplated as part of the urban renewal process but they are not regarded as exclusive techniques. It was almost two hundred years ago that Marie Antoinette is supposed to have said "let them eat cake", and she has been considered uncommonly stupid ever since. But she did not advocate that bread, even stale bread, be destroyed or withheld from the poor. There are people today who apparently believe that the housing conditions of the poor can be advanced by the destruction of their homes or by the enforcement of provisions which make it impossible for landlords to offer them inferior accommodation.

Property maintenance standards and occupancy codes have their place in urban renewal schemes, and must be adopted by local governments if the quality of accommodation is to be restored and maintained. The municipalities must also adopt programs for the improvement of municipal facilities in renewal areas. A further incentive to the maintenance and improvement of privately owned dwellings in renewal areas is the knowledge that the whole area is subject to uniform standards of private upkeep and public services. This knowledge should help eliminate some of the investment disincentives that derive from the external environmental impact on individual property values. Finally, the availability of insured NHA mortgage loans should facilitate the financing of major improvements and make the sale and transfer of properties more fluid.

Yet are all these factors taken together really capable of making good housing available for most of the present residents of these areas? The present tenants and owners of such housing may be basically unable to afford the costs of occupying the improved accommodation at acceptable densities. If so, they will have to move out, and if alternate accommodation is not available at prices they can afford, they will extend the area of blight into other parts of the city.

Our federal legislation may be defective in that the rehousing requirement is imposed explicitly only where residents are forced to move because of public acquisition and clearance of existing housing. This implies that those who merely have to improve their property, at their own expense, and maintain it in acceptable condition and at acceptable densities, can somehow afford to do so. This seems unlikely. If renewal policies really do result in a genuine improvement in the quality of private housing and a reduction of congestion, then it seems likely that the refurbished housing will be occupied by higher income people after renewal. Therefore, many of the original residents will be displaced. There is no requirement in the federal legislation that rehousing plans be prepared for this kind of displacement. The federal legislation, of course, does not preclude such programs.

In conclusion then, the improvement of properties, and the enforcement of maintenance and occupancy codes involve a displacement of people as does the process of expropriation and clearance. To the extent that provision is not made for the rehousing of all the low-income people displaced by renewal, the act of renewing one blighted area may serve merely to extend others.

Conclusion

This analysis has been confined largely to residential urban renewal, and only passing reference has been made to commercial and industrial blight and to the role of the city core or central area in modern metropolitan centres.

It is often lamented that the central business district of many large cities is suffering from a flight of valuable assessments to the suburban fringe and from a failure of new retail and other commercial assessments to locate at the centre of growing cities. This problem is quite separate from the housing problems posed by residential slums. But the strengthening and revitalization of urban centres also represents an important part of the objectives of federal renewal measures.

The imperfections of the urban land market make it particularly difficult for private enterprise to mount large scale coordinated commercial and retail redevelopment projects in and near the central business districts of large cities. The fragmentation of land ownership makes it difficult to assemble sizeable land holdings on which to base integrated developments. The private developer is exposed to the danger of being forced to pay exhorbitant prices to hold-out property owners. The same difficulty does not arise in the urban fringe to as great an extent, so that this imperfection of the market tends to discriminate against the city centre. The availability of federal renewal aids to the municipality, which help to finance the use of expropriation powers to assemble land, does something to redress this balance, and it is expected that urban renewal policies will lead to dramatic new developments of considerable scale at or near the urban central business districts.

The rationalization for federal support to such an objective takes one rather beyond housing questions and could well form the subject of another paper. Certainly issues of national self esteem are very much involved. Anyone who has watched developments in downtown Montreal and Toronto over the past few years becomes aware that while the developments there are local, and for the most part privately financed, their physical scale and drama places them quickly among our most important national symbols. Such issues, therefore, cannot be excluded from the conduct of federal urban renewal policies. In its forlorn and desperate concern about symbols of national identification, it is fitting enough for Canada to seek to develop dazzling and distinctive cities, but a more formidable achievement in real terms and a more compelling sign of national distinction would be the provision of safe and commodious housing for all its citizens.

10 The Concept of Regional Government and a Proposal for Ontario

D. C. Rowat

The Problem of Identifying Regions

In the research and writing on the concept of the "region", it is hard to see a connecting link between the work that is being done by the economic geographers and that of the political scientists. It is also difficult to find a focus for discussion, because those who use the term often mean different things by it. We use it indiscriminately for a geographic area of any size and at any level of government all the way from world regions to municipal regions. Many geographers and economists seem to be searching for sets of clearly defined geographic areas that are in some way "natural". But surely the meaning of "region" must vary with the use to which the concept is put. A political scientist would ask: Is "region" a useful concept for government? Are there such things as natural *political* regions?

Looking back historically, the basis for natural political boundaries, if any, apparently has been community of interest based in turn on two main factors. One factor is urban concentration. Throughout history, from the earliest city-states, the urban area has been a basis for political organization. The other factor is geography. For political organization beyond the city, natural geographic boundaries have had considerable influence. They have created differences of language, culture, economic conditions and so on, which have formed the basis for political boundaries. However, these boundaries usually have been ill-defined, unstable and frequently shifting. Only the modern nation-state has had sharply defined geographic boundaries.

How "natural", then, are the geographic boundaries of modern nation-states? No doubt there has been some influence of geography, language, culture and economy in the creation of these boundaries. Yet there are tremendous variations in area and population among the nations of the world, ranging all the way from several small nations of less than one million to the huge geographic area of China, containing 700 million people. Moreover, many nations contain a great variety of languages, cultures and economic resources. Also, a glance at a map of the world will show that many of the boundaries dividing nations are straight lines, obviously drawn arbitrarily on a map and in no sense "natural". Look at the dividing line between the USSR and Eastern Europe, or at the straight lines, arbitrarily drawn, between the United States and Mexico, and between the United States and Canada. Obviously, there is little that is "natural" about the boundaries of many nation-states other than an emotionally based feeling of community among the population within those boundaries. The intensity of their feeling may vary from one nation to another, from one individual or area within the nation to another, and from one period to another.

This arbitrariness of boundaries is also true within federations. There is little logic in the size, population or boundaries of the states or provinces in a federation. It is true that the state boundaries in India, Switzerland and the USSR seem to be based mainly on geography, language, history and other "natural" factors. But the state boundaries in Western Germany, the United States, Australian and Canada are for the most part arbitrary straight lines or squares. In Canada, geography is the main basis for the boundaries of the Maritime provinces and British Columbia, but not of the other provinces. Take Newfoundland and Labrador, for example; not much logic there. The Prairie provinces are arbitrary rectangles, while Ontario and Quebec are a queer mixture of geographic boundaries and arbitrary lines. Even admitting that geography has played a considerable part in defining these boundaries, it has not dictated the size of provinces. As we all know, there are enormous differences in size and population among the provinces. If boundaries are dictated by geography, then one should ask: Why is Prince Edward Island a province, but not Montreal or Vancouver Island? Clearly, there is not much logic, not much that is "natural" in a geographic sense, about most of Canada's provincial boundaries.

Moving down to the municipal level, in most provinces one finds the same arbitrariness of boundary and geographic area for the rural municipalities. In keeping with the concept of the city-state, municipal boundaries are drawn around urban concentrations. But they vary tremendously in population, all the way from Montreal with about one million, to the smallest village. A further complication is the two-tier system of municipal units in Ontario and Quebec. These provinces have a double layer of municipalities, the top level being the county governments. Some county areas no longer fit modern social and economic conditions. Another complicating characteristic of this two-tier system is that the cities have been excluded from the boundaries of the county municipalities. This is not true, for instance, of most cities in Great Britain or in many states of the United States.

Now, given these illogical boundaries and differences in size and population for nations, for states or provinces within federations, and for municipalities, what sense can be made of the concept of "natural region"? What political level are we talking about when we refer to the region? Are we talking about the supranational level (for example, Western Europe), the sub-national level (say, the Prairie provinces), or the sub-provincial level? At the sub-provincial level, are we talking about urban metropolitan areas, counties, or areas larger than counties, such as eastern Ontario? Because it is doubtful whether there *are* such things as "natural" regions apart from political units, apparently there is no easy way of answering these questions.

Are the economic geographers looking for a single set or level of natural regions? If so, these regions may cross-cut the political boundaries of any level because the political units are so "unnatural". To deal with such regions might involve working with several existing levels of government. In terms of political reality, then, is it of much use to "discover" such regions? Or, do the economic geographers conceive of a hierarchy of natural regions, one set within another? If so, it is clear that these regions would not coincide at all with the "unnatural" political boundaries at any level. It is very unlikely, therefore, that one would conveniently find a hierarchy of natural regions *within* political boundaries — one set at the sub-national level and another set below this at the sub-provincial level.

Yet economic geographers and others often talk as though it is possible to do so. We speak of the five sub-national economic regions of Canada, and Messrs. Camu, Weeks and Sametz have recently "discovered" sixty-eight regions at the sub-provincial level.[1] But have we not simply created these two concepts of the region because it has been administratively useful to do so? Why would it not be just as logical and "natural" to find between these two extremes of five and sixty-eight, a set of about twenty regions, based on the middle-sized provinces, with Ontario and Quebec each divided into four or five regions? The answer is that such regions are not badly needed for purposes of economic and social analysis; several provincial governments of this size already exist, and full statistical information is regularly collected on a provincial basis. Similarly at the lowest level, local governments and census districts already exist. So it is "natural" to find larger geographic-economic regions which provide for a level of analysis between the municipality or census district and the province.

---

[1] P. Camu, E. P. Weeks and Z. W. Sametz, *Economic Geography of Canada, With an Introduction to a 68-Region System*, Macmillan, Toronto, 1964.

Few people realize how arbitrarily defined the Camu-Weeks-Sametz regions are. In the first place, they are restricted to provincial boundaries and often follow illogical county and census district boundaries. More surprising is that the number of regions for Ontario and Quebec, ten each, was determined by the coding system developed for automatic data processing. The number was limited to ten because there are only ten integers between thirty-nine and fifty in the case of Quebec, and forty-nine and sixty in the case of Ontario. This means that the regional economic planning councils in Ontario have been set up for areas which were created mainly to suit the convenience of the computer. Similarly, the number of economic zones within a region is restricted to ten by the coding system. It is hardly likely that natural regions would be made up of groups of no more than exactly ten economic zones, and it is therefore no more likely that Ontario and Quebec have ten economic regions than that they have fifteen, twenty or five. Moreover, sociological and other factors were given a weight of only 10 per cent, and the authors themselves tell us that "the main principle of operation has been to obtain approximate conjunctions of recognized economic units with combinations of statistical units".[2] In short, artificial regions were created of a convenient but arbitrary size for the purpose of aggregating data and analyzing economic activity below the provincial level. They cannot claim to be truly "natural" regions for purposes of economic planning, administration or government.

Are there, then, such things as "all-purpose natural" regions? It seems to be true that economic activity and cultural influence spread out in increasing concentric circles from urban centres. Using the analogy of waves created by stones dropped in a scattered fashion over water, some economic geographers therefore believe that the way to find natural regions is to find the limits of the "waves" of influence by drawing boundaries along the lines where the waves from different urban centres collide. But there are two criticisms of this analogy. Urban

---

[2] *Ibid.*, p. 265.

centres vary greatly in size, so that the strong waves from a large city (stone) may override the weak waves from a town (pebble), and it becomes difficult to find the lines where the waves collide. A more serious criticism is that urban centres send out a great many waves of different kinds and intensity. These travel different distances and meet the corresponding waves from other urban centres at different points. So it becomes impossible to draw a single line around an urban centre's area of influence, and one is left with a complex overlay of regions representing the boundaries of influence of different economic and social factors. Therefore, except possibly for metropolitan areas, there seems to be little prospect of finding within a country a single set, or a hierarchy of sets, of regions which represent a "natural" bunching of social and economic activities in areas other than politically defined ones. However, once a set of regions has been decided upon (that is, their general number and size has been determined), the economic geographer can help to define precise boundaries by trying to group together natural factors.

Criteria for Political Regions

Following this gloomy view of the prospect of finding natural regions, the question is what sense or use political scientists can make of the idea of a political region. In other words, how does one know whether a regional level of government is needed? To answer this question, four main criteria may be applied in choosing governmental areas in a democracy.

One of these has already been mentioned: the area chosen must encompass people who have a feeling of common interest. This seems to have been the basis for political boundaries throughout history. But it is a very vague concept. If one is thinking of creating a new regional government, how does one measure "community of interest"? How does one know where it begins and ends? Indeed, how does one even identify it? Secondly, the administrative ease and efficiency with which one level of government can deal with another level is an important criterion. This, in turn, depends upon the number of units at the lower level. For instance, in Ontario there are close to 1,000 municipalities. Therefore, the provincial government in its dealings with the local governments has, in administrative jargon, a "span of control" of about 1,000 units. Thirdly, and this is the criterion stressed most frequently in studies of local government, the governmental unit must encompass enough population and wealth to finance and administer efficiently the modern battery of services expected of it. The fourth and most important criterion is decentralization. The political system must avoid excessive centralization. It may therefore be desirable to create lower level units of government to increase the number of centres at which political decisions are made, thus keeping the political system pluralized. If real political decisions are to be made by these units, however, they cannot be merely administrative divisions; they must have elected representatives and they must be relatively independent of the higher level. As a convenient shorthand, these four criteria will be referred to as the interest, intergovernmental, efficiency and decentralization criteria.

Let us examine the interest criterion at greater length, because it is rather vague and is perhaps the most difficult to understand. In attempting to apply this criterion to the possible need for regional government at any level, one must ask: Is there a community of interest which has not found expression? This community of interest may be based on geographic, economic or cultural factors. One example is the postwar move toward the integration of Western Europe. A community of interest seems to exist there which has no corresponding political organization. Similarly in Canada, there may be a community of interest in the Atlantic or prairie regions which is not adequately expressed because there is no corresponding regional unit of government. There are also identifiable regions of this kind in the United States, like the South and the Corn Belt.

A serious problem in attempting to apply this criterion is that the existing political system may prevent the expression of these "other-based" interests — interests which are geographically based, but not on the boundaries of the existing political units. J. E. Hodgetts has suggested that in Canada the parliamentary system of government may have had this effect at both levels of government.[3] The strictness of party discipline may prevent the adequate expression of other-based interests through the existing party system. In federal politics one thinks of the break-away political parties based on the prairies. At the provincial level, the strictness of party discipline in Ontario, for example, may be preventing the expression of strong interests based on eastern Ontario or northeastern Ontario. The research problems involve such questions as: How do we know when or where such communities exist? What are their geographic limits? May the community of interest be based only on objective factors, such as the transportation pattern or the centre of economic influence, or must it be based also on a strong, subjective feeling of community? How clear-cut must these factors be to warrant a regional unit of government? One can easily see that the concept of community of interest is almost impossible to apply operationally.

Another complicating point is that over a period of time a political unit will create its own community of interest. The nation is the most obvious example. The national government reinforces the concept of the nation and the feeling of nationalism. Similarly in a federal system, the provincial boundaries mark out and create communities of interest within those boundaries. Thus, although one can provide for an existing community of interest by creating a political unit for it, one can also create a community of interest by creating a political unit. Is the latter type of community feeling less genuine?

In discussing regional government, since it is unlikely the provinces will join to create multipurpose regional governments, let us concentrate our attention on the level below the

---

[3] J. E. Hodgetts, "Regional Interests and Policy in a Federal Structure", *Canadian Journal of Economics and Political Science*, Vol. 32, February 1966, pp. 1-14.

province. This level is closely related to the city and to the problem of how far the city's influence extends beyond the built-up area. Here it is difficult to confine one's attention within the boundaries of a single province. A metropolitan area may cross provincial boundaries. Ottawa-Hull is a prime example. This example is further complicated by the fact that it is also the federal capital, and therefore problems of constitutional jurisdiction between the federal and provincial levels of government are involved.[4] Metropolitan areas may even cross international boundaries. Windsor-Detroit is a good example. Indeed, the Greek planner, C. A. Doxiadis, who was attached to a planning group in Detroit, claims that the whole Great Lakes area is one gigantic international megalopolis centred on Detroit, with the Canadian extension including Toronto, Montreal and Quebec City.[5] In thinking about regional government in relation to urban concentration, then, one sees that economic and social influences do not stop at provincial boundaries. The attendant problems can be solved only by intergovernmental, even international, cooperation.

An important consideration regarding the need for regional government at the sub-provincial level is the size and population of a province. The need will also be greater in a province with a large number of small rural municipalities. So we must start analyzing this problem with some of the elementary facts about the structure of local government in Canada. The accompanying Table 10-1, which is a simplified version of one in the Canada Year Book 1966, shows the number of units of each type of local government in each province.

Note that only Quebec and Ontario have a second tier of local government, the county municipality. Also, only Montreal, Toronto and Winnipeg have metropolitan authorities, and only the latter two have a genuine second tier of metropolitan-wide government. Since then, B.C. has created a system of regional authorities. The most useful column

---

[4] See the author's report, "The Proposal for a Federal Territory for Canada's Capital", in Ontario Advisory Committee on Confederation, *Background Papers and Reports*, Toronto, 1967, Vol. 2.

[5] *Time*, November 4, 1966.

TABLE 10-1

MUNICIPALITIES IN CANADA, BY PROVINCE

as at January 1, 1965

	Cities	Towns	Villages	Rural[1]	Second-Tier Counties	Metro. Corpns.	Total
Newfoundland	2	60[2]	51	—	—	—	113
Prince Edward Island	1	7	17	—	—	—	25
Nova Scotia	3	39	—[3]	24	—	—	66[3]
New Brunswick	7	20	1[3]	15[3]	—	—	43[3]
Quebec	65	180	325	1110	75[6]	Montreal	1756
Ontario	32	157	159	590	38	Toronto	977
Manitoba	9	36	41	110[4]	—	Winnipeg	197
Saskatchewan	11	121	364	296	—	—	792
Alberta	9	89	167	485	—	—	313
British Columbia	32	8	58	32	—	—	130
Total Incorporated	171	717	1183	2225	113	3	4412

1 Rural municipalities are designated by different names in the different provinces; excludes local improvement districts except for 18 in Ontario.
2 Includes 11 rural and local improvement districts operating under the same Act.
3 Excludes village service commissions and local improvement districts.
4 Includes 5 suburban municipalities.
5 Includes 26 county municipalities.
6 Includes Inter-Urban Corporation of Ile Jésus (which became City of Laval in 1965).
Source: Based on Canada Year Book, 1966, p. 97.

from our point of view is the one labelled Rural. It illustrates the great variations in the size and number of rural municipalities in proportion to provincial population. New Brunswick, of course, has now abolished its rural municipalities. But even before abolition of these municipalities, New Brunswick, and Nova Scotia as well, had a relatively small number in proportion to provincial population (fifteen and twenty-four respectively). This compares with nearly 600 in Ontario and over 1,100 in Quebec. However, these large numbers are partly compensated for by the second-tier counties. Manitoba and Saskatchewan, too, have a very large number of small rural municipalities in proportion to population (about 100 and 300, respectively). It is in the very large populous provinces and in those which have the largest number of rural municipalities that the case for a regional level of government is likely to be strongest. However, a convincing case can also be made for regional government in provinces which have relatively large rural municipalities — as was attempted for Nova Scotia some years ago.[6] Even though some criteria of the report do not apply as neatly there, the others (especially "decentralization") are important enough to carry the argument.

Compared with the number of states in a typical federation, one cannot help being impressed with the tremendous number of units of local government in each province — in Quebec over 1,700 and in Ontario nearly 1,000. In Saskatchewan, which is much smaller in population, there are close to 800. Yet the largest federation, the United States, has only fifty states. Switzerland has twenty-two, and the typical number is about ten, as in Canada, Western Germany, and also in the most recent proposal for Nigeria. Australia has only six. In short, a much greater gap exists between the municipal and provincial levels in Canada than between the state and central governments of most federations.

---

6 Donald C. Rowat, *The Reorganization of Provincial-Municipal Relations in Nova Scotia*: A Report Prepared for the Government of Nova Scotia by the Nova Scotia Municipal Bureau, Halifax, 1949, Parts 3 and 4.

Sub-provincial Region Building

Having looked briefly at the factual situation across Canada, let us now try to apply the four criteria to the sub-provincial level to see what is needed. Are there communities of interest going unexpressed? Considering the large number of local units and the consequent gap between the provincial government and the municipalities, there may be communities of interest at the regional level which cannot be expressed in Ontario, Quebec and the western provinces. Now that New Brunswick has abolished its rural municipalities, there may soon be communities of interest going unexpressed in New Brunswick.

A special problem in applying the interest criterion is that there are metropolitan areas nearly everywhere in Canada which have spilled over the boundaries of the central city. Each is a single, built-up area with a community of interest which can no longer be expressed through the existing governmental machinery, except where a metropolitan government has been created as in Toronto and Winnipeg. The speed of urban growth in the twentieth century has rendered obsolete the drawing of a boundary around the community of interest represented by the build-up area. Adjacent areas will in the foreseeable future become urban. Where does the metropolitan area stop? It seems to shade into the countryside. Not only that, but cities are growing into other cities, resulting in galaxies of cities in certain parts of the world, such as the northeastern United States and the Los Angeles area. In Canada, south central Ontario is a good example. So it is often difficult now to draw a line around the community of interest of even an urban area.

Considering the second criterion, ease of intergovernmental communication, let us try to apply the idea of the span of control, which is a convenient sort of rubric or rule of thumb in public administration. Administrative writers claim that, because the number of possible relationships rises with the number of units in geometric progression, a superior unit can deal with only a small number of inferior units. The number that early writers tended to favour ranged from six to twelve units. Later writers have contended that in many situations the span of control can be much larger than this and work successfully.[7] However, 1,000 and 1,700, as in Ontario and Quebec, are simply too many units for a higher level of government to deal with. Furthermore, the counties are not a real buffer between the provinces and the municipalities. It is not a system in which the province delegates power to the county and then the county delegates power to the munici- pality; it is a system in which the province deals directly with both levels. Although the other provinces which do not have this second tier have smaller total numbers of units, one could still argue that they have far too many for effective inter- governmental communication. This argument probably does not apply to Prince Edward Island or New Brunswick. Nor does it apply with much force to Nova Scotia, which has only sixty-six units.

Let us now apply the criterion of efficiency. Are the existing municipal units big enough to finance and provide govern- mental services efficiently? Here we must first decide what population is "big enough". The minimum efficient size for financing and providing local services has grown in the twentieth century for a number of reasons. First, the efficient size has increased with the rise in the standard of services provided and the consequent increase in cost, which small units cannot afford. Also, it has grown with the development of specialization. Many people advance the principle that a unit should be big enough to hire at least one full-time expert in each service being provided. Certainly some services require even more. For instance, a fully manned health unit would require at least one full-time doctor and probably several full-time nurses. So the question can be asked: Is the unit big enough to enjoy the full benefits of specialization? Clearly most rural and small urban municipalities in Canada are too

---

[7] Luther Gulick, "The Division and Coordination of Work", in Donald C. Rowat (ed.), *Basic Issues in Public Administration*, Macmillan, New York, 1961, p. 55.

small to meet this criterion. Finally, the tremendous improvement in transportation makes it much easier to travel and communicate from one side of a large geographic unit to the other. The size of the old school district was based on the distance that a young child could conveniently walk to school. It was also based on the one-teacher, one-room school before the days of specialization in teaching. Thus, one could go through the range of services that have in the past been provided and that could in the future be provided by a local level of government, and conclude that the existing units simply are not large enough to finance and administer efficiently the full range of services.

What then, is the minimum efficient size? This is a disputed point. It no doubt varies from one service to another. A number of experts, especially in the social services and education, have argued that the minimum efficient size for a multipurpose unit is a population of about 50,000 with an absolute minimum of about 30,000.[8] Some of the existing municipalities, especially among the cities, are beyond these minima, but most municipalities are not. The result has been provincial centralization of services. Since the local units have been unable to finance or provide many services efficiently, the province has felt duty-bound to supply them, either directly or by controlling local standards. The local units have declined in importance as decision centres, since the vital decisions are now being made at the provincial level. This, of course, works directly against the decentralization criterion.

Is the solution to this problem enlargement of the municipalities? Probably not. Many of them are small urban centres — villages and towns with clear-cut communities of interest. Abolishing them in order to create larger units would interfere with the criterion of a political basis for expressing com-

---

[8] See, for example, G. F. Davidson, *Report on Public Welfare Services*, Nova Scotia Royal Commission on Provincial Development and Rehabilitation, Halifax, 1944, p. 52. The most recent expert support for the 50,000 figure comes from the United States President's Commission on Law Enforcement and Administration of Justice, for administering police forces; see *Time*, March 24, 1967, p. 22.

munity of interest. Politically, one should not simply create large new municipalities that would gobble up the villages and towns. The alternative solution, which is contained in my report to the government of Nova Scotia, is to create a second tier of regional governments to include the villages and towns. In accordance with the decentralization criterion, these governments must have elected councils with considerable independence from the provincial government. They must not be mainly units of provincial administration with the regional council only advisory, as in the Michener proposal for Manitoba.[9]

Even where there is no obvious community of interest at the regional level, this solution is desirable because most municipalities are so ill-equipped to finance and administer many modern governmental services that the intergovernmental, efficiency and decentralization criteria can be met only by the creation of regional units. Clear regional communities of interest would of course be a strong additional, but not a necessary, factor to justify the creation of regional governments.

Because of the division between urban and rural municipalities in Canada, the problem arises of including the cities in the regions. Clearly cities below 50,000 in population are not large enough to finance and administer some local services efficiently, but the larger cities are. Great Britain has carved out only the very largest cities as one-tier county boroughs, and even quite large cities are in a two-tier system with strong county governments sitting above them. Some experts in Britain feel that even the largest cities should come under a reorganized system of regional government based on the counties.[10] Unfortunately, Ontario and Quebec long ago made

---

9 Manitoba Royal Commission on Local Government Organization and Finance, *Report*, 1964; summary and comment by Dennis A. Young, *Canadian Public Administration*, Vol. 8, March 1965, pp. 24-35.

10 See, for example, W. A. Robson, *Local Government in Crisis*, Allen and Unwin, London, 1966; and Derek Senior, "The City Region as an Administrative Unit", *Political Quarterly*, Vol. 36, January-March 1965, pp. 82-91.

the decision to carve out all cities separately from the second-tier counties. In the past, this may have been satisfactory for cities of over 50,000. However, because of the rapid modern growth of such cities, even this is no longer desirable. Growth beyond their existing boundaries must now be controlled by an authority which encompasses the growth areas also, for both planning and governmental purposes. In the past, annexation by the city has always been "too little and too late".

For urban areas with populations greater than about 150,000, annexation or consolidation are not desirable solutions for another reason. An urban area with a population beyond about 150,000 is nearly always made up of a central city and several satellite centres representing geographically based communities of interest within it. To consolidate such an area under a single city government wrongly assumes that the area is an undifferentiated blob, and prevents these communities of interest from being adequately expressed. This is the great virtue of the two-tier metropolitan system, as evidenced by Toronto and Winnipeg. Such a system also fits the criterion of decentralization. Unfortunately, because of the gigantic size of some of our modern cities, even local governments can sometimes be too highly centralized. Large urban areas should therefore have their own two-tier structures of local and metropolitan or regional government.

Assuming, then, that a regional level of government which includes cities is desirable, what size should the regional units be? How many should there be? Here it is extremely difficult to make any clearly rational decision. Because the criteria are vague, they do not provide a firm guide. Our only clear guide, as has been suggested, is that the minimum efficient population is about 50,000. If in any province the creation of regions with an average population of 50,000 would result in fewer than ten, regional government is probably unnecessary, except for metropolitan areas. Therefore, provinces with populations under 500,000 may not need a second tier of regional government. New Brunswick, Prince Edward Island

and Newfoundland are near this range. However, in New-foundland even the lowest level of rural municipalities is weak, and, as mentioned, New Brunswick is actually abolishing its existing one-tier rural counties. The decentralization criterion is not much in evidence in these provinces.

The best prospects for the adoption of regional government, then, lie in other provinces. Nova Scotia and the Prairie provinces have decentralized many of their provincial services into administrative regions, so that it would be relatively easy to delegate these to a regional level of municipal government. British Columbia has already created the beginnings of a regional system of government,[11] and the idea is now being actively discussed in Quebec and Ontario.[12]

A Proposed Regional Scheme for Ontario

The problem of regional size is most puzzling in Quebec and Ontario because of their large size and population. Ontario will be taken as an example and a tentative proposal attempted based upon the guidelines advanced above.

Using the minimum efficient size of 50,000 as the average population, there would be more than one hundred regional units in Ontario. Obviously, there would be too many units for the province to deal with even after the regional level of government had been created. And at a population of only 50,000 the regional governments would be too close to their constituent units; the services at the two levels would probably overlap too much. Also, it is very likely that between the regional level and the provinces there would be interests based on larger regions, such as eastern or northwestern Ontario, which

---

11 Legislation in 1965 provided for the creation of Regional Districts, with Boards composed of representatives from the councils of the member municipalities.

12 W. H. Palmer, "Concepts of Regional Government", *Municipal World*, Vol. 75, November 11, 1965, pp. 343-344; Association of Ontario Counties, "A Model Regional Government", *Municipal World*, Vol. 75, December 12, 1965, pp. 372-378.

would go unexpressed. The size and number of units, then, must be determined some other way.

Suppose there were only ten regions. Roughly, they would average 700,000 in population. Ontario has already created ten economic planning regions, so one naturally wonders if this would be an appropriate level for regional governments. The author's view is that 700,000 is a tremendous population for a regional unit of government. There would no doubt be a gap in community interests below that level. Keep in mind that unless one is proposing a third tier of government above the counties, regional government at this level assumes that the county governments are to be obliterated. Yet their hundred-year existence has in many cases created strong county-based communities of interest. The obliteration of these units may easily leave a serious gap in the representation of communities of interest below the regional level. Further, ten powerful regional governments would probably be serious political rivals of the provincial government. Hence the province would be chary about creating regional governments with any real independence. It would not have the same fears about smaller units.

It appears, then, that the number of regions should fall somewhere between our two extremes of one hundred and ten. Let us now consider the existing county system as a potential base for regional government. Their number, thirty-eight, is large but perhaps not excessive. In the past, the counties have not been a suitable level of regional government mainly because they have been weak, with few services to perform. They have very few powers, and practically none over the local units within them. Could they not be strengthened enough to make them correspond to the regional governments that we are discussing?

A difficulty with this proposal is the exclusion from the counties of all the cities and seven of the largest towns. Only about half of the people in the province live within the municipal counties, and their average population is only about 75,000.

Even if the thirty-eight county governments were so strengthened that the province did not have to deal directly with the
municipalities within them, it would still have to deal directly
with the counties plus the forty-odd cities and towns, about
eighty units in all. This comes close to our previous figure
of one hundred, and would probably be an excessive number
for efficient intergovernmental communications. More serious,
many independent urban units would still be below the
minimum efficient size of 50,000. Also, cities are natural
regional centres of service and influence for their surrounding
counties, and, as mentioned previously, large cities nowadays
expand and shade into the countryside. Clearly then, if the
counties are to be made the basis for regional government,
they must be reorganized to include the cities.[13]

This reorganization would, of course, create a tremendous
change in the character of the county governments. It would
give them jurisdiction over the cities as well as over the
towns, villages and townships. Since their councils would
include a large proportion of representatives from the cities,
the councils would become much more conscious of the urban
need for controlled development. At the same time, many of
the services provided in the big urban centres could at last
be made available, through regional administration, to the
surrounding countryside.

But what should be done about the large metropolitan
areas, of which there are several in Ontario? For reasons
already given, those over about 150,000 in population should
not be consolidated into one city. Nor should they be carved
out of the surrounding county if this can be avoided, because
in most cases the remainder of the county would be too
truncated to make a viable unit. Also, the metropolitan areas
are spreading faster than the smaller cities, and are most in

---

[13] The Ontario Legislature's Select Committee on the Municipal Act and
Related Acts has also made this proposal; see its *Fourth and Final
Report*, March 1965, Part 2; also, Ralph W. Krueger, "Tangled Admin-
istration: Organization for Regional Development" in John B. Fother-
ingham, *Transition: Policies for Social Action*, McClelland and Stewart,
Toronto, 1966, pp. 96-98.

need of controlling the development of their potential suburbs. Yet they soon grow beyond any boundary that is drawn
around the existing built-up area. A county level of regional
government, then, seems ideal for them. They would become,
in effect, urban or "metropolitan" counties, much like metropolitan Toronto, and consolidation of the whole built-up area
would be unnecessary.

In most cases, the large metropolitan areas in Ontario are
surrounded by a single county which is small enough to be
an effective planning and governmental unit for the built-up
and potentially urban area within it. This seems to be true
of the Hamilton, Windsor, London and Kitchener areas. In
the case of Ottawa, the province is now creating a regional
government based on Carleton county but also taking in
part of Russell county on the east. The remainder of Russell
will be too small to be viable and would have to be joined
with a neighbouring county. A metropolitan county government for the Niagara area would require joining the counties
of Lincoln and Welland; one for the Burlington-Oakville area
would require joining Halton and Peel. In addition, there
may be a case for carving out the Burlington-Oakville area
as a separate urban county and joining the northern portions
of Peel and Halton into a single county, as the Peel-Halton
study has proposed.[14] In order to create a metropolitan county
for the Oshawa-Whitby area, the northern part of Ontario
county could be joined with Victoria, having Lindsay as its
regional centre. Similar metropolitan governments might also
be created for the Lakehead and Sudbury.

Thus with only relatively minor adjustments of boundaries,
the main metropolitan areas could easily be included within
the regional-county system of government. Since their population would be overwhelmingly urban, they could be separately
designated as "metropolitan" or "urban" counties or regions,
and given special powers of urban government. There would
thus be about ten such metropolitan regions.

---

[14] Ontario Department of Municipal Affairs, *Peel-Halton Local Government Review*, 1966.

Some of the counties are small in size and have especially small populations with no city centre. In several cases, therefore, one could join together contiguous counties to form regional units. Thus one might reduce the number of non-metropolitan units to about twenty-five. As an added refinement, but at considerable political cost, one could relocate boundaries that seem to cut across closely integrated social and economic areas. Thirty-five units would not be an unmanageable number, because in accordance with the decentralization criterion, the regional governments should be relatively independent and not closely supervised by the province. They, not the province, should deal with the municipalities below them. Summing up, then, it is here proposed that the counties and cities be joined together as the basis for a new system of regional government in Ontario.

Conclusion

Let us conclude with a general question about the proposal. Are the needs and situations of the various areas of the province now so different that one can no longer apply a uniform system such as county government or the regional system proposed? The Ontario provincial government seems to be attacking the problem as if each area required a quite different structure of local government. At the request of particular localities it has been commissioning studies of individual areas. These areas have been based mainly on urban centres, but the size of the area studied has depended on local requests for inclusion. Eight such studies have been initiated, and four of them have been completed: the Murray Jones study of the Ottawa area, the Mayo study of Lincoln and Welland counties, the Plunkett study of Peel and Halton counties, and the Hardy study of the Lakehead.[15] Three of

15 Ontario Department of Municipal Affairs, *The Ottawa, Eastview and Carleton County Local Government Review*, 3 vols., 1965; *Niagara Region Local Government Review*, 1966; *Peel-Halton Local Government Review*, 1966. *Exploratory Statement*, 1966; *Lakehead Local Government Review*; *Research Report*, 1966, and *Lakehead Local Government Review*, 1968.

these studies — by Jones, Mayo and Hardy — have already proposed a second tier of metropolitan or regional government. The other studies are of the Waterloo, Muskoka, Brantford and Hamilton areas.

Although the provincial government makes frequent mention of regional government, the meaning of the term is rather vague. It is not clear whether provincial officials mean the county, a new level above the county, a uniform pattern for the whole province, or merely selected two-tier metropolitan governments.[16] In recent provincial pronouncements the term for metropolitan government has been changed to regional government. For example, the new government proposed for the Ottawa area on February 1, 1967 by the Minister of Municipal Affairs was described as a regional government.[17] Yet, except that it would take in a large rural area which is only potentially urban, it is not very different from the metropolitan Toronto scheme. If the provincial government continues to initiate area studies and one by one sets up metropolitan or regional governments for the areas studied, it may eventually achieve somewhat the same general pattern of regional government as proposed in this paper. But it will be a very expensive and time-consuming process. It would be far cheaper and much faster to study the whole scheme of regional and metropolitan government at one time. The result would be a less complex and more logical scheme of regional government throughout the province.

---

[16] See especially Premier John Robart's speech in the debate on the Speech from the Throne, Ontario Legislature, *Debates*, February 2, 1967, pp. 166-169.

[17] *Ottawa Citizen* and *Ottawa Journal*, headline stories, February 2; and Mr. Spooner's speech, "Ottawa, Eastview and Carleton County Local Government Review", February 1, 1967, mimeo.

Conclusion

11 Approaching the Urban Unit: Some Conclusions and a Beginning

N. H. Lithwick
Gilles Paquet

This volume has attempted to perceive the nature of the city from a more comprehensive perspective than is open to any single discipline. We set our sights at a distant goal — namely, a view of the urban unit as a total phenomenon. While we moved in that direction, the distance covered is slight in comparison to the distance remaining. This set of papers examines a variety of aspects of the total phenomenon, but the examination has been conducted primarily from the unique perspective of the individual contributors. At some points, and particularly in the first section, some cross-disciplinary dialogue emerges. But, by and large, the volume is multi-disciplinary. Nevertheless, we consider it as more than a simple stock-taking. The language of the specialist is now clearer, and the direction and possibilities of each discipline can be fitted into a broader conceptual framework. The papers thus provide a variety of starting points for the rational pursuit of knowledge about the Canadian urban reality.

It is useful in this concluding note to point out the gaps that we have not tried to fill and to offer some explanation for our omissions. The sins of commission might also be briefly assessed. Then we shall turn to the question of urban policy. In the first instance we must indicate the reality and seriousness of the urban problem. Then we can evaluate the efforts being made at the political and administrative levels to meet this problem. If nothing else, the reader cannot help becoming aware of the gaping policy vacuum in this area in Canada. Finally, we shall try to use the discussions in this volume as a starting point for a more appropriate approach to the problem. By appropriate we mean not only the most efficient technical solutions, but also the politically operational ones.

These views on urban policy might serve as a useful independent statement at a time when a leap into some form of large scale urban policy institution seems to be imminent — the Economic Council of Canada has devoted a full chapter to the urban problem in its Fourth Annual Review, and scuttlebut has it that the federal government is considering a Department of Urban Affairs.

Omissions and Commissions

This volume is a sampler, containing papers by specialists in diverse disciplines on a variety of urban issues. They do not purport to be survey articles. In addition they vary immensely in scope. Some are perhaps unduly restrictive. Some are almost entirely methodological. Our intention was to force the reader to become aware of the many ways of dealing with the urban unit. A side effect has been to provide substantive information on a number of aspects of the Canadian urban scene that have not yet been analyzed with sufficient care.

In addition we have chosen to broaden the context of the urban problem by including several papers that might be more appropriately considered to lie at the crossroads of urban and regional studies. For geographers and political scientists as well as economists, the two problems are not completely divorced. This can be seen by reviewing the literature in urban economics and urban geography. The case is strengthened by the general consensus that the neglect of the relationship between city and region accounts for the failure to explain the dynamics of both.

If what we have included appears as a fruit salad, what we have not dealt with might be perceived as the whipping cream. We have not included, for example, any contributions by city planners, by engineers or by municipal administrators, all of whom dominate the current urban scene. For each of these groups, one can think of a variety of urban issues which they would be competent to discuss. Let us examine them in turn in order to provide our reasons for bypassing them.

Planners are first and foremost integrators and thus they function by necessity at the cross-disciplinary level. But their techniques of problem solving are largely heuristic, because of the complete absence of analytical schemes capable of integrating the urban reality. As a result we felt that their contribution to our particular discussion would not at present be substantial. Indeed, their success largely awaits a better understanding of the elements of that reality. With the appropriate artillery, we might then enter into a dialogue with regard to the optimum way to integrate these elements in the pursuit of our urban objectives.

As for engineers, we must underline the importance of the contribution they have made to the understanding of urban problems. Our initial inquiries suggest it is possible they have had as much impact on the design of cities as have city planners. The location of watermains and sewers is at least as crucial as the specification of zoning by-laws in the structuring of the urban landscape. We had hoped to include one facet of this field — namely, transportation studies — but the engineering side itself is so complex that it must be considered independently in a separate analysis of the physical technology of the urban unit.

Finally, we felt that municipal administrators could not add very much to this rather abstract discussion of a research framework. Their comparative advantage lies in the detailed knowledge of the organizational and institutional operations of municipalities. At this level we are not sufficiently informed to carry on meaningful discussion.

The Urban Crisis in Canada

Our examination of the nature of cities comes at an opportune time. Many issues have arisen in the past decade or so, both in Canada and in the United States, regarding the functioning of the city. As a result the public has become aware of an "urban crisis". Our interest in urban studies was triggered by this centripetal process, and these papers were assembled to permit the segregation of particular issues on the basis of a rational analysis. Let us examine, then, the nature of this urban crisis and how well we are equipped to handle it, given the state of the arts in urban studies.

The fundamental source of the urban crisis is the process of urbanization itself. For a host of perfectly rational private economic reasons, the population has concentrated in the cities in ever-increasing proportions. The consequent social costs have grown so fast that by the time they were recognized they required solutions sufficiently drastic to implant a crisis mentality. Thus, increasing population density has created our slum crisis, our pollution crisis, our unsafe city streets. At the same time, this process has led to our accelerating sub-urban sprawl, creating our transportation crisis, our municipal revenue crisis, our municipal service crisis and our housing crisis.

Despite these general points, we know very little about the process of urbanization in Canada and about the structure and functioning of our cities. This cannot be ascribed simply to a total lack of relevant literature. Recent surveys[1] in the United States have revealed that a substantial amount of detailed work has been produced in the last half century, and that a lot of work is currently under way which should provide the appropriate tools for solving the urban problem. Much of this detailed work is still somewhat disintegrated. Urban studies can be compared to a pool into which all sorts of people have jumped from many spots on the bank. Still

---

[1] For example, see P. M. Hauser and L. F. Schnore (eds.), *The Study of Urbanization*, Wiley, New York, 1965.

we have accumulated a certain stock of knowledge about approaches to the urban phenomenon.

If the techniques are available, how can one explain the unwillingness of research workers to enter this field? How can one explain the great paucity of work currently being done in Canada? A handful of sociologists, a few geographers and a sprinkling of economists constitute the elusive army waging what James Q. Wilson has called "the war on cities".[2] We contend that this is a gross misallocation of intellectual resources. At the beginning of the 1960's property tax revenue, which constitutes more than 90 per cent of local revenues in Canada, represented more than 5 per cent of national income, more than 46 per cent of the total tax revenue of local and provincial governments, and some 16 per cent of the total tax revenue of all governments.[3] This order of magnitude should have attracted the attention of academics and policy-makers alike. In fact, in the Canadian scholarly journals and in the few journals of opinion there is scarcely any acknowledgement of an urban crisis. Economists know that a large array of services have been municipalized over the last quarter of a century. That is, a large number of services have acquired a certain degree of publicness and local governments have been saddled accordingly with new responsibilities. This has led to serious strains on municipal finances and to difficult provincial-municipal relations. Political scientists are aware of the problem of the optimal administrative structure required to fit the pattern of collective needs with their different and changing degree of publicness. But all this seems to be restricted to discussions over cups of coffee.

Several processes are at work that militate against serious urban research. The first is the peculiarity of the Canadian bureaucracy which feels that its own expertise far exceeds that elsewhere, so that no dialogue is required. If to this we add a miser's approach to internal research effort, a withholding of

---

[2] James Q. Wilson, "The War on Cities", *The Public Interest*, No. 3, Spring 1966.

[3] D. Netzer, *Economics of the Property Tax*, Brookings Institution, Washington, 1966, p. 12.

relevant data and a reluctance to permit program evaluation, the contribution of this segment of our research establishment toward solving the urban dilemma must be judged as negative. Certainly the relevant governments are aware of some of the problems, for both federal and provincial governments have become deeply involved in urban renewal, low-rental housing, mortgage financing and so forth. But the failure to do the serious hard work is strikingly evident. Most programs appear to have been strung together on an *ad hoc* basis. For example, it is extremely difficult to find the rationale for the Central Mortgage and Housing Corporation's urban renewal policy. Its criteria for allocating funds to this activity are equally obscure. The goals and objectives of provincial departments of municipal affairs seem to be even more elusive.

If the bureaucrats have closed mouths, the academics have closed minds. In no other country is so much effort devoted to doing and redoing the same tasks. In economics, the magic areas are growth, trade, money and econometrics, and woe to him who strays from the fold. The well-meaning cite the lack of research funds, which is surely a fiction in the urban context.

If the researchers are not doing the work, one reason might be that the urban crisis has not really stimulated public concern. An essential ingredient seems to be missing for a full recognition of the urban problem. There must be a perception of the problem of our cities by the population at large. This perception has been emerging in the United States since the early 1960's. The first two problems are general: the "psychological" problem created by new high expectations; and the "technical" problem of public nuisances, scarce public resources and fiscal imbalance. Moreover, the American urban problem has an additional component — the explosive Negro and immigrant lower class ghettos.[4] This third aspect has captured the imagination of the public and has led it to raise the other two problems. The physical, economic and sociological cities have become a centre of interest for all the

---

[4] Wilson, *op. cit.*

journals of opinion, and ever since the Moynihan Report on the instability of the Negro family, the majority of Americans (who are living in cities) have been made increasingly aware of urban problems. This has even led President Lyndon Johnson to deliver a special message to the Congress on improving the nation's cities. Because this third factor does not exist to the same extent in Canada, it is unlikely that the problem will as easily move the public. Moreover, Canada is faced less with an *absolute* crisis (whatever it may mean) than with a problem of *relative standards*. Our cities may well be "in better shape than most cities of the world, with the possible exception of a few in Northern Europe" but if "people are beginning to say that they won't accept them any longer", this creates the so-called crisis.[5] Without this explosive third aspect to our urban problem, the crisis component has not yet become apparent; our cityscape has simply been deteriorating without anyone worrying unduly about it.

If there were public recognition of the problem, demands for urban research would be forthcoming. But the public cannot exercise these demands effectively in the Canadian context, despite the reality of the crisis. We must therefore integrate this diffuse field of knowledge in order to spell out precisely the urgency of the crisis. Only thus will the public become conscious of its deteriorating environment. Once the public begins to demand solutions, policy recommendations can be formulated. Such integration has to be effected at the cross-disciplinary level.

In the United States institutions for cross-disciplinary research already exist, such as the MIT-Harvard Joint Center for Urban Studies. Symptomatically, only very recently have such creatures emerged in Canada. It is only fair to say that no institution has produced much yet but embryos of integration are already developing in Canada at Toronto, York, McMaster, and Carleton Universities, Waterloo, and at the Université de Montréal.

---

5 D. P. Moynihan, "Is There Really an Urban Crisis?" *Challenge*, Vol. 15, No. 2, November-December 1966.

Therefore, while some of the tools have already been developed, it is possible that the Canadian urban problem will not be articulated as clearly as the American. It lacks the critical ghettoing dimension and the expertise to recognize, analyze and articulate the problem is relatively less developed. However, the interest generated by the idea of a Department of Urban Affairs, the allocation of a chapter in the Fourth Annual Review of the Economic Council and the emergence of a few centres with a definitely cross-disciplinary approach to urban issues, may produce some public demands. Therefore it might be an opportune time to comment on the need for a rational urban policy.

Evaluation of Current Public Policy

A discussion of urban policy currently being implemented in Canada requires little space. There is in fact no such thing. Constitutionally the municipalities are creatures of the provincial governments and as such cannot entertain any rapport with the federal government. This has not barred the federal government from developing policies tending to deal with particular urban problems. Ever since the Dominion Housing Act of 1935 and more particularly since the introduction of the National Housing Act of 1944 and the establishment of Central Mortgage and Housing Corporation in 1945, the federal government has been active in the field of urban development. Since the Second World War the forms that this intervention has taken have varied greatly, from sharing in mortgage loans, constructing homes for veterans and building low-rental housing in partnership with provincial governments, to the insurance of mortgage loans and urban renewal activity via land assembly projects. These bits and pieces have nowhere been fitted into a consistent urban policy. Indeed, the home construction program appears more and more to conflict with the urban renewal home destruction program. These activities cannot be evaluated here, but it should be noted that the indirect intervention of the federal government has always been on a limited scale and has proceeded through devious routes. Furthermore, its role will be eroded significantly by the recent creation of a series of provincial housing corporations.

The provincial governments have had different experiences. Some provinces have done little. Others, such as Ontario, have attempted to set up a system of legal rules for subdivision and housing development permitting the Department of Municipal Affairs to guide urban growth by giving it the power to police the integrity of the master plan. In this case, many decisions as to subdivision activities, long a political football for municipal councils, have been more or less removed from the realm of politics. Any corrigendum or alteration to the master plan of a city has to be approved by the Department of Municipal Affairs, and thus the provincial government can supervise the process of urban growth and enforce some of its preferences.

A variety of policy instruments are available to policymakers. Our own research into municipal taxation and expenditure reveals that a multitude of additional instruments could easily be developed should the need arise. The problem is not so much a deficiency of policy instruments as the complete absence of a consistent policy framework.

It might be argued that municipal governments are solely responsible for urban policy and that the role of higher-level governments, because they have been ineffective, should be terminated. However, the intervention of higher-level governments has many possible rationales. While jealousy of their powers may explain the provinces' concern, the literature contains two very convincing arguments for higher-level government (federal and provincial) intervention. One pertains to demand and the other to supply.

On the demand side, one of the key questions has to do with what the people want. In recent years, the literature has demonstrated that the urban problem could be considered in terms of fiscal incidence. The city as an economic organism is supplying collective-consumption goods, and the problem is to determine the factors affecting the demand for such goods and the mechanism through which such demand is channeled.[6] Without reviewing this literature, we may note that as the city grew it began supplying not only non-private goods but also collective-consumption bads or nuisances like pollution and congestion. Since individuals could be assumed to have no taste for these nuisances, the problem was to determine the intensity of distaste for such nuisances and the strength of preferences for city goods.

This question led to numerous discussions which have raised fundamental issues about "what people really want". Some like D. J. Elazar have suggested that "whatever changes the American people seem to be seeking, they are not directed toward the enhancement of the facilities that lead to an urbane or citified life, but rather to the introduction in the city of qualities associated with the rural life". According to him, "the American urban place is pre-eminently an 'anti-city' ".[7] This naturally raises some questions as to the reality of the urban crisis. Elazar suggests that Americans have decided in fact to take "the economic advantages of the city while rejecting the previously inevitable conditions of citified living".[8] According to Elazar, therefore, the urban crisis stems from a refusal to accept these conditions.

The problem might, however, be more than a gross mis-reading of the preferences of the citizens. It may be that the "urbanist" has blown his own particular preferences out of proportion. Elazar continues, "there is a great deal of evidence to indicate that most models of improvement proposed for the American city are nothing more than projections of the desires of certain articulate minorities . . . ."[9] Taking into considera-

---

6 See A. Williams, "The Optimal Provision of Public Goods in a System of Local Government", *Journal of Political Economy*, Vol. 74, No. 1, February 1966; J. B. Cullingworth, *Restraining Urban Growth: The Problem of Overspill*, Fabian Research Series No. 211, London, January 1960. Also A. Breton, "A Theory of the Demand for Public Goods", *Canadian Journal of Economics and Political Science*, Vol. 32, No. 4, November 1966.

7 D. J. Elazar, "Are We a Nation of Cities?" *The Public Interest*, Vol. 4, Summer 1966.

8 *Ibid.*

9 *Ibid.*

tion non-private goods and nuisances, and the need to recognize "hidden" preferences of the citizens, a central government which attaches some weight to the goal of *equality* and *equity* will naturally find it desirable to intervene. On the demand side therefore the intervention of higher level government has a distributive connotation.[10]

On the supply side, the technological character of the services that a city renders makes intervention by a central government necessary here also. The nature of these services precludes the possibility of important continual productivity increases.[11] This technological characteristic tends to push up the real cost of such activities. This means that the expenses of the municipality have to be increased just to maintain the standards of city life over time. If one adds to this the costs of externalities and so on, one can see that the Baumol argument in favour of transferring resources from the productivity generating sectors strongly supports the interventionist position.

As we have seen the central government has been intervening since the 1930's, and the results are not impressive. Indeed the operations of higher level governments have created what Moynihan has called a "crisis of confidence".[12]

The public has perceived that the active role of higher-level governments has not led to substantial achievements. In part this is due to the ostrich-like behaviour of the bureaucracy, which buries policies that are deemed by it to have failed, even though the failure might have been due to bad judgment and even though much can be learned from the failure. As a result, the public has developed a cynical attitude toward the value of urban policy, without realizing that most of its failures are due to bad management and not to inappropriate ideas.

---

10 An argument has been put forward by Walter Heller, *New Dimensions of Political Economy*, Norton, New York, 1967, Ch. 3, for public interference at this level.

11 See W. J. Baumol, "Macroeconomics of Unbalanced Growth: The Anatomy of Urban Crisis", *American Economic Review*, Vol. 57, No. 3, June 1967.

12 D. P. Moynihan, "A Crisis of Confidence?" *The Public Interest*, No. 7, Spring 1967.

Toward a National Urban Policy

If we accept the argument that federal and provincial participation in the formulation and promulgation of urban policy is justified, then we must decide what form this participation might take. At present there is no machinery in operation. Furthermore, given the limited perception of the problem, it is too early to design such machinery. Nevertheless, our past discussion suggests what first steps must be taken by the higherlevel governments.

Urban Research

It is vital that resources be made available through some central research agency to enlarge the scope and scale of serious urban research, in an effort to uncover the basic nature of the urban reality. To the extent that this work will be most relevant at the interdisciplinary level, appropriate institutions must be encouraged and if necessary created. An advisory group consisting of project directors could integrate these efforts so as to avoid duplication and to maximize the free flow of knowledge. The latter would be greatly enhanced by a large scale data development program, since the absence of accurate municipal data is perhaps the greatest stumbling block to satisfactory research.

Urban Problems

Policy can be framed only in the light of society's preferences. To elicit these is particularly difficult in Canada because we have nothing akin to United States commissions and committees which permit open public discussion. We could, however, establish a Senate Committee on Urban Affairs to hold public hearings and provide it with sufficient resources to call for briefs by experts on relevant matters. This would provide a forum for the determination of society's objectives with regard to the urban problem and its priorities. In other words, the urban goals would be established. A continuing committee would guarantee an adjustment of the goals as society's preferences shift.

Urban Policy

The previous two programs set out the realities and the desires facing us. To relate the two is the role of urban policy. What is needed is a joint federal-provincial body capable of integrating all policy instruments in all related fields, from transportation to housing. The prototype might be the Tax Structure Committee, although a ministerial committee would be preferable for setting policy. Strong links with the research advisory group and the Senate Committee would guarantee the relevance of their work, and would ensure constant re-evaluation of all policy moves.

In fact there is no reason why a permanent Senate Committee on Urban Affairs could not be given terms of reference broad enough to include both regional and urban problems. Appropriate weight could then be given to these particular goals which the government now considers as *given*.

These institutions may appear to constitute a parallel government. In Western economies there is a shift toward the executive, and our legislative bodies which are non-experts and non-interventionist will have to accept the streamlining of certain institutions.[13] However, before attempting to create these new institutions, more must be learned about the problem. This book has attempted to bring together certain facts about urban life in Canada. It can, however, be only the first of a series of studies to uncover the many facets of the complex urban reality. If, indeed, the urban problem is going to be the most important faced by our society in the second half of the twentieth century, our effort here can be interpreted as an attempt to make the future a matter for public choice.[14]

---

13 A. Shonfield, *Modern Capitalism*, Oxford University Press, London, 1965.

14 Bertrand de Jouvenel has been suggesting for years that the question of finding ways to make the future a matter of public opinion is one of the most important problems of the political process.

Bibliography

Alexandersson, Gunnar. *The Industrial Structure of American Cities*; a geographic study of urban economy in the United States. University of Nebraska Press, Lincoln, Nebraska, 1956.

Alonso, William. *Location and Land Use: Toward a General Theory of Land Rent*. Harvard University Press, Cambridge, 1964.

Andrews, R. B. *Urban Growth and Development*. Simmons-Boardman Publ., New York, 1962.

Applebaum, W. and Cohen, S. B. "The Dynamics of Store Trading Areas and Market Equilibrium", *Annals of the Association of American Geographers*, Vol. 51, pp. 73-101.

Babcock, R. F. *The Zoning Game*. The University of Wisconsin, Madison, 1966.

Banfield, E. C. (ed.). *Urban Government: a reader in politics and administration*. Glencoe Free Press, New York, 1961.

Bartholomew, H., assisted by Jack Wood. *Land Uses in American Cities*. Harvard University Press, Cambridge, 1955.

Barton, A. H. "The Concept of Property-Space in Social Research" in P. F. Lazarsfeld and M. Rosenberg (eds.), *The Language of Social Research*. Free Press, Glencoe, Ill., 1955.

Beckmann, M. J. "Some reflections on Lösch's theory of location", *Regional Science Association, Papers and Proceedings*, Vol. I, N1-N9, 1955.

Beckmann, M. J. "City Hierarchies and the distribution of city size", *Economic Development and Cultural Change*, Vol. 6, pp. 243-248, 1958.

Berry, Brian J. L. "A note concerning methods of classification", *Annals of the American Association of Geographers*, Vol. 48, pp. 300-303.

Berry, Brian J. L. "City Size Distribution and Economic Development", *Economic Development and Cultural Change*, Vol. 9, pp. 573-588, 1961.

Berry, Brian J. L., Barnum, H. G. and Tennant, R. J. "Retail Location and Consumer Behavior", *Regional Science Association, Papers and Proceedings*, Vol. 9, pp. 65-106, 1962.

Berry, Brian J. L. and Garrison, W. L. "A note on central place theory and the range of a good", *Economic Geography*, Vol. 34, pp. 304-311, 1958.

Berry, Brian J. L. and Garrison, W. "Alternate Explanations of Urban Rank-Size Relationships", *Annals of the American Association of Geographers*, Vol. 48, No. 1, 1958.

Berry, Brian J. L. and Meltzer, Jack (eds.). *Goals for Urban America*. Spectrum, Englewood Cliffs, N.J., 1967.

Berry, Brian J. L. and Pred, Allen. *Central Place Studies: A Bibliography of Theory and Applications*. Regional Research Institute, Philadelphia, 1965.

Berry, Brian J. L., Simmons, J. W. and Tennant, R. J. "Urban Population Densities: structure and change", *Geographical Review*, Vol. 53, pp. 389-405, 1963.

Bunge, W. *Theoretical Geography*. Lund, 1962.

Chapin, F. Stuart and Weiss, Shirly F. *Urban Growth Dynamics in a Regional Cluster of Cities*. Wiley, New York, 1962.

Chapin, F. Stuart and Weiss, Shirly F. *Factors Influencing Land Development*. University of North Carolina, Chapel Hill, N.C., 1962.

Clark, Colin. "Urban Population Densities", *Journal of the Royal Statistical Society*, Series A, Vol. 114, pp. 490-496, 1951.

Clark, P. J. "Grouping in spatial distribution", *Science*, Vol. 123, pp. 373-374, 1956.

Crawford, K. G. *Canadian Municipal Government*. University of Toronto Press, Toronto, 1954.

Davis, O. A. and Whinston, A. B. "The Economics of Complex Systems: The Case of Municipal Zoning", *Kyklos*, Vol. XVII, No. 3, 1964.

Deutsch, Karl *et al. Political Community and the North Atlantic Area.* Princeton University Press, Princeton, 1957.

Duncan, O. D. *Metropolis and Region.* Resources for the Future, Washington, 1960.

Elison, L. M. *The Finances of Metropolitan Areas.* Michigan Legal Publications, Ann Arbor, 1964.

Ely, R. T. *Characteristics and Classification of Land.* Ann Arbor, Michigan, 1922.

Gans, Herbert J. *The Urban Villagers.* The Free Press of Glencoe, New York, 1962.

Garrison, W. L. "Towards simulation models of urban growth and development", *Land Studies in Geography*, Vol. 24, pp. 92-108, 1962.

Gertler, L. "Studies on Urban Shadow Phenomenon in Three Ontario Communities", Conservation Council of Ontario, Resources for Tommorow Conference, 1961.

Greenhut, M. L. *Plant Location in Theory and Practice: The Economics of Space.* University of North Carolina Press, Chapel Hill, N.C., 1956.

Haas, Ernst. *Beyond the Nation State.* Stanford University Press, Stanford, 1964.

Haas, Ernst. "International Integration. The European and Universal Process", *International Organization*, Vol. XV, 1961.

Haggett, Peter. *Locational Analysis in Human Geography.* Edward Arnold, London, 1965.

Hodgetts, J. E. "Regional Interests and Policy in a Federal Structure", *Canadian Journal of Economics and Political Science*, February 1966.

Hoover, E. M. *The Location of Economic Activity.* McGraw-Hill Book Co., New York, 1948.

Isard, W. *Location and the Space Economy.* Jointly by Technology Press of MIT and Wiley, New York, 1956.

Isard, Walter *et al. Methods of Regional Analysis: An Introduction to Regional Science.* MIT Press, Boston, 1960.

Kaplan, H. *The Regional City.* C.B.C.

Kaplan, H. *Urban Renewal Politics: Slums Clearance in Newark.* Columbia University Press, New York, 1963.

Krueger, Ralph W. "Tangled Administration: Organization for Regional Development" in John B. Fotheringham,

Transition: Policies for Social Action, McClelland and Stewart, Toronto, 1966.

Lange, O. *Wholes and Parts*. Pergamon, Warsaw, 1965.

Langlois, Claude. "Problems of Urban Growth in Greater Montreal", *Canadian Geographer*, Autumn 1961.

Lösch, A. *Die raumliche Ordrung der Wirtschagt*. Translated by W. H. Woglom and W. F. Stolper as *The Economics of Location*. Yale University Press, New Haven, 1954.

Lösch, A. "The Nature of Economic Regions", *Southern Economic Journal*, Vol. 5, pp. 71-78, 1938.

Lowenstein, L. K. *The Location of Residences and Work Places in Urban Areas*. Scarecrow Press, London, 1965.

Lowenstein, L. K. "The Location of Urban Land Uses", *Land Economics*, Vol. 39, November 1963.

Mayer, H. M. and C. F. Kohn (ed.). *Readings in Urban Geography*. University of Chicago Press, Chicago, 1959.

Meyer, J. "Regional Economies: a survey", *American Economic Review*, Vol. 53, pp. 19-54, 1963.

Muth, R. F. "Economic Change and Rural-Urban Land Use Conversion", *Econometrica*, Vol. 29, pp. 1-23, 1961.

Muth, R. F. "The Spatial Structure of the Housing Market", *Regional Science Association, Papers and Proceedings*, Vol. 7, pp. 207-220, 1962.

Netzer, D. *Economics of the Property Tax*. Brookings Institution, Washington, 1966.

Ostry, S. and Rymes, T. *Regional Statistical Studies*. University of Toronto Press, Toronto, 1966.

Pfouts, L. W. *The Techniques of Urban Economic Analysis*. West Trenton, N.S., Chandler-Davis, 1960.

Philbrick, A. K. "Principles of Areal Functional Organization in Regional Human Geography", *Economic Geography*, Vol. XXXIII, 1957.

Philbrick, A. K. "Areal Functional Organization in Regional Geography", *RSAP*, 3, 1957.

Pitts, F. R. (ed.). *Urban Systems and Economic Development*. University of Oregon, Eugene, 1962.

Ponsard, C. *Economie et espace: essai d'intégration du facteur spatial dans l'analyse économique*. Sedes, Paris, 1955.

Rannells, J. *The Core of the City*. Columbia University Press, New York, 1956.

Rawson, Mary. *Property Taxation and Urban Development.* Urban Land Institute, Washington, 1961.

Rowat, Donald C. (ed.). *Basic Issues in Public Administration,* Macmillan, New York, 1961.

Rowat, Donald C. *Your Local Government.* Macmillan, Toronto, 1955.

Sayre, W. and Kaufman, H. *Governing New York City.* Russell Sage Foundation, New York, 1960.

Smith, Robert H. T. "Methods and Purpose in Functional Town Classification", *Annals of the Association of American Geographers,* Vol. LV, September 1965.

Stone, L. O. *Urban Development in Canada,* Dominion Bureau of Statistics, Ottawa, 1968.

Subcommittee on Urban Affairs of the Joint Economic Committee U.S. Congress. Hearings. *Urban America: Goals and Problems.* 90th Cong. First Session, Sept. 27, 28, Oct. 2, 3, and 4, 1967. Washington, G.P.O.

Subcommittee on Urban Affairs of the Joint Economic Committee U.S. Congress. Materials Compiled and Prepared. *Urban America: Goals and Problems.* Washington, G.P.O., August 1967.

Thompson, Wilbur R. *A Preface to Urban Economics.* Johns Hopkins, Baltimore, 1965.

Thompson, Wilbur. "Toward a Framework for Urban Public Management" in Sam B. Warner (ed.), *Planning for a Nation of Cities.* MIT Press, Cambridge, 1966.

Tiebout, Charles M. *The Community Economic Base Study.* Supplementary Paper No. 16, Committee for Economic Development, December 1962.

Turvey, R. *The Economics of Real Property.* George Allen and Unwin, London, 1957.

Vining, R. "Delimitation of economic areas: statistical conceptions in the study of the spatial structure of an economic system", *Journal of the American-Statistical Association,* Vol. 18, pp. 44-64, 1953.

Wehrly, M. S. and McKeever, J. R. *Urban Land Use and Property Taxation.* Urban Land Institute, Technical Bulletin No. 18, 1952.

Wingo Jr., Lowdon. *Transportation and Urban Land.* Resources for the Future, Washington, 1961.

Index